Share & Care
The Story of the Nova Scotia Home
for Colored Children

Share & Care
The Story of the Nova Scotia Home for Colored Children

Charles R. Saunders

NIMBUS
PUBLISHING

© Copyright Charles R. Saunders, 1994

94 95 96 97 98   5 4 3 2 1

All rights reserved. No part of this book covered by the copyrights hereon may be reproduced or used in any form or by any means—graphic, electronic, or mechanical—without the prior written permission of the publisher. Any request for photocopying, recording, taping, or information storage and retrieval systems of any part of this book shall be directed in writing to the Canadian Reprography Collective, 379 Adelaide Street West, Suite M1, Toronto, Ontario, M5V 1S5.

Nimbus Publishing Limited
PO Box 9301 Stn A
Halifax, NS B3K 5N5
(902) 455-4286

Design: Arthur B. Carter, Halifax
Cover photo: Bob Brooks
Printed and bound in Canada

Nimbus acknowledges the support of the Canada Council and the N.S. Department of Culture.

Canadian Cataloguing in Publication Data
Saunders, Charles R.
Share & care
ISBN 1-55109-065-1
1. Nova Scotia Home for Colored Children—History.
2. Blacks—Education—Nova Scotia—Dartmouth—History. I. Title.
LC2862.D37S38 1994   371.97'960716225   C94-950022-4

*This book is dedicated to
everyone who was, is, or will be
a resident of the Nova Scotia Home for Colored Children*

NSHCC children dressed for an outing in the early 1960s.
(Courtesy Donna Byard Sealey)

Contents

1 Beginnings: 1605-1908 — 3
- Exploration and Slavery — 3
- The Black Loyalists — 5
- Exodus to Sierra Leone — 8
- The Maroon Interlude — 9
- The Black Refugees — 10
- Father Richard Preston — 14
- Achievement in Adversity — 17

2 "Therefore Be It Resolved...": 1908-1921 — 21
- Children in Need — 21
- A Pastor's Cause — 24
- A Change in Vision — 29
- Kinney and Bauld — 30
- The Groundwork is Laid — 33
- The "Greatest Day" — 39

3 Years of Consolidation: 1921-1940 — 47
- Setting Standards — 47
- Daily Life — 53
- One-Room Education — 57
- Life on the Farm — 61
- Musical Youth — 62
- A Memoir — 65
- The "Little Colony" — 67

4	**The Winds of Change: 1940-1960**	**73**
	J.A.R. Kinney's Passing	73
	Another Passing	75
	The Second Kinney Generation	78
	The Farm's Heyday	80
	Bauld School Days	85
	Rev. Donald E. Fairfax	89
	Noel Johnston's Shopmobile	93
	New Ground	96
5	**The Old Order Ends: 1960 - 1973**	**103**
	The Calm Before the Storm	103
	White Children at the Home	110
	Separate and Unequal	113
	The Last School Closing	117
	Down Off the Farm	120
	The Kinneys Depart	123
	Mary Paris	128
	Gone Too Soon	132
	The Foster Home Problem	134
	Edie Gray's Children	142
6	**A New Attitude: 1973-1979**	**147**
	The Mandate Changes	147
	From Superintendent to Director	151
	New Directions	154
	A New Board	159
	Selecting a Site	165
	Second Opening	169

	The Strike	172
	Aftermath	178
7	**Picking Up the Pieces: 1979-1991**	**183**
	The Post-Strike Period	183
	A New Director Arrives	187
	More Problems	189
	Programs and Promises	192
	A Woman's Touch	197
	The Newest Matron	200
	Renewal and Remembrance	202
	The Old Home	204
	The Board	209
8	**The Home Today**	**217**
	Continuing Tradition	217
	What's in a Name?	220
	Daily Life in the 1990s	226
	The Children	231
	In the System But Not of It	233
	The Future of the Home	239
	Afterword	**249**

What Band That Sunday Morning?:
Helen Creighton and the Home for Colored Children

Beloved Reader

As you disturb these leaves
Lushly parting before your eyes,
They shiver before your sweet breath.

In your passage, your pilgrimage,
From beginning to beginning,
Remember you will also be leaves,

Frail blossoms upon the wind—
Then these leaves in another hand.

George Elliott Clarke

Introduction

Upon my arrival at the Nova Scotia Home for Colored Children in 1980, I knew I had discovered a legacy that begged to be recorded. As I stood in the parking lot on that bright August day and wondered which of the many doors I would enter, I was overcome by this piece of black history to which I was about to provide leadership. To be honest, I was a little bewildered, for I was standing on hallowed land.

Then a little boy ran up to me and asked the make of my car. From a window, a staff member pointed towards the office. My task had begun in earnest.

During my early years as Executive Director, it was very difficult to connect the achievements of the Home's forebears with its present programs because of an absence of adequate records. Since the files on hand seemed rather sparse, I spent a great deal of time gathering records, notes and stories from near and far.

It was during this process that I made the decision to write a history of the Home. It was a story that had to be told. It occurred to me that I could accomplish the task in about six months.

I could not have been more wrong. Ten years have elapsed after those thoughts passed through my head.

During that decade, through a federal Secretary of State grant, we gleaned every piece of information that we could find about this Home. Countless interviews have taken place with former residents, staff, board members, volunteers, friends and family of the Home.

However, it was not until I had the opportunity to go to Toronto to meet with Mr. Ross Kinney III, grandson of the Home's first Superintendent, that our project truly began. Entrusted with two personal albums of Kinney family memorabilia and the good wishes of Ross, I knew we were finally on our way to the preservation of the history of this great institution. Indeed, it was the Kinney family who had embodied this unique orphanage for two generations.

To prevent damage to any of the original photos, I immediately had copies made of the collection's contents. At some point, the Home must consider setting up an archive, as some of the early pictures, stories and clippings are truly precious memories that should not be lost to the ravages of time. We owe this to our black youth.

Almost from the outset, my vision and thirst for the completion of a work for generations of black families past and present was supported by Althea Tolliver, current Supervisor of the Home. Having co-written an earlier book on the black communities of Nova Scotia, Mrs. Tolliver's input was invaluable.

As the research progressed, David Langille, a commercial-artist-turned-theology-student, joined the Home's staff as an on-call worker. His interest in the graphic design of the book and contact with local publishing houses helped to carry the project one step further.

What Mr. Langille learned in his attempts to market the book was that if it were to be published professionally, it would have to be written by a person who combined literary skills with a genuine understanding of the black perspective. That view was confirmed by Ms. Dorothy Blythe of Nimbus Publishing, who showed an early interest in the book, encouraged its development, and eventually chose to publish it.

Enter Charles Saunders, well-known black columnist for *The Daily News*, a local newspaper. Having published three black-oriented novels, as well as non-fiction books on Africville and the black boxers of the Maritimes, Mr. Saunders became our main catalyst.

With financial support from the Nova Scotia Department of Tourism and Culture and the federal Department of Multiculturalism and Citizenship, Mr. Saunders assumed the task of writing the story of the Nova Scotia Home for Colored Children and attacked the project with enthusiasm and commitment.

To increase our potential readership, two other literary figures were invited to participate in the project. Mr. Clary Croft, a noted folklorist, was asked to share some of the late Dr. Helen Creighton's tales of her involvement with the Home and its legendary annual School Closing concerts.

Another was award-winning poet George Elliott Clarke, who was commissioned to tell the Home's story through verse.

The literary team was falling into place.

The memory of Mrs. Margaret L. Wright (1943-1992), the Home's former Administrative Secretary, is inherent in this story. An eighteen-year employee of the Nova Scotia Home for Colored Children, Mrs. Wright was the spouse of Charles Wright, a former Home resident and current employee. Mrs. Wright was responsible for the typing and proofreading of several earlier versions of this manuscript. She was also a valuable resource person who had had long-time intimate contacts with many former residents, staff and board members. She considered this work to be a labor of love. She is sadly missed by all.

The publication of *Share & Care: The Story of the Nova Scotia Home for Colored Children* represents a monumental achievement. We feel the Home's long history parallels the many trials and tribulations endured by Nova Scotia's black population. It is very important to preserve a place in history for this institution that was built by blacks for their own people.

We hope this story will find its way into your schools, libraries and other centres of education so that it may be told time and again for generations to come.

We owe a great deal of gratitude and respect to our founders, former residents, staff, board members, volunteers, supporters and friends who have made this institution a source of pride for all to see.

Wilfred A. Jackson, B.A., M.S.
Executive Director
Nova Scotia Home for Colored Children

Preface

I came into this story when I picked up the telephone one day in August 1991. On the other end was a young man named David Langille. David was working at the Nova Scotia Home for Colored Children that summer, and he was calling to ask if I'd be interested in helping to prepare a manuscript of the Home's history.

I'm a "come-from-away," which is how Maritimers refer to those who were not born in this part of Canada. However, even though I'd only been living in Halifax for six years, I was well aware of the existence of the Nova Scotia Home for Colored Children. But the institution was little more than a name to me; I didn't know very much about its history.

I gave David a non-committal response. I was considering another venture then, and there was no way I could do both at the same time. Not long after I heard from David, that other venture fell through. In retrospect, I'm glad it did.

After getting back in contact with David, I arranged to see him and the manuscript and materials that had been compiled to date. David dropped by my house with a box filled with photocopies of old pictures and newspaper clippings related to the Home, as well as a two hundred-page compilation of the research that had been done to date.

David and I didn't know each other. But he sure knew how to get me hooked on the project. As I scanned the pages of the compilation, I saw a microcosm of black Nova Scotian history.

Once I started looking through the materials in that box, I didn't want to stop. The story of the Home unfolded before me through headlines dating back to the earliest years of this century. Faces in old photographs beckoned, urging me to recount the stories they had to tell of how the Nova Scotia Home for Colored Children was founded more than seven decades ago to address a need in the black community.

It was an urge I couldn't have resisted even if I had wanted to. Before long, I told David I was on board. After that, I spoke with Wilfred Jackson, the Home's Executive Director, and Althea Tolliver, Child Care Supervisor, both of whom had been working on the project for several years. We all agreed that my job would be to turn the materials they had given me into a publishable manuscript. Funding would be provided through the federal Secretary of State Department, and I was also fortunate enough to receive an Experienced Author's Grant from the provincial Department of Tourism and Culture.

And so my journey to the Home began. As I immersed myself in the material Wilf had been gathering since 1984, I began to appreciate the tremendous amount of work that had already gone into the project, and the true significance of the Home emerged from those pages.

The NSHCC was a positive development for the black community decades before the current trend toward "self-help." It represented cooperation among blacks and whites well before the heyday of the civil rights movement. And it is an institution that has adapted to major changes in child-care philosophy and social conditions that have forced others like it to close their doors.

I was well aware that it would take a great deal of effort on my part to do justice to the project the NSHCC administration had placed in my hands. Little did I know, however, that two years would pass before I finally turned the last draft of the manuscript over to Dorothy Blythe of Nimbus Publishing.

Those two years had their ups and downs. The September 1991 meeting I had with Wilf and Althea became the first of many. That was one of the ups. No one could ask for better cooperation and assistance. Not only were they willing to provide as much interview time as I needed, they also went out of their way to find archival materials without which this book's contents would have been greatly diminished.

Another up was the interviews I conducted with current and former NSHCC staff members and residents. Some of the latter had not been associated with the Home for many years, yet they were more than willing to share their experiences. The names of those with whom I spoke are listed in the Acknowledgements. This book could not have been written without their help.

What were the downs? Well, in a project like this, research begets more research. There has to be a cutoff point somewhere, but every time a deadline loomed, something more had to be done. Even today, I can still think of other people I'd like to talk to, more documents I'd like to locate, other old newspapers I'd like to read on microfilm; new directions I'd like to explore.

But the journey has to end sometime, and that time has arrived. Along the way, the Nova Scotia Home for Colored Children became my Home, as it has been for everyone whose lives it has touched. Hopefully, by the time you finish this book, the NSHCC will be your Home, too.

Charles R. Saunders
August 31, 1993

Acknowledgements

A work on the scale of *Share & Care* is the product of many hands, minds and voices. Although my name occupies the author's position on the title page, the help of those others made its publication possible. As you read this book, please remember their names. They have helped to make history.

Share & Care is a story rather than a history. For that reason, references to sources are provided directly in the text rather than in separate footnotes. Those sources include newspaper and magazine articles, taped interviews, telephone conversations, minutes from various African United Baptist Association annual meetings and several boxes of documents from the NSHCC, along with two thick albums of clippings collected by the late Ida Kinney.

The materials the NSHCC provided also included brief histories of the Home written by Rev. Donald E. Fairfax and Wayne Kelsie.

Two excellent books on black Nova Scotian history are *Beneath the Clouds of the Promised Land* by Dr. Bridglal Pachai and *The Immigration and Settlement of the Black Refugees* by John Grant.

The excerpt in my text from Sir Alexander Cochrane's War of 1812 proclamation came from Grant's book. Other historical references, including the quote from Muriel States on Henry G. Bauld, J.A.R. Kinney's declaration of race pride, and the Earl of Dalhousie's evaluation of the Black Refugees, came from *Beneath the Clouds*.

Wilfred Jackson, who had worked on this project for eight years before handing it over to me and worked closely with me during my two-year tenure, deserves special credit. Althea Tolliver also gave me much of her time and arranged for me to speak with four of the Home's residents in the course of my research. I also thank those residents, whose privacy has been ensured through the use of pseudonyms. Some former residents and others have also been given pseudonyms for the same reason.

Other members of the Home's staff who kindly consented to interviews were the late Margaret Wright, long-time office secretary; maintenance man Freddie Sparks (who has since retired); maintenance man Charlie Wright and Office Manager Jocelyn Boyd, both former residents of the Home; Child Care Supervisor Patricia Mugridge; and child-care staffers Sheila States, Hank Simmonds, Beverly Wyse and Hope Hume.

Past staff members who were interviewed include former Executive Director Bob Butler; former NSHCC Social Worker Sheila Lucas; and ex-Child Care Supervisors Veronica Marsman (also once a NSHCC resident), Sherry Bernard and Cherry Paris.

I was fortunate enough to contact several former residents of the Home, some of whom lived there in the 1920s and 1930s. Others are of more recent vintage. One, Larry Leigh, was interviewed before I became involved in the project. Others include George Bernard, Sr., Phyllis Lucas, Alfie White, Larry Leigh, Tracy Dorrington, Alisa Stevens, Robert Loppie, Kim Covey and Jocelyn Boyd, who is now the Home's Office Manager.

Four former teachers at the NSHCC's Henry G. Bauld School participated in the project. Gertrude Tynes and the late Patricia Riley were interviewed before my involvement, and I spoke with Noel Johnston and Donna Byard Sealey. In addition, Shirley Morgan contributed a written account of her time at the school.

Present and former NSHCC Board members interviewed by me include Jack MacNeil, Wayne Adams, Donna Smith, Rodger Smith, Rev. Donald E. Fairfax, Rev. Donald D. Skeir, Gus Wedderburn, Alice Croft and James Harper. The late Rev. William P. Oliver was interviewed prior to my involvement.

Special thanks are due to Ross and Patricia Kinney for the use of information from their family albums and for taking the time to talk with me about their experiences and perspectives on the Home.

Frances Harper provided valuable information about her grandfather, the late James Bundy, who was the Home's chauffeur and maintenance man. Trevor Townsend and Bill Greatorex of the Nova Scotia Community Services Department helped by showing how the Home fit into the province's care-giving network. Edith Gray shared warm memories of the Home residents she cared for as a foster parent. Bruce Johnson shared memories of his late mother, Mayola Johnson, who was the Home's cook for two decades. Joan Jones shared her experiences in the Home's Black Awareness program in 1980.

Last but not least, I wish to thank my friend George Elliott Clarke for the poetry that enhances this book, and my literary colleague Clary Croft for contributing a view of the Home through the eyes of the late folklorist Dr. Helen Creighton.

A non-fiction book can only be as good as its sources, and the sources for *Share & Care* were the best. They are to be congratulated for their contributions.

Slave Days

    Whips snarled and cursed God's sweet air and gashed flesh
To raw redness in those days, those slave days,
When iron was clamped to wrists, ankles, and necks,
In rebel colonies whose cannon barked
"Liberty! Liberty!," but whose law books
Tore child from parents, and cast all in chains.
    In those days, those slave days, blood crimsoned dawn
And dusk; the sun and moon hid their faces.
But God hears prayer! Some slaves stole their freedom,
Mustered to the King, became Black Pioneers,
Ethiopian troops, Black Loyalists,
Flourishing arms against Yank slaveholders.
    Magnificent, they confounded their foes,
Found Nova Scotia freedom in those days.
They fathered citadels, mothered churches,
While slavemasters crumbled in dust and fire.
Don't you see what a little faith can do?
Don't you see? — Slave days are over!

George Elliott Clarke

Beginnings: 1605-1908

1

Exploration and Slavery

To understand and appreciate the circumstances that led to the founding of the Nova Scotia Home for Colored Children, it is necessary to take a long look in the mirror of time, back to the origins of the province's black community.

That story begins in the early seventeenth century, when seagoing adventurers from Europe were exploring two great continents that were new to them but were an ancient home to the aboriginal inhabitants. One of those explorers was the Frenchman Pierre du Gua de Monts. In what is now Nova Scotia, De Monts founded the settlement of Port Royal in 1608. His party later included a black man with a Portuguese surname, Mattieu da Costa, who acted as an interpreter between the French and the Micmac, the local aboriginal population.

Although da Costa was probably the first black man to set foot on Nova Scotian soil, his presence was only transitory. Permanent black settlers arrived later, along with the French

Mathieu Da Costa, as played by actor Tracey Connell in the film *Fields of Endless Day*.

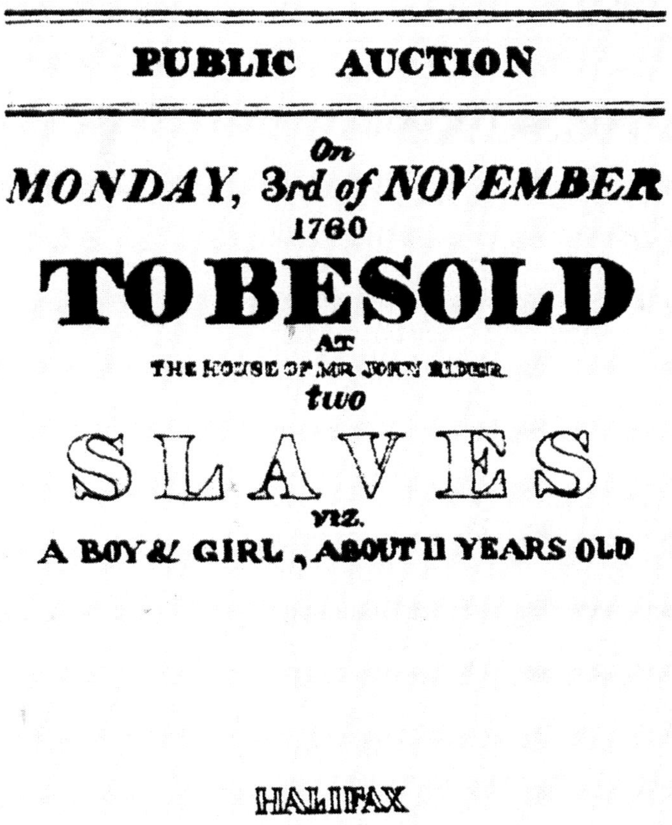

PUBLIC AUCTION

On MONDAY, 3rd of NOVEMBER 1760

TO BE SOLD

AT THE HOUSE OF MR JOHN RIDER

two

SLAVES

VIZ.

A BOY & GIRL, ABOUT 11 YEARS OLD

HALIFAX

Slave auction poster.

and English colonists who competed for the land that belonged to the Micmac.

Some of the early black inhabitants were free, including one on Cape Sable Island who bore the suggestive name of La Liberté. Others were slaves or servants "indentured for life," who did domestic, agricultural and artisan work. Still others were former slaves who had bought their freedom or been granted manumission by their owners. Regardless of individual status, the number of blacks in Nova Scotia remained small. But that small, struggling population was the ancestral source from which the black community of later times arose.

The slave experience in early Nova Scotia and other parts of Canada differed in some ways from that of the brutal plantation system that developed in England's southern colonies. The Nova Scotian economy did not depend on the use of massive amounts of cheap, involuntary labor. But the differences were only a matter of degree, not kind.

Slaves in Nova Scotia were still considered property rather than people. They could be bought and sold like merchandise or livestock. Slave auctions in Halifax were recorded as early as 1752, only three years after the founding of the city. Depending upon the temperament of the owner, slaves could be beaten with whips, or treated with the "kindness" usually reserved for a favorite pet or draft animal.

Although some Nova Scotians opposed slavery on moral grounds, the system's status quo persisted well into the eighteenth century. Some prominent citizens, including the first Presbyterian minister in the province, were slaveowners.

Toward the end of the century, an event occurred that would forever alter the course of history in North America. That milestone was known as the American Revolution, which lasted from 1776 to 1783.

The Black Loyalists

When the thirteen American colonies successfully revolted against England and seceded from the British Empire, the repercussions of the rebels' victory affected Nova Scotia, which had remained faithful to the Crown. Many like-minded residents of the former colonies fled north to Canada after the Revolutionary War ended in 1783. These exiles were known as Loyalists, and a large number of them were black.

The story of the Black Loyalists is the tale of a gamble that failed on one level, yet succeeded on another. During the course of the American Revolution, the British governor of Virginia, Lord Dunsmore, issued a proclamation promising freedom to any slave who fought for the Crown. At the same time the rebel commander-in-chief, General George Washington, refused to allow blacks to fight in the American forces. The fact that Washington and many of his contemporaries owned slaves may have influenced his decision.

Several thousand blacks accepted Lord Dunsmore's offer, forming units with names like the Ethiopian Regiment and the Black Pioneers. Eventually, Washington reversed his earlier stance and opened American ranks to blacks as well, with the promise of freedom as a reward for success. Blacks fought with distinction on both sides of the Revolutionary War in the hope that their efforts would earn the liberty they desperately desired.

When the rebels finally won the war, the Black Loyalists found themselves in a precarious position. They had gambled that the British would defeat the rebels, and had fought hard to achieve that end. But in the wake of the Crown's surrender, the victorious American slaveowners demanded the return of their human property.

The British, realizing their moral obligation to those who had heeded Lord Dunsmore's appeal, offered to evacuate Black Loyalist families to other parts of the Empire, an option that was also available to whites who were being persecuted for supporting the wrong side in the rebellion.

Some Loyalists—mostly white—headed south to Jamaica and other British possessions in the Caribbean. Others—white and black—sailed north to Nova Scotia. Their arrival would change the face of the province.

Between 1783 and 1784, 30,000 Loyalists arrived in Nova Scotia, tripling the colony's population in less than a year's time. This large contingent of immigrants included approximately 3,500 blacks who were free under the terms of the Dunsmore proclamation, and 1,232 blacks who came involuntarily as the property of slaveowning ex-Americans.

The Black Loyalists were determined to carve out new lives for themselves in their northern refuge, and many of them were well-equipped to do so. Their occupations ranged from blacksmith, tailor, carpenter and baker to domestic servant and farm hand. Unfortunately, the playing field upon which the black newcomers were expected to compete was far from level. They soon discovered that many obstacles stood between them and their goals.

One obstacle was the fact that Nova Scotian society condoned slavery, however small the scale within which it had been practiced prior to the Loyalist immigration. Tension between Black Loyalists and the slaveowners was inevitable. The existence of a productive population of free blacks would have seriously undercut the rationale behind what some Americans called "the peculiar institution" of involuntary servitude.

The massive influx of white and black evacuees also strained the colony's resources to their limits. Land had to be surveyed and parcelled out, provisions had to be distributed, employment had to be found. The needs of white soldiers and landowners were quickly accommodated, but Black Loyalists found themselves relegated to the eighteenth-century equivalent of the "back of the bus."

Although the British promised all Loyalists, regardless of color, land grants and up to three years of rations to tide them over until they became self-sufficient, most blacks received no land and less than a year's rations. And the scant acreage some blacks did manage to obtain tended to be isolated and unproductive.

Thus, the still-hopeful Black Loyalists settled into places with names such as Birchtown and Chedabucto, Preston and Little Tracadie, Shelburne and Annapolis, and, of course, Halifax. Some tried to cultivate the rocky, sandy soil of their meager land allotments. Others worked as farm hands and domestics. Still others attempted to follow the trades they had practiced before the Revolution, only to meet with stiff resistance from white counterparts who believed their own livelihood was threatened by the lower wages paid to blacks.

Sometimes that resistance became violent. In 1784 a race riot erupted in Shelburne. A mob of unemployed whites drove the blacks out of town, and then descended on the neighboring black settlement of Birchtown and burned several homes there.

As the years in Nova Scotia mounted, so did the privations. The Loyalist dream of freedom and equality turned into a nightmare of poverty and oppression. Rev. Boston King, a preacher who had been an officer in the Black Pioneers during the war, wrote the following account of the conditions his people faced:

> *Many of the poor people were compelled to sell their best gowns for five pounds of flour in order to support life. When they had parted with all their clothes, even to their blankets, several of them fell down dead in the streets, thro' hunger. Some killed and ate their dogs and cats; poverty and distress prevailed on every side.*

Still, the Black Loyalists persevered. Religion became the source of their strength. Boston King was only one of several extraordinary black leaders who emerged from the crucible of the black church. Separate churches were established throughout North America when it became clear that black worshippers were not welcome in white congregations.

Rev. David George, a Baptist minister from South Carolina, founded six churches in Black Loyalist settlements. When one of his churches was destroyed in the 1784 Shelburne riot, George held camp meetings in the surrounding woodlands. Moses Wilkinson, although blind and lame, preached the Methodist gospel at Birchtown; Thomas Brownspriggs and Joseph Leonard were black Anglican ministers. The tendency to turn inward in the face of rejection by the larger society was to be repeated throughout the history of the black community.

The military was another source of black leadership in the late eighteenth century. Colonel Stephen Blucke of the Black Pioneers received 200 acres of land near Shelburne and eventually established a school for blacks in the area.

Another soldier, Sergeant Thomas Peters, petitioned tirelessly for land and political rights for his people in both Nova Scotia and the newly created province of New Brunswick. His quest for justice carried him all the way to England and back.

Black women also contributed to the survival of the Loyalists. Catherine Abernathy, for one, established a school in Preston, a community that would grow in significance as the years passed. She also assisted her husband, Adam, in his Anglican ministry.

Despite their best efforts, as well as those of white friends and sympathizers, by the end of their first decade in Nova Scotia, the Black Loyalists appeared to have lost their gamble for a better life in Canada. The summers were short, the winters long, and future prospects looked bleak. For some, the solution to their problems appeared to lie in yet another sea voyage, and yet another gamble.

Exodus to Sierra Leone

In 1790 a black visitor from Nova Scotia arrived at the busy docks of London, England. This traveller, Thomas Peters, carried a petition from more than 200 black families in Nova Scotia and New Brunswick, families who had diligently collected the funds necessary to pay his passage.

The petition laid out a litany of broken promises and shattered dreams. In part it read:

> *That some part however of the said Black people are earnestly desirous of obtaining their due allotment of land and remaining in America, but others are ready and willing to go wherever the wisdom of Government may think proper to provide for them as free subjects of the British Empire.*

Peters and his petition soon came to the attention of Granville Sharp, a prominent figure in the British movement for the abolition of slavery. One aspect of the abolitionists' efforts was the establishment of a West African colony called Sierra Leone, to be settled by free blacks.

To the African-born Peters, Sierra Leone sounded like an excellent alternative to Nova Scotia. He soon struck an agreement with the Sierra Leone Company to recruit Black Loyalists to populate the fledgling colony.

Peters returned to Canada to persuade his people to undertake yet another voyage. He was followed in 1791 by John Clarkson, a white agent of the Sierra Leone Company. Together, Peters and Clarkson convinced nearly 1200 blacks to sign up for resettlement in Africa.

Ironically, the Sierra Leone effort met with opposition from some white Nova Scotians who objected to the loss of cheap and easily exploited labor. Others supported the effort, believing blacks would be better off in a faraway country of their own.

On January 15, 1792, fifteen ships departed from Halifax Harbor to transport free blacks to Africa—an ironic reversal of the usual traffic in slaves to the Americas. Those ships carried nearly half of the Black Loyalists who had cast their lot with the British nearly two decades before. They also took away many Loyalist leaders.

Thomas Peters...gone.
Adam and Catherine Abernathy...gone.
David George...gone.
Boston King...gone.
Joseph Leonard...gone.

Only Colonel Stephen Blucke remained behind, and he died under mysterious circumstances a short time after the others' departure.

When the migrants arrived in Sierra Leone, they found a new set of tribulations awaiting them. The indigenous Africans objected to the colonists' presence, and the newcomers also faced hunger, lack of housing, and disease. Still, the Loyalists established a settlement called Freetown and embarked on a rocky road that would eventually lead their country to independence in 1961.

Some say the Sierra Leone migration deprived Nova Scotia of the "best and brightest" of the Black Loyalists. But that view unjustly dismisses the courage and perseverance of those who elected to stay and build a community in Canada. They were the ones who had looked at the land they lived on and saw endless green pine forests and clear, cold lakes and meadows adorned with wildflowers like splashes from God's paintbrush.

And they made a vow: "Here we stay."

Those persistent people, along with the hundreds of slaves still held by white Loyalists, comprised the second root stock of Black Nova Scotia.

The Maroon Interlude

July of 1796 saw the arrival of a unique group of black immigrants from the British Caribbean colony of Jamaica. These newcomers were called Maroons, a Spanish term meaning "runaway slave."

From the time African slavery was introduced in Jamaica, black bondsmen and women escaped from their plantations and took refuge in the mountains deep in the island's interior. For more than one hundred years, these escaped slaves and their descendants had been waging guerrilla warfare against those who sought to put them back into chains.

By 1738, peace treaties were signed between the Maroons and the Jamaican colonial government. The Maroons were granted freedom under certain conditions, one of which was a requirement to return runaway slaves who had made their way to Maroon communities.

One group, called the Trelawney Town Maroons, refused to return runaways. War between them and the colonial government broke out in 1795, and a short time later the Trelawney Towners were forced to surrender.

Not long after the Maroons laid down their arms, they found themselves herded onto ships bound for exile in Nova Scotia. Approximately 550 of them disembarked in Halifax in July 1796. Almost immediately, the Maroons turned preconceived Nova Scotian beliefs about blacks upside down.

As an organized, cohesive unit, the Maroons dealt with the Nova Scotia

The Jamaican Maroons waged guerilla warfare against British slave owners in the 18th century.

government from a position of strength. They did most of the construction work on the fortifications that became known as the Halifax Citadel, and they lived together in Preston, which had been virtually abandoned after the Black Loyalist migration to Sierra Leone.

The Maroons did not adapt well to life in Canada. Climate was an obvious source of discontent; less obvious were government efforts to break up their community and alter the lifestyle they had developed in the mountains of Jamaica. After four contentious years in Nova Scotia, the Maroons decided they would prefer to settle elsewhere.

"Elsewhere" turned out to be Sierra Leone. The Maroons arrived there in 1800. In one of history's great ironies, they came just in time to help put down a rebellion initiated by their predecessors, the Black Loyalists.

Although the Maroons' sojourn in Nova Scotia was short, it was also highly symbolic. Possibly, a few of them stayed behind and left descendants. To this day, many black Nova Scotians claim Maroon ancestry.

However, the legacy of the Maroons was more a matter of pride and spirit than family ties. Their courage, solidarity and fierce independence provided an example Nova Scotian blacks would never forget.

The Black Refugees

After the departure of the Maroons, the black community settled into a period of consolidation. Churches deserted by preachers bound for Sierra Leone found new clergy. Schools found new teachers. Children who had never known the lash of slavery grew up virtually side by side with those who had. Beleaguered by racism and stricken by poverty, the blacks were nonetheless becoming entrenched in Nova Scotia, whether the rest of the province liked it or not. And there were more to come.

In the years since the Revolution, the United States and Great Britain had shared an uneasy co-existence, with Canada caught in the middle. Although Great Britain was involved in a major European campaign against Napoleon during most of the early 1800s, the upstart American ex-colonies remained a thorn in the English Lion's paw. And the Americans believed their independence was compromised by the existence of British colonies in Canada, and by the British policy of seizing sailors from American ships and forcing them into the Royal Navy.

Thus, from 1812 to 1815, Britain and America fought their second—and last—war against one another. Canada was heavily involved in that war, as were blacks on both sides of the border.

In many ways the War of 1812 echoed the Revolution. As before, British strategists attempted to undermine the American economy by offering freedom to black slaves who escaped to Crown lines. A proclamation by British Vice Admiral Sir Alexander Cochrane read in part:

Black fugitives waiting on the shore of Maryland's Chesapeake Bay for a British ship to take them to freedom.

This is therefore to give notice that all persons who may be disposed to emigrate from the United States with their families, be received on board of His Majesty's ships or vessels of War, or at the military posts as may be established upon or near the coasts of the United States, when they will have their choice of either entering into His Majesty's sea or land forces, or of being sent as free settlers to the British possessions in North America or the West Indies where they will meet with all due encouragement.

Although Admiral Cochrane's appeal was not directed specifically toward blacks, the meaning of the phrase "as free settlers" could not have been mistaken by slaves eager to break their bonds.

Again, as in the previous century, blacks were asked to choose between the promises of the Americans and the British. Slaves and ex-slaves alike fought bravely on both sides of the battle lines. Cochrane himself enlisted 500 into an all-black corps called the Colonial Marines.

By 1815 the war had ended in a stalemate. The United States retained its independence, and Great Britain retained its Empire, of which Canada remained an important part.

And, once again, black Americans who had gone over to the British side found they had backed the wrong horse. Once again, it became incumbent upon the British to honor their pledges and provide a refuge for escaped slaves and soldiers.

For all the similarities between the situation of the Black Loyalists of 1783 and their counterparts of 1813-1815, there were also significant differences. Whereas most of the black veterans of the Revolution chose to migrate to Nova Scotia, those of the War of 1812 went to Trinidad. Also, the Black Loyalists had been accompanied by a larger group of whites who were like-minded in their devotion to the British Crown, allowing the races to share at least one common cause.

There was no such circumstance in 1815. During America's thirty years of independence, the notion of allegiance to the British Crown had been virtually eradicated. The Loyalist philosophy had become a relic of the past. No mass movement to Canada of politically alienated whites occurred in the wake of the War of 1812. The blacks who went north at that time were simply escaping slavery, nothing more—and that, in itself, should have been viewed as an understandable motive for emigration.

However, the Black Refugees arrived in Nova Scotia as an isolated, unwanted group. Approximately 1,200 came from the Chesapeake Bay area of Maryland during 1813-1814, while the war was still in progress. Some even sailed on the same British warships that had participated in the burning of Washington, D.C., the American capital.

Another contingent of 800 came from Bermuda after the conclusion of hostilities. Smaller groups continued to trickle in as late as 1816. Although some landed in New Brunswick, the majority settled in Nova Scotia.

Although there was a need for cheap labor in Nova Scotia during the war years, the Black Refugees found their welcome as cold as the climate. The Lieutenant-Governor of the province, Sir John Sherbrooke, received a petition from the House of Assembly asking for an end to black immigration. Although Sherbrooke dismissed the petition, most Black Refugees experienced a taste of things to come immediately upon arrival, when they were quarantined on Melville Island, a prisoner-of-war camp in the North West Arm near Halifax. After undergoing processing on the island, the Refugees were free to seek whatever employment was available, or to settle on land grudgingly provided by the Nova Scotia government.

Almost 1,000 Refugees ended up in Preston, where they joined the Black Loyalists and possibly a few leftover Maroons. Other Refugee settlements included Hammonds Plains, Beech Hill (which later became Beechville), and Campbell Road (which later became Africville). Another settlement was established in Loch Lomond, in neighboring New Brunswick.

The new arrivals were expected to carve out their own foothold in the Maritime economy. However, several obstacles stood in their way. The land on which they settled was often unproductive. The end of the war created an economic decline and a corresponding squeeze in the labor market. And there was also prejudice to contend with. Given those obstacles, the condition of the Refugees deteriorated soon after they arrived.

In 1816 the new Lieutenant-Governor of Nova Scotia, the Earl of Dalhousie, assessed the Black Refugees as follows:

Permit me to state...plainly that little hope can be entertained of settling these people so as to provide for their families and wants—they must be supported for many years—Slaves by habit and education; no longer working under the dread of the lash, their idea of freedom is idleness and they are therefore quite incapable of Industry.

Dalhousie was expressing a common theory of his time. And some blacks, driven to despair by dire circumstances, may well have matched his stereotype. Others, however, gritted their teeth and did what they had to in order to survive. They cleared the land, planted crops, worked as artisans and craftsmen, performed menial labor and prayed for better times to come.

In 1841, Lieutenant-Governor Viscount Falkland received a petition that stated:

Petitioners are Refugees...being placed by Government upon ten acre lots, of poor land, many of them including swamps and likewise entirely barren & unproductive, and none of them sufficient to yield subsistence for a family however skilled and industrious.... But few white men in this country seldom make a living upon ten acres even of good land.

The petitioners, who were from the Preston area, asked for title to their land and a chance to obtain better acreage. Although their words refuted the earlier claims of Lord Dalhousie, the document was shelved.

The Refugees constitute the third root of the black Nova Scotian community. Within a generation, they merged with the Loyalists and the remaining slaves to form the core ancestral population over the remainder of the nineteenth century.

Father Richard Preston

As the War of 1812 faded into history, the small Nova Scotian black community struggled through the rest of the nineteenth century. Its men labored as farmers, carpenters, lumbermen, miners and blacksmiths. Women worked as domestics, seamstresses, weavers and midwives and many sold farm produce in town markets. With schooling rarely available, children entered the labor force at an early age. Life was difficult for everyone in the 1800s, but blacks bore the additional burdens of prejudice and discrimination.

One moment of rejoicing during those years occurred on August 1, 1834, the day slavery was abolished throughout the British Empire. By that time, slavery in Nova Scotia had already withered on the vine. Its practice had long become more trouble than it was worth. But in 1834 there might still have been a few elderly blacks who had arrived as slaves with the Loyalists half a century before. These few would have had ample reason to celebrate the official end to their involuntary servitude.

Of more immediate significance to the future of the black community was the arrival in 1816 of a young escaped slave from Virginia named Richard Preston. Preston knew his mother had emigrated to Nova Scotia as a Refugee, and he had come to the province to seek her out. He found her in the Preston settlement.

The similarity in the names of the man and the community was coincidental, but perhaps also an omen. Having found his mother, Richard Preston decided to remain in Nova Scotia. Through his religious leadership, the black community developed the strength it needed to endure the many hardships that lay ahead of it.

Soon after his arrival in the province, Preston became involved with

Rev. Richard Preston, founder of the African United Baptist Association.
(Courtesy Black Cultural Centre for Nova Scotia)

Rev. John Burton, Moderator of the Maritime Baptist Association. Eventually, Preston became the first black delegate to that association. But prejudice extended even into houses of worship; many white parishioners refused to allow blacks into their churches or, if they did, forced them to sit in separate pews. In that regard, nothing much had changed since the days of the Loyalists.

In anticipation of the establishment of their own Baptist church where they could worship without undergoing such humiliation, black parishioners gathered funds to send Preston to England for religious studies. Preston arrived in Liverpool, England, in 1831, and a year later he received his ordination from the West London Baptist Association. He also raised enough money to build a black church in Halifax.

On April 14, 1832, the Cornwallis Street Baptist Church—known to this day as the Mother Church—opened its doors under the pastorship of Reverend Preston. Two years later, he led his congregation in a hymn of rejoicing on Emancipation Day:

Sound the loud timbrels
O'er Egypt's dark sea,
Jehovah hath triumphed,
His people are free.

Over the next twenty years the minister, who became known to one and all as Father Preston, visited black communities throughout the province and was instrumental in the establishment of eleven more churches.

Preston's crowning achievement came in 1854, with the founding of the African Baptist Association, later renamed the African United Baptist Association (AUBA). Thirty-six delegates from twelve churches met at Granville Mountain to form what remains the largest and most influential organization in the history of black Nova Scotia.

Seven years later, Father Preston died. His leadership had given the scattered, isolated and poverty-stricken black communities some much-needed cohesiveness.

Some have criticized the separate churches and schools Preston and other black leaders developed, calling them exercises in "self-segregation" that further isolated the community. Those institutions were separate by necessity, not choice. With blacks systematically excluded from white churches, schools and other establishments, there was no other alternative. Preston and his contemporaries did not adhere blindly to a doctrine of "separate but equal." For them, it was a matter of "separate or nothing."

This tradition of self-reliance and solidarity within the community extended well into the next century, and was one of the factors that led to the establishment of the Nova Scotia Home for Colored Children.

Achievement in Adversity

Several nineteenth-century black Nova Scotians overcame the odds against them to make noteworthy achievements. In Annapolis Royal, Rose Fortune became North America's first black policewoman; she also established her own baggage and trucking businesses. And Dr. William Harvey Goler of Halifax became a professor of history and president of Livingston College in North Carolina.

On October 28, 1859, William Edward Hall, the son of a Black Refugee, was awarded the Victoria Cross for his heroism at the Shah Nujeef Mosque during the Sepoy Rebellion in India. Hall, who grew up in Hantsport, Nova Scotia, had taken to the sea at a young age. Before joining the British Navy as an Able Seaman, Hall had seen service in the U.S. Navy.

As a British sailor, Hall fought in the Crimean War during the early 1850s. Later, he joined the crew of his ship, the *Shannon*, in the siege of the town of Lucknow during a military revolt in India. Single-handed, Hall fired the cannon that breached the walls of one of the rebel strongholds, the Shah Nujeef Mosque.

William Hall, V.C.

As a result, Hall became the first black and only the third Canadian to receive the British Empire's highest military honor. After leaving the Royal Navy in 1876, Hall retired to a farm in the Annapolis Valley, where he died in 1904.

Another black Nova Scotian who gained renown abroad was George Dixon, who had been born in Africville. At age 16, Dixon left Halifax to pursue a boxing career in Boston. Four years later, in 1890, he became the first black fighter to win a world championship when he knocked out Nunc Wallace in eighteen rounds for the vacant bantamweight title. Dixon later won the world

James Robinson Johnston, the first black lawyer in Nova Scotia and the originator of the idea of a Home for Colored Children.
(Courtesy Black Cultural Centre for Nova Scotia)

featherweight title as well, thus opening the door for the many black champions who followed in boxing and other sports.

Closer to home, history was made in 1898 when a young man named James Robinson Johnston became the first black graduate of the Dalhousie University Law School in Halifax. Johnston was a member of a distinguished family that included his grandfather, Rev. T. Thomas, and his uncle, Baptist activist Peter McKerrow.

After graduation, Johnston pursued further legal studies under Mr. Justice Russell and J.T. Bulmer. In 1901 he opened his own practice, specializing in criminal and military law. The *Halifax Herald* once described him as "an ornament to the bar," "a good lawyer" and "a pre-eminent citizen." He became involved with the Conservative Party and achieved some influence in political circles.

Johnston was also active in the affairs of the African United Baptist Association. At the Cornwallis Street Church, he served as superintendent of the Sunday school and as church clerk. He also founded the Baptist Youth Provincial Union. In 1906 he assumed the clerkship of the AUBA upon the death of Peter McKerrow.

As a leader in the black community, Johnston thought long and hard about the continued impoverishment and marginalization of his people, especially the children. The AUBA also expressed concern. The deplorable conditions that existed in black communities across the province were a constant topic of discussion in meetings of the Association's Education and Mission committees.

Johnston keenly observed developments south of the border, paying particular attention to the work of noted educator Booker T. Washington. In 1881, Washington had founded Tuskegee Institute in Alabama, an agricultural and industrial school that provided a practical and skill-oriented education for blacks.

The success of Tuskegee and other black self-help schools in the United States led Johnston to present a momentous proposal to the AUBA in 1908. The proposal called for the establishment of a Normal and Industrial Institute for black children in Nova Scotia. In those days, "Normal" was a designation given to schools that provided teacher training. Hampton Institute in Virginia, which had influenced the development of Tuskegee, provided the model for Johnston's dream.

Johnston could not have been unaware of the poor educational facilities available to blacks in the province. He had been fortunate to receive excellent schooling, but the majority of his contemporaries had not. Many black children did not attend school at all, and most of those who did went to segregated institutions. One such institution was the African School, founded in Halifax in 1836. Others were funded by church groups and the province. Despite the best efforts of teacher and pupils alike, however, the level of education for most Nova Scotian blacks remained inadequate. During a time when a sense of social responsibility for neglected and unwanted children was beginning to work its way into public consciousness, blacks remained on the outside looking in.

These and other factors influenced Johnston to approach the AUBA with an alternative to the existing situation in education and children's services. With the AUBA's acceptance of his proposal, the seed from which the Nova Scotia Home for Colored Children would one day grow was firmly planted.

Vision

James Robinson Johnston,
a lettered voice
orating in the wilderness,
dreamt of a refuge,
a Normal
and Industrial Institute.

Every work of Beauty
is born in a dream.

With Puryear, he prayed
for black artisans
and architects
to carve from the wilderness
of Western civilization
a home.

George Elliott Clarke

"Therefore Be It Resolved...": 1908-1921

2

Children in Need

James Johnston's proposal for a Normal and Industrial Institute for young black Nova Scotians could not have come at a more opportune time. The late nineteenth and early twentieth centuries were not the best of times to be a neglected child, especially a black one. Children of the poor and working classes were expected to begin earning their own keep at an early age. When economic pressures became too difficult for families to bear, some of these children were literally left by the wayside.

At the same time, however, sympathy for the causes of humanitarianism and social justice had been on an upswing during the second half of the 1800s. In Nova Scotia, several institutions for the maintenance of those considered helpless and hopeless were established. Among them were denominational orphanages, such as Saint Mary's Convent Orphanage, founded by the Roman Catholic Church in 1849. In 1857 the Protestant Orphan's Home was established and, ten years later, Saint Paul's School for Girls opened its doors.

The government also joined the institutional trend, erecting the Halifax Poorhouse in 1867. Prior to that time, the indigent had been housed in a ramshackle, chronically overcrowded structure that could not meet the needs of the hundreds of inmates it received each year, no matter how many times it was expanded.

Children who were destitute but not necessarily orphans also needed care. To address that need, several specialized institutions emerged, such as the Halifax Industrial School, founded in 1865 and intended as a home for boys who did not fit into the public school system. The Halifax Infants' Home was established in 1875. St. Patrick's Home, a training and industrial school for delinquent Roman Catholic boys, opened in 1885. These institutions were followed by the Protestant Orphans' Home and the Maritime School for Girls, both located in Truro.

In 1880 the provincial government passed a law that empowered the Society for the Prevention of Cruelty to Animals (SPCA) to deal with the abuse and neglect of minors. By 1888, almost 70 percent of the cases handled by the SPCA involved children rather than animals. Overwhelmed by duties it didn't consider part of its original mandate, the SPCA pressed for the establishment of an organization to deal solely with the needs of children.

Under that pressure, the Children's Aid Society came into being through the efforts of Judge R.H. Murray, Secretary and Solicitor of the SPCA; and Ernest H. Blois, the first provincial Superintendent of Neglected and Delinquent Children.

Yet for all this impressive outpouring of the milk of late nineteenth-century human kindness, one group remained untouched by the flow: Nova Scotia's black population.

Scattered and segregated, the people of the black communities had always relied on each other for support. The church and extended family provided the safety net to which those who needed help could resort. However, given the endemic poverty of those communities, situations beyond the capacity of their resources invariably arose. Parents died, accidents occurred, money ran out. Some families buckled and split apart under the duress exerted by racism and discrimination. One additional mouth to feed sometimes became one too many.

When unfortunate predicaments occurred, the children of black communities needed the same assistance that was readily available to their white counterparts in similar circumstances. However, for the majority of orphaned or abandoned black children, the doors to the Catholic and Protestant orphanages and industrial schools were slammed shut by the hand of segregation. In keeping with the tenor of the times, most social welfare institutions operated on a strict "whites only" basis.

The extended family provided a great deal of support for blacks in the early 1900s.
(Courtesy Public Archives of Nova Scotia.)

A black child in need who could not be cared for by relatives within the community faced the grim options of homelessness or placement in a poorhouse or adult mental asylum. Indeed, as a cost-cutting measure, some municipalities housed the indigent and the mentally ill under a single roof. Despite the good intentions behind the organization of the poorhouses, or "county homes" as they were sometimes called, most of them were unfit for human habitation, let alone the care and shelter of neglected children. And the mental institutions offered even worse circumstances.

Needless to say, such environments were far from conducive to the healthy development of children of any color. The fact that innocent boys and girls could be subjected to this type of treatment is a stark indication of the continued low esteem in which the black community was held—a holdover of the attitudes earlier expressed by Lord Dalhousie concerning the plight of the Black Refugees.

The need for an institution like the Home for Colored Children was urgent for education in general and the care of indigent minors in particular. Once again, the black community faced the same choice it had earlier confronted concerning religious and educational facilities: "Separate or nothing."

James R. Johnston refused to be satisfied with "nothing." If the doors to the white institutions were closed and barred, he believed it was up to the black community to establish an alternative of its own. A year after Johnston tabled his plan for a black industrial school, an important ally arrived to stand by his side.

A Pastor's Cause

In 1909, Reverend Moses B. Puryear emigrated from Harrisburg, Pennsylvania, to become pastor of the Cornwallis Street Baptist Church in Halifax. Rev. Puryear was an activist minister, deeply committed to community development. He was also an adherent to the Booker T. Washington doctrine of practical, industrial education as the best vehicle for black progress. And he was familiar with Hampton Institute, the model Johnston had chosen for his own proposal.

In Rev. Puryear, Johnston found a natural partner and supporter for the hard work necessary to lay the ideological and physical foundations for the most ambitious project black Nova Scotians had attempted to date. The resources of the black community, meager though they were, needed to be mobilized. And, despite the tradition of self-reliance blacks had developed out of necessity, assistance from outside the community had to be solicited.

Over the next five years, Johnston and Rev. Puryear worked tirelessly toward the fulfillment of their common goal. In the meantime, the need for the proposed institute became more acute, as the following contemporary account indicates:

Back in the spring of 1913, a colored mother died, leaving an infant child, and a husband who was on the high seas. Few friends did this little Mother have, and, after vainly trying, there seemed to be no Institution that would receive this motherless Colored Baby. When it became known, many of the best citizens of Halifax became thoughtful and asked questions.

In the following year another mother died, leaving a large family, and a husband that did not seem to care. Again a place was sought for the children, and no door could be opened for them, because of their color, but the Poor House, known as the City Home. This did not seem just a proper place for the rearing of children...all efforts to overcome this condition were of no avail.

In another case that occurred in 1914, a black baby named Arthur MacDougal Scott was born in the Victoria General Hospital in Halifax. Within a few days of the birth, Baby Arthur's mother died of diphtheria. No relative came to claim him, and none of Nova Scotia's Protestant orphanages would agree to take him in. Later, a Catholic institution agreed to accept him. Baby Arthur died before his first birthday.

Sadly, cases like these were far from unusual, and they underscored an urgent need. Later in 1914, Johnston and Rev. Puryear received permission to present their particulars for the proposed institute to the Nova Scotia legislature, which tabled the matter for further discussion.

Rev. Puryear also called a meeting at the Halifax Board of Trade chambers to gather support from all Nova Scotians for the new institute, which would function as both an industrial training school and a shelter for orphaned and abandoned children. As a result of that meeting, the proposal gathered a great deal of momentum.

Early in 1915 a stunning setback occurred when Johnston was murdered by his brother-in-law during a family dispute on March 3. At Johnston's funeral, the streets between the Cornwallis Street Baptist Church and Camp Hill Cemetery were lined with mourners of both races. The procession included members of the Nova Scotia Barristers' Society and the AUBA, symbolizing the two principal concerns of his life.

Despite the untimely death of a man who was potentially the greatest black Nova Scotian leader since Richard Preston, the drive to establish the institute he had conceived went on. The fulfillment of Johnston's dream came to be seen as the best possible tribute to his memory.

Now the burden fell squarely on the shoulders of Moses Puryear. And those shoulders proved far from wanting. A committee was formed to petition the government to incorporate the institute. Members of the committee included Rev. Puryear, J.A.R Kinney, W.F. de Costa, Robert H. Murray, Ernest H. Blois, Henry G. Bauld and H.V. Weir.

A month after Johnston's death, the Nova Scotia Legislative Assembly passed an Act to incorporate "The Nova Scotia Home for Colored Children." Section 2 of the Act empowered the Home to:

> *purchase, take and hold real and personal estate and may sell, convey, lease, mortgage or otherwise dispose of same, and may invest any money that may come into their hands for the use and benefit of the said corporation, as may be deemed advantageous to the said corporation, for the purpose of securing and selecting and establishing lands and buildings for the care, education, and training of the members of the Afro-American race.*

The legislation also enabled the proposed Home to act as a children's aid society "for matters affecting the children of the coloured race, and to receive and keep the same under their care pursuant to the provisions of the 'Children's Protection Act, 1912'."

Having obtained official provincial blessing, Puryear's next step was to bring the matter of the institute to the AUBA once again, this time at its annual convention in September. During the course of the convention, the following resolution was adopted:

> WHEREAS *there is no institution for the Industrial, Domestic and Business training of our young men and women;*
>
>   AND WHEREAS *it is the duty of the Race to produce its own leaders who shall be architects to carve our place in Western Civilization;* THEREFORE BE IT RESOLVED *that we, the African United Baptist Association, endorse, by moral and financial aid, the proposed institution to be known as the Industrial School of Nova Scotia for Coloured Children.*

This resolution marked a major step forward from the AUBA's 1908 endorsement of Johnston's initial idea. At that time, the AUBA had only accepted in principle the idea of an industrial school for Nova Scotian blacks. Now the most influential organization in the black community had decided to commit its time, energy and money to transform the idea into reality.

Two more years of groundwork were needed, years during which the First World War raged in Europe, with its attendant diversion of manpower and resources. Many black Nova Scotians served in the No. 2 Construction Battalion, a military unit formed in response to blacks' insistence upon being allowed to serve their country despite persistent efforts to prevent them from doing so.

The unit's contribution to Canada went unrecognized until July 1993, when a memorial plaque was unveiled at the site of its old headquarters in Pictou, Nova Scotia.

On October 12, 1917, the Home received its first Board of Trustees. The President was Henry G. Bauld, with R.H. Murray as Secretary and G.R. Hart as Treasurer. Other members included Rev. Puryear, Ernest H. Blois, C. Strickland, Charles Coleman Blackadar, John Murphy, Thomas P. Johnson and J.A.R. Kinney.

The Home's Board was one of the first interracial directorates ever to operate in the province. Rev. Puryear, Kinney and Johnson were the black members. Kinney was an employee of Wm. Stairs, Son and Morrow, Ltd., a ship chandlery company with interests in forestry and mining. Johnson, county councillor from Preston, was the first black elected official in Nova Scotia.

The rest of the Board members were white. Some had previously served on the committee that had asked the government to incorporate the Home. Blackadar owned the *Acadian Recorder*, a Halifax newspaper, and had previously been involved in charitable activities such as the Home for Aged Men and the Anti-Tuberculosis League. Murphy and Strickland were bank managers.

Once the Board was formed, events began to accelerate. The Trustees' first task was to locate a site for the institute. Eventually they selected a vacant building owned by the Halifax Industrial Boys School in the North End of the city. Well aware of the considerable expenses involved in renovating and equipping the structure, which was little more than a cottage, the Trustees approached Halifax City Council with a request for a $500 grant.

In a letter to Council dated October 29, 1917, the Board provided the following summary of its efforts to date:

We have been fortunate in securing a most desirable building, belonging to the Industrial School, on most generous terms. The building is conveniently located, and surrounded with very attractive grounds. We have also been fortunate in getting in touch with a matron who comes very highly recommended to undertake this work.

The Halifax Board of Control acted quickly and submitted its recommendation to City Council on November 1:

The Board of Control submit herewith a report from Controller Murphy recommending a grant from the City of $500.00 towards a home for neglected coloured children. The recommendation is unanimously submitted to the City Council for approval with the amendment in place of the suggestion that the amount be included in next year's estimates, that the City Solicitor be instructed to draft legislation empowering the City to make such a grant.

On November 8, City Council approved the grant. Further contributions to the preparation of the building included $100 from Wm. Stairs, Son and Morrow, Ltd. and $25 came from black businessman George Roache.

The prospective matron to whom the Trustees' letter to City Council referred was Miss Julia Jackson, a Philadelphian recruited by Rev. Puryear. Miss Jackson came to Halifax on November 15, a week after the city's grant was finalized. Her qualifications for the position were excellent, and great enthusiasm greeted her arrival.

At a reception held in her honor at the Cornwallis Street Baptist Church, Miss Jackson spoke at length about the impact the newly formed institute would have on the present and future development of neglected, destitute and orphaned black children. She was certain the Home would produce children capable of occupying meaningful and prosperous positions in the black community and in society as a whole. These opinions echoed those of the AUBA in its 1915 resolution, as well as the guiding principles of Johnston and Rev. Puryear.

A November 17 article in the *Halifax Evening Mail* stated that Miss Jackson was very impressed by the sympathetic attitudes of the prominent citizens of Halifax. Miss Jackson also placed emphasis on the importance of aid from concerned citizens of the immediate and neighboring areas.

By the first week of December the Home was ready for its official opening. The building was secure, its Matron was in place and public support was high. Then a disaster of epic proportions struck the city of Halifax.

From the time of its founding, Halifax had been a major seaport for commercial and military shipping. In the midst of the First World War, the presence of naval craft carrying live ammunition in Halifax Harbor was natural and expected. Standard safety measures prevailed. But on December 6, all precautions came to naught when the French munitions ship *Mont Blanc* collided with a Belgian relief freighter, the *Imo*.

In the resulting explosion, the North End of Halifax and parts of neighboring Dartmouth and Bedford were flattened, leaving thousands of people dead or injured. The sheer force of the Halifax Explosion remained unmatched by any other manmade blast until the first atomic bomb was detonated during the Second World War, twenty-eight years later.

One of the casualties of the disaster was the little cottage in the North End that was about to become the Home for Colored Children. With her prospective place of employment now a shattered ruin, Julia Jackson returned to Philadelphia, lucky to be alive to tell her story. Had the Home been opened only a few weeks earlier, Miss Jackson and the children who may have been under her care would certainly have been among the dead and wounded.

Four years of regrouping and rebuilding would be needed before James Johnston's dream became a reality.

A Change in Vision

The Explosion caused such tremendous damage and destruction in Halifax that the number of homeless residents skyrocketed. Families disintegrated, children wandered aimlessly through rubble-filled streets, and the jails, mental hospitals and poorhouses were pressed into service to provide shelter for a traumatized population. The capacity of those facilities soon surpassed their breaking point. The need for immediate relief was acute.

To assess the predicament of the city's children, a committee of prominent citizens was formed. Its chairmanship fell to Ernest Blois, who was still superintendent of neglected and delinquent children. As mentioned in Janet F. Kitz's book on the Explosion, *Shattered City*, the committee believed that "'Coloured or feeble-minded orphans' constituted a special problem that would have to be dealt with."

In the wake of the disaster, the idea of an institution to provide for the educational needs of black youth dropped further down the list of the province's priorities. Still, the Home's Board of Trustees held a series of emergency consultations to assess the damage and plan ahead.

As early as December 19, the Board appointed a committee consisting of H.G. Bauld, J.A.R. Kinney and R.H. Murray to meet with Premier G.H. Murray. The purpose of the meeting was to discuss future plans for the Home and a possible relocation.

Because of a concentration of black families in the North End, the Explosion had dramatically increased the number of black children in need of shelter and care. Even if the original facility were rebuilt, it would be much too small to fulfill the increased demand for its services.

Accordingly, Premier Murray instructed the committee to seek a larger site, preferably in a farming area, and to report back once a suitable property had been found. That process took slightly more than a year to complete.

In the meantime a serious rift had developed among the Trustees. Rev. Puryear had always viewed the institute primarily as an educational alternative, a training ground for future generations of productive citizens who would uplift the black community. Although Rev. Puryear was certainly not one to turn a blind eye to the plight of parentless children, he viewed the care and shelter of such children as a secondary function of the institution. Practical education that would provide marketable skills was the primary goal.

That vision had been shared by James Johnston and had motivated the effort that had resulted in the cottage and the high hopes the Explosion had obliterated. Now the Trustees were leaning more toward an emphasis on shelter rather than education, with the Home becoming an orphanage rather than a normal and industrial institute. And that was a shift in direction Moses Puryear could not in good conscience abide.

Unable or unwilling to compromise his principles, Rev. Puryear submitted his resignation as pastor of the Cornwallis Street Church in 1918, ending an eventful nine-year ministry. He returned to the United States and died four years later in Germantown, Pennsylvania, which was then a suburb of Philadelphia.

The two leading forces in the quest to establish the Home had now departed, one through death, the other through disappointment. In the years following the tragedy of the Explosion, two new leaders—J.A.R. Kinney and H.G. Bauld—stepped forward to guide the Home along a different route from the one James Johnston had conceived.

Facing page - The 1919-1920 Executive Committee for the AUBA included three men instrumental in the establishment of the Home: J.A.R. Kinney (back left), Thomas Johnson (front left), and Rev. A.A. Wyse (front middle). The others are Rev. W.N. States (back right) and Rev. W.A. White (front right).

Kinney and Bauld

In her book *A Brief History of the Colored Baptists of Nova Scotia*, Pearleen Oliver described James Alexander Ross Kinney as "perhaps the most outstanding layman ever to enter our work." The work to which she referred involved the AUBA and the Home for Colored Children, with which the Kinney name will forever be associated.

Born in Yarmouth, Nova Scotia, in 1878, Kinney moved with his parents, James and Charlotte, to Halifax two years later. Like Johnston, young Kinney journeyed successfully through the city's public education system. In 1897 he became the first black graduate of the Maritime Business College. Immediately upon graduation, Kinney was hired as advertising manager by the Wm. Stairs, Son & Morrow company. He would hold that position for the next twenty-six years.

Kinney was also active in the affairs of the Cornwallis Street Baptist Church, which he joined at the age of 14. Within the church, he served as

accountant and head of the Efficiency Committee and he also served two terms as Clerk of the AUBA. It was through his church activity that Kinney became involved in the long and difficult process of establishing the Home. He served on all the committees and delegations that existed before and after the Explosion, and was also a member of the original Board of Trustees.

When Rev. Puryear departed, the burden of leadership passed to Kinney, and he accepted it whole-heartedly. Although Kinney was not as unbending on the concept of practical education as Rev. Puryear, he held similar views concerning the need for black progress and advancement.

Henry Gibson Bauld, first NSHCC Board President.

In a speech Kinney delivered at the AUBA's convention in September 1918, he summed up his social philosophy: "I will in all these ways aim to uplift my race, so that to everyone bound to it by ties of blood, it shall become a bond of ennoblement, and not a byword of reproach." Kinney practiced what he preached. The *Sunday Leader*, a Halifax newspaper, referred to him as the "King Pin" and "live wire" of the black community. And he was never afraid to confront the establishment.

A 1916 newspaper article recounts a showdown between the Halifax Board of Control and a delegation from the Afro-Canadian Improvement League that consisted of E.L. Cross, Rev. J.P. Stevens and Kinney. The delegation presented the Board with a protest relating to a sign at a market building that read: "For Colored People Only—Free Lunch Today."

Kinney "claimed that it was a discrimination against colored citizens, and should not be exhibited in the citizens' public market." The Mayor said the sign had been "put up without his orders" and he assured the delegation "it would not happen again."

That incident was an impressive example of the clout Kinney wielded. It's doubtful many other North American blacks of the early 1900s—a time when most blacks found it more prudent to be neither seen nor heard—could have pried this kind of public apology from a white mayor.

For all his pride and passion, however, Kinney did not stand alone in his efforts to organize the Home. By his side stood Henry Gibson Bauld, a prominent Halifax businessman and Liberal provincial legislator.

Bauld had succeeded his father, William, in the management of a wholesale grocery firm called Bauld Gibson and Company, later known as Bauld Brothers. His association with the Home began with the committee that petitioned the government to incorporate the Home in 1915. In 1917 he was elected president of the Home's Board of Trustees, a position he would hold for the next thirty-three years.

The relationship between Bauld and Kinney was one of friends and equals, not mentor and subordinate as was usually the case between whites and blacks at that time. Bauld recognized Kinney's abilities as an administrator and fund-raiser, and Kinney in turn accepted Bauld's unbiased commitment to the Home. When Kinney passed away in 1940, Bauld paid him the following tribute: "A finer character could not, in my opinion, be found in Nova Scotia."

This mutual respect formed the cornerstone of a building and fund-raising campaign unprecedented in the history of the province.

The Groundwork is Laid

The establishment of the new Home presented a much greater challenge than had the purchase of the now-demolished cottage in North End Halifax. Land had to be located and bought, a building had to be erected, staff had to be hired. The provincial government had agreed to purchase a suitable property, but the rest was the responsibility of the Trustees and the community, black and white alike.

In early February 1919, Reverend Arthur A. Wyse, pastor of the Preston–Cherry Brook Baptist churches, informed the Board that a property near the Preston Road was available. Rev. Wyse, a native of Lake Loon, Nova Scotia, had served as a Licentiate preacher for twenty-two years before becoming ordained in 1915. He lived to an advanced age and in 1951 he officiated at the baptizing of sixty-five candidates from Cherry Brook, a record for the largest single baptism ever held in the AUBA.

The site, known as the MacKenzie property, consisted of 211 acres of farmland, of which twenty-five were already arable. It was located about six miles from Dartmouth and was close to the largest concentration of blacks in the province.

The government dispatched a representative named Daniel A. Moser to determine the suitability of the site. Liking what he saw, Moser secured an option to purchase the property. With Premier Murray's approval, the land was bought and deeded to the Home.

Rev. Arthur A. Wyse.
(Courtesy Black Cultural Centre for Nova Scotia)

With the purchase of the land, the first major hurdle had been cleared. Many more would follow.

Ernest Blois, who was the provincial Director of Child Welfare and a member of the Home's Board of Trustees, consulted closely with an architect named B.J. Patterson in the design of the facility. Kinney, whose efforts on behalf of the Home were tireless and persistent, was another design consultant.

In the meantime, a comprehensive, province-wide fund-raising campaign began under the leadership of Kinney, Rev. Wyse and prominent members of the Halifax business community. Kinney began by securing a pledge from the AUBA to donate projected contributions of $200 to the Home Fund. The Association's member churches were also urged to solicit collections on an individual basis. The ties between the AUBA and the Home became so strong that a report from the Home is to this day a regular part of the Association's annual meeting.

Black financing for the Home also flowed in from bake sales, rummage sales and sales of quilts and other crafts. Every contribution, however great or small, was accepted by Kinney's canvassers.

Significant support from leaders of the white community was forthcoming as well. Among others, Lieutenant-Governor MacCallum Grant,

Premier Murray and his successor, Acting Premier E.H. Armstrong, Senator William Dennis and Halifax Mayor John S. Parker provided moral patronage and practical advice.

Advertising for the Home Fund circulated throughout the province's media and trade publications. Mayor Parker issued the following appeal, dated August 22, 1919, under the headline "Let Us All Chip in And Give the Fund For The Colored Children A Boost":

> FELLOW CITIZENS: *The people of Halifax have always shown a hearty interest in every worthy cause that has presented itself. Do not let the colored citizens feel we are not interested in them. Laying aside all other considerations, let us realize that little lives are at stake.*
>
> *There is a crying need at this time for the establishment of such a Home. It will settle city and town problems throughout Nova Scotia—it will arrest misunderstandings, and do for a portion of our fellow-citizens what they are unable to do for themselves.*

Church fund-raising poster for the NSHCC.

WE ASK YOUR HELP

It will be no Burden to Raise the $5000 Needed by the Nova Scotia Home for Colored Children. If Each Christian Man or Women in this Province who can Afford it Will Mail to us Immediately $1.00, $2.00 or $5.00

Believing that we will find the greatest human interest and sympathy among the 200,000 Christians of the Maritime Provinces we are making our appeal for funds to the Baptists, Methodists Episcopalians and Presbyterians through the medium of their own Church Paper.

The great need for this Institution was the urge that caused us to open last year before sufficient funds were raised to finish the building and equip it, but we have been well repaid by the results accomplished in caring for the 20 little ones that have come to us during the year.

The Nova Scotia Home for Neglected and Orphan Colored Children is a Worthy Charity

which can be placed alongside of all other Welfare Work, it is supervised by the Government, and directed by a competent Board of Management. The Nova Scotia Home for Colored Children may be regarded as a home Mission effort in which all Christians can share with a feeling of mutual interest, as this Institution is undenominational.

The Nova Scotia Home For Colored Children Needs $5000

IF 5,000 of the 200,000 members of the Christian churches would mail to us $1.00 the amount would be raised, or 2,500 of the 200,000 would give $2.00, or 1,000 of the 200,000 would give $5.00.

WHAT WILL YOU GIVE?   **Please Act Quickly**   **MAIL YOUR GIFT TODAY**

ADDRESS ALL CORRESPONDENCE TO JAS. A. R. KINNEY, Secretary, 42 Kings Place, Halifax, N. S. REMIT BY EXPRESS M. O., P. O. ORDER OR CHEQUE, MADE PAYABLE TO A. B. MITCHELL, Treas.

ALL MONIES WILL BE THANKFULLY RECEIVED AND PROMPTLY ACKNOWLEDGED

HENRY G. BAULD, M. P. P., President.   A .B. MITCHELL, Treasurer.   JAS. A. R. KINNEY, Secretary.

The merit of the effort cannot be gainsaid. This has been recognized by many of our best citizens as reflected in the handsome gifts they have made.

The Home must be built. Ten thousand dollars must be raised. Let everyone chip in something, whether large or small, and make up the amount quickly.

Above - John Parker, Halifax Alderman and Mayor. As Mayor, Parker was an enthusiastic fund-raiser for the NSHCC.
(Courtesy Public Archives of Nova Scotia)

Facing page - NSHCC fund-raising poster showing a white child.

In other advertisements and circulars, Mayor Parker reminded citizens that "our gifts are sent to Asia, Africa, and the Isles of the Sea, while right AT HOME we have an object to subscribe to. Now it's the Colored Children's turn."

One poster, asking "Every Christian Church in the City and Throughout the Province" to help raise $25,000 for the Home, hedged its bets. Along with a line drawing that showed what the building would look like upon completion, it displayed a photo of a white infant.

Despite a tinge of paternalism consistent with the social climate of the early 1920s, the appeals touched a sense of fair play that had previously been conspicuously absent in Nova Scotia's race relations.

The "Colored Children's turn" had indeed come. But they would take that turn in an institution separate from those that accommodated whites.

At the AUBA's annual meeting in September 1920, a truly impressive report on the progress of the Home project was read. The building was already under construction, and a total of $40,000 had been raised, $1,000 of which was guaranteed by the AUBA itself. Only $350 of that guarantee had been met thus far, but the fund-raisers were confident the rest would be made up soon. An ambitious plan to raise $2,000 per year from the black communities for the Home's upkeep was put forward as well.

Much of the labor involved in the construction of the Home was provided by residents of North Preston, East Preston, Cherry Brook and Lake Loon. They felled trees and dug up stumps so the foundation of the building could be laid. With their own hands, they excavated the foundation

"THEREFORE BE IT RESOLVED..."

Every Christian Church In the City and Throughout the Province Is Invited and Urged To Take Up a Collection To Help Raise

$25,000

For the Home for Colored Orphan and Neglected Children.

"As ye did it unto the least of these, ye did it unto me,"

are familiar words of the Great Nazarene.

The Institution is undenominational. Any child sent by the Superintendent of Neglected and Delinquent Children for the Province, or by a Children's Aid Society will be received.

$25,000 IS THE SUM REQUIRED TO PROVIDE THE BUILDING AND THE NECESSARY EQUIPMENT, AND FOR THIS WORTHY CAUSE WE ASK YOUR GENEROUS SUPPORT.

A CHEQUE FROM YOU WILL MAKE HIM RICHER, AND WILL NOT IMPOVERISH YOU.

Please mail to Mr. George R. Hart, Treasurer, 30 Kent Street, Halifax.

The Campaign Committee For The Home For Orphan and Neglected Children

JAMES A. R. KINNEY, ROOM 5, CITY HALL.

Phone Sackville 3144.

Martha Harris, Matron at the time of the Home's opening.

and mixed and poured cement for the walls and footings, and they made many of the interior fixtures and furnishings. Using skills handed down from Loyalist and Refugee ancestors, the community completed an endeavor that would have filled their ancestors' hearts with pride.

The final blueprints for the building were prepared by George A. Ross and Robert H. MacDonald, the architects who planned much of the rebuilding of Halifax after the Explosion.

Donations from outside the community were also helpful. For example, bedding, linen and other furnishings were generously supplied by the Nova Scotia Furnishing Company of Halifax.

Another method of raising funds was "bed endowments," through which a group or individual could sponsor a bed at the Home for a minimum of $40. A pamphlet published after the opening listed the following "bed endowment" donors from the black and white communities:

> *J.J. Scrivens & Sons; Mahons Limited; Chronicle Publishing Co.; Alderman Johns Murphy; Mr. & Mrs. D.M. Owen; Citizens of Halifax, White; Citizens of Halifax, Colored; Carmania Lodge; I.O.G.T., New Glasgow; Zion Church, Truro; Zion A.M.E. Church, Halifax; Cornwallis Street African Baptist Church, Halifax; Victoria Road A.B. Church, Dartmouth; Cherrybrook A.B. Church; Hammonds Plains A.B. Church; Inglewood A.B. Church; Gibsons Woods A.B. Church; Preston East A.B. Church; No. 2 Construction Battalion, Yarmouth Boys.*

As the year 1921 began, the imminent opening of the Home became a highly anticipated event throughout the province. As a January 15 newspaper article put it:

> *The Nova Scotia Home for Colored Children, six miles out from Dartmouth, on the Preston Road, is about completed, and will very soon be handed over for occupation.*

The colored people of this city, and the province generally, are to be congratulated on the establishment of this splendid institution, which so soon shall enter upon its career of philanthropic usefulness and which will help to round off the circle of such agencies for good work and benevolence in Nova Scotia.

By March, sufficient construction had been completed to allow the Home to open on an unofficial basis. The Trustees hired a new Matron, Mrs. Martha Harris of New York City, who had been recommended by the Russell Sage Foundation.

Born in Hamilton, Ontario, Mrs. Harris was a graduate of the Hamilton Collegiate Institute and the Lincoln Hospital in New York. Not only was she a registered nurse, she also possessed experience as a social worker for the New York Urban League, which had recommended her for the Colored Home position. Prior to her arrival in Nova Scotia, she had supervised a convalescent home in White Plains, New York.

Although the official opening of the Home was not scheduled until June 6, Mrs. Harris began taking in urgent cases soon after her arrival in Nova Scotia. By opening day, twelve children were already under her care.

The Home's work had begun quietly. But its formal inauguration would be an historic event, complete with all the pageantry and ceremony such an occurrence deserved. As the front-page headline of the June 8 *Sunday Leader* newspaper proclaimed:

The Formal Opening by Lieutenant Governor Grant Was an Epoch Making Day For The Colored Race of the Maritimes—It Betokened a Bond of Sympathy Rare on This Continent

The "Greatest Day"

The formal opening of the Home coincided with the second convention of the Congress of Nova Scotia Colored Women, to be held at the Victoria Road Baptist Church in Dartmouth. Ladies from black communities throughout the province were expected to attend the event.

Invitation from The Trustees of the Nova Scotia Home for Colored Children

Invitation to the Home's official opening.

A year earlier, the province had hosted a Canada-wide Congress of Colored Women, the first such gathering in the nation's history. The current one, however, would focus on provincial concerns. Both congresses were sponsored by the AUBA's Ladies Auxiliary, an organization that began four years earlier at the famous "Meeting at the Well" in East Preston, when Mrs. C.S. McLearn gathered the first group of women ever to attend an Associational assembly.

The AUBA Ladies Auxiliary had also worked tirelessly to raise funds for the Home. A Ladies Auxiliary for the Home was also established prior to the informal opening. The founding executive included Mrs. James A.R. Kinney, President; Mrs. Wellington N. States, Vice President; Mrs. Maggie Upshaw, Secretary; Mrs. Joseph H. Saunders, Treasurer; and Mrs. Bessie Davidson, Assistant Secretary. Mrs. Davidson was elected in place of the original holder of the office, a Mrs. Lindsay. Most of the women in the Home's Auxiliary were also members of the AUBA's counterpart.

A 1921 newspaper report credits the Ladies Auxiliary as being "instrumental in making the tag day concerts and opening ceremony on June 6 such a success." The report went on to say: "During the coming year these ladies will co-operate with the Board of Directors to make the home carry out its intended functions."

```
PROGRAMME
GRAND MAY FAIR
In Aid Of
THE NOVA SCOTIA HOME FOR COLORED CHILDREN
DISTINGUISHED PATRONAGE
Trinity Hall, Cogswell Street, May 1 to 6, 1922
Under the Auspices of
THE LADIES' AUXILIARY FOR THE HOME
Tea served daily from 5 to 7 p.m.    Refreshments 5 to 10.30
```

The Home's Ladies' Auxiliary was instrumental in fund-raising efforts.

Between the Colored Women's Congress and the opening of the Home, the weekend of June 4-7 promised to be highly eventful. And it fully lived up to that promise.

On the fourth, which fell on a Saturday, the cities of Halifax and Dartmouth held a Tag Day to help raise the additional $2,000 needed to "clean off all charges outstanding, and commence a worthy activity free of debt," according to a contemporary newspaper report.

The next day, Reverend Wellington N. States of the Victoria Road Church preached a stirring sermon to the delegates of the Colored Women's Congress. That Sunday also featured gospel music concerts by a choir consisting of "the pick of the finest colored singers of Nova Scotia." The choir performed at the Casino Theatre in Halifax and the St. James Presbyterian Church in Dartmouth, and the songs on its programme included: "I Will Extol Thee," "Ethiopia," "Awakening" and "A Song of Victory." A "silver offering" of 25 cents for the Home Fund was collected at both venues.

Finally, on the afternoon of June 6, a moment that had been thirteen years in the making came to pass. At approximately 2:30 p.m., a crowd the *Halifax Herald* estimated at 3,000 gathered at Knox's Farm for a procession that would march three-quarters of a mile to the grounds of the Home. It was the largest single assembly of blacks in Nova Scotia since the arrival of the Loyalists back in 1783. A substantial number of whites also attended the ceremony, providing an unprecedented show of support for an undertaking by their black neighbors.

Well before the time the ceremony was to begin, the roads leading to the Preston area were jammed with travellers of both races. Although it cost 50 cents to travel from Dartmouth to the Knox Farm, Bauld Brothers, Ltd. provided free transportation in its motor trucks.

At 3:00, Private Arthur Wyse, son of Rev. A.A. Wyse and Grand Marshal of the procession, led the march to the Home. Behind him marched the Salvation Army Band, followed by the executive of the African United Baptist Association and the local Masonic order. The Fife

The Home as it appeared on Opening Day, June 6, 1921. Photo attributed to Nova Scotia folklorist Helen Creighton.
(Courtesy Public Archives of Nova Scotia)

Facing page - Various photos from Opening Day.
(Courtesy Public Archives of Nova Scotia)

and Drum Band of the Industrial School also participated.

Then came a succession of carriages containing dignitaries such as Lt. Governor Grant; Acting Premier E.H. Armstrong; Mayors John Parker of Halifax and I.W. Vidito of Dartmouth; C.C Blackadar of the Home's Board of Directors; Rev. M.P. Montgomery, moderator of the Baptist Association; and Rev. C.A. Stewart, Presiding Elder of the African Methodist Episcopal (A.M.E.) Church.

The Boy Scouts and Girl Guides of the A.M.E. provided an honor guard as the procession arrived at the stage that had been built for the speakers and the musical performers.

Sacred music consecrated the opening of the Home, with songs performed by a select choir that had helped to raise funds just the day before. A final "jubilee" was sung by a special chorus of elders of "seventy and eighty years of life." These elders were the grandchildren of the Black Refugees and the great-grandchildren of the Black Loyalists—truly a living link to their community's origins and a bridge between the generations.

Then the speeches began, with H.G. Bauld acting as master of ceremonies. Scriptures and prayers were read by Reverends J.W.A. Nicholson and A.A. Wyse. The Lieutenant-Governor officially declared the Home to be open and emphasized the tremendous needs for which it was now responsible. He also acknowledged the hard work and dedication displayed by all the individuals who had been instrumental in the funding and establishment of the Home.

Acting Premier E.H. Armstrong stated that the Home was the first of its kind in Canada, and that Nova Scotia had thus posed a challenge to other provinces to provide similar facilities for needy black children.

Other speakers included Halifax Mayor Parker; Dartmouth Mayor Vidito; Rev. E.S. Mason, Superintendent of the Baptist Home Missions of Wolfville, Nova Scotia; C.C. Blackadar; and Rev. Montgomery, President of the African Association.

All the speakers underscored the importance of the occasion. However, it was the eloquence of J.A.R. Kinney, then Secretary of the Board of Directors, that came closest to capturing the day's true meaning when he called it "the greatest event in the history of the colored people of Nova Scotia."

Others agreed, although for different reasons. Under the headline "IDEAL HOME FOR COLORED CHILDREN OF NOVA SCOTIA," the *Church Echo* newspaper made the following observation:

To the little bright-eyed, curly-haired children, now inmates of the Home, it was certainly a day long to be remembered, for in the years to come they

"THEREFORE BE IT RESOLVED…"

THE SUNDAY LEADER

HALIFAX, SUNDAY, JULY 10, 1921

Panorama View of Nyasa Southern at the Formal Opening of the Colored Orphans Home Near Preston

Mrs. Martha G. Harris, Matron, and Miss Agatha Murphy of the Staff of the Colored Orphans' Home Recently Opened Near Preston

The Girl Guides of Zion African Methodist Episcopal Church who, with the Boy Scouts, Acted as a Guard of Honor at the Formal Opening of the Colored Orphans' Home

The Nova Scotia Home for Colored Orphans, Near Preston, Halifax County, Which Was Formally Opened June 6th by His Honor Lieut.-Governor Grant of Nova Scotia, the First Institution of its Kind in All Canada

Facing page - Poster advertising fund-raising concert for the NSHCC.

will tell about the great Governor of the Province who shook hands with them, patted them on the head, and smiled and spoke kindly to them.

A concert by the Salvation Army Band followed the speeches, and the Ladies Auxiliary served refreshments from a large booth constructed for that purpose. The programme ended with more gospel music in an unfinished wing of the building. Three hundred people stayed on to continue the celebration.

In the final hour of daylight, the last participants made their way back to their homes and farms or rode to the ferry terminal in Bauld Brothers trucks, satisfied that they had been part of a milestone event in the history of the province.

The next day, the Colored Women's Congress convened at the Victoria Road Church. Papers were presented on topics such as "Woman's Worth," "A New Day," "Home Influence" and "Woman's Part in the Progress and Development of the Race."

Martha Harris, Matron of the Home, read a paper on the practical topic of "Sanitation and Hygiene." Unfortunately, she did not get the chance to implement her ideas. Only a few days after the Home's official inauguration, Mrs. Harris was forced to resign her position because of health problems.

Her departure foreshadowed the many ups and downs the Nova Scotia Home for Colored Children would face throughout its existence.

"THEREFORE BE IT RESOLVED..."

CASINO
THEATRE GOTTINGEN ST.

TOMORROW

SUNDAY
4 p. m.

A High Class Sacred Concert by 50 Selected Singers From the Choirs of the Principal Colored Churches in Nova Scotia.

Beautiful Sacred Anthems, Solos, Duets, Quartets—deeply spiritual renditions by voices noted for richness and harmony.

Held In Connection With the Opening of the Nova Scotia Home For Colored Children.

A Silver Offering of 25c Will Be Accepted

Programme

1. Anthem—"I Will Extol Thee."
   Combined Choirs
2. Solo—Selected.
   Mrs. (Rev.) W. N. States
3. Anthem—"Exalt Him."
   Truro Choir
4. Solo—Selected.
   Mrs. (Rev.) W. C. Perry
5. Number—"Ethiopia."
   Zion A. M. E. Choir
6. Chorus—"Onward Christian Soldiers."
   Combined Choirs
7. Quartette—Selected.
   V. R. B. C.
8. Solo—Selected.
   Miss Louisa Byard
9. Chorus—"Awakening."
   Combined Choirs
10. Solo—"A Crown of Life."
    Mrs. W. M. Samuels
11. Number—"Forward."
12. Piano—"Nearer My God to Thee."
    Miss Todd
13. Solo—"Prayer Perfect"
    Miss M. V. Mallard
14. Chorus—"A Song of Victory."
    Combined Choirs

Pianist—Miss M. Symonds.

Violin—Mr. Chas. A. Allison.

Hymn for Portia White

the white bathing moon
    watches itself in the sea:
        all black and handsome.

George Elliott Clarke

Years of Consolidation 1921-1940

3

Setting Standards

The unexpected departure of Martha Harris was not the only difficulty the Home faced after its formal opening. Despite the best efforts of fundraisers from both the black and the white communities, the institution was still operating under the burden of a deficit.

The first problem was solved through the hiring of Mrs. Sadie Steen. Like Mrs. Harris, Mrs. Steen had graduated as a registered nurse from Lincoln Hospital in New York. She was a schoolteacher as well.

Unfortunately, the Home's financial problems were not so easily remedied, and the deficit continued through its first two decades of operation. The problem wasn't helped by the delay of some municipalities in making the payments needed to support the children they sent to the Home.

Not long after the opening, James

Sadie Steen, Matron of the NSHCC.

Kinney undertook the position of Superintendent of the Home. The post represented an addition to his other responsibilities as Secretary of the Board of Directors.

With characteristic energy and discipline, Kinney devoted himself to the development of the Home. In *A Brief History of the Colored Baptists of Nova Scotia*, Pearleen Oliver described him as a "perfectionist" who "struggled to bring everything and everyone with whom he worked up to his standards."

And his standards were high, both for himself and his community. The following quotation attributed to Kinney in a pamphlet published shortly after the formal opening of the Home summarizes his philosophy:

> *I ask you to help support the Home for Colored Orphans and Neglected Children because responsible citizenship entails duties and obligations as well as rights and privileges. When my race or any other group of the community demands equality of citizenship they must be prepared to render the same service that other citizens render. We must make our contribution toward the public good in some form or other just as the other members of the community do.*

Kinney's standards extended to the white community as well. When the Halifax School Board announced a plan to establish a separate school for blacks within the city on the pretext of relieving overcrowding, Kinney categorically denounced the notion in a letter to the editor of the *Halifax Evening Mail*. He took the School Board to task for advocating segregation, noting that the matter had been "decisively cleaned up by legal process" forty years earlier.

In 1884 the Nova Scotia House of Assembly had amended its education measures to provide that "colored pupils shall not be excluded from instruction in the public school in the section or ward in which they reside." The implication was that black children were not totally relegated to segregated instruction, and these pronouncements had enabled Kinney and James Johnston, among others, to attend predominantly white schools.

Kinney also pointed out the shortcomings of a segregated education system in general: "Educational authorities know quite well that colored schools in districts not a stone's throw from the city of Halifax have been without teachers for periods as long as two years, owing to lack of them." Far from the acquiescence many black leaders exhibited at that time, Kinney ended his argument on a confrontational note: "Be careful, gentlemen, how you proceed, for history records that wherever justice has been denied and duties evaded, retribution invariably follows."

Some may claim the position Kinney took in his letter was self-contradictory. After all, he represented an institution that was itself segregated. However, the Home was conceived as the best solution available to problems that originated in the segregation imposed by the majority; and in his letter, Kinney was reminding the majority that in the few instances in which the walls of segregation were torn down, they should not be put up again.

For all his unyielding diligence, high standards and perfectionism, there was another, softer side to J.A.R. Kinney, a side that emerged when he walked among the residents of the Home. His kindness and concern for the children in his charge were legendary. Despite his reputation as a hard-nosed businessman, he often dug deep into his own pocket to provide for the children's needs.

J.A.R. Kinney, NSHCC Superintendant, as he looked during the 1930s.
(Courtesy Nova Scotia Home for Colored Children)

By March 1922 the Home had received twenty children, of whom three had been discharged. In a pamphlet commemorating the informal opening, entitled: "On March 11, 1922, We Were One Year Old—Just A Crawling Infant," progress was reported, but also mentioned was the need for further work to expand the building and to engage a teaching staff that was "competent in all branches."

June 6 marked the formal first anniversary of the institution. The Home Grounds hosted appropriate Founders' Day ceremonies, including addresses by H.G. Bauld and

Reverends A.A. Wyse and W.A. White. Music during the day was provided by the boys of the Halifax Industrial School, and there was also an evening concert by the "Star colored troupe" and McNally's orchestra.

Some lighter moments also occurred, as the following newspaper account of a hiking competition reveals:

Only four men entered the hike from the Dartmouth post office to the front door of the Home, but it was one of the best hikes held hereabouts, and was won by Gordon Beals in one hour and ten minutes. The contestants, Gordon Beals, Henry Bundy, Harvey Beals, and Cecil Pleasant made a great race. At the King Street Baptist Church, Bundy took the lead of a yard, and he was closely followed by Gordon Beals and it was neck and neck practically for the six miles until Bundy took a lead at Knox's farm of about three yards, but was followed so closely by Beals that he fell exhausted by the Home gate, but picked himself up and staggered to the finishing line and received second prize. Harvey Beals beat out Cecil Pleasant after four miles, but the finish was close. The ladies race was won by Sarah Grant, second Maggie Walsh.

Nettie Martin Kinney, wife of J.A.R. Kinney.

By the fall of 1922, much of the construction mentioned in the Home's March publication had been completed. An "ell" containing new Matron's quarters, an eight-bed dormitory, a large sewing room and a bathroom had been added. The barn was relocated, new facilities for cattle were constructed, a carriage shed was built and the farmhouse that came with the property was renovated. Electric lighting was also installed.

However, the Matron, Mrs. Steen, tendered her resignation after only fifteen months of service and returned to New York on October 1. Mr. and Mrs. John Desmond, who had managed a farm at Tracadie, Nova Scotia, were hired as housekeeper and caretaker.

The Home had weathered its first year well. However, 1923 would be a time of changes: some positive, others unfortunate.

Tragedy struck James Kinney a double blow that year when his wife, Nettie Martin Kinney, and a young daughter named Edna both fell ill and passed away. With two surviving children—13-year-old J.A.R., Jr. and infant Dorothy—to care for, Kinney continued to commute daily between his family home in Halifax and his Home in Westphal. Ten years later, a cottage was built on the grounds of the Home as a residence for the Kinneys.

The year 1923 also marked the hiring of Mrs. Myrtle Elizabeth Fowler to replace Mrs. Steen as Matron. A native of New Glasgow, Nova Scotia, Mrs. Fowler resided in Halifax and was a member of the Cornwallis Street Church. Unlike her pre-decessors, the new Matron held her position for a remarkable thirty-one years. During much of that time, Lavinia Tolliver served as Assistant Matron.

Elizabeth "Nanny" Fowler, long-time NSHCC Matron.

Mrs. Fowler bore responsibility not only for the diet, clothing and medical care of the children; she was also in charge of domestic services and staff personnel. Beyond that, she served as the focal point for needs above and beyond the basics. She provided for those needs so well that she became known within the Home as "Nanny" Fowler.

Like Kinney, Mrs. Fowler was committed to the progress and advancement of her people. Although she is remembered as a strict disciplinarian, former Home resident Phyllis Lucas remembers a softer side.

Mrs. Lucas was brought to the Home from Saint John, New Brunswick, at age 12 in 1939. Her parents had both died, and social service authorities would not allow her grandmother to work and look after the child at the same time.

She recalls journeying from Saint John to Halifax with her social worker. James Bundy, the Home's driver, picked them up and drove them to the NSHCC. When she arrived, she didn't want to stay and began to shed tears when it became clear that she would not be going back to Saint John.

"Mrs. Fowler looked at the social worker and said, 'They cry when they come and they cry when they go,'" Mrs. Lucas recalls. "And then Mrs. McGee, my social worker, left. I was still crying, and I was taken into a sitting room, where there were other children. After a while, the other children were called to dinner, but I was told to stay. Being a child, I thought to myself, 'They must not feed you on the first day.'"

James Bundy, with grandson Wayne Bundy.
(Courtesy Frances Harper)

"What I didn't know was that Mrs. Fowler had arranged for me to eat in the staff room with the 'big girls.' So I did eat that day. But I still cried enough to fill a river."

Eventually, Mrs. Lucas became the Home's bookkeeper and worked closely with Mrs. Fowler.

"She was a kind woman, and she was good to me," she says. "She would sometimes use physical chastisement. But there is a difference between discipline and cruelty. Mrs. Fowler was never cruel."

Of her six-year stay at the NSHCC, Mrs. Lucas says: "It was a beneficial experience. I always say the best bread and butter I ever had was at the Home." After leaving the Home, Mrs. Lucas remained in Nova Scotia and now lives in Dartmouth.

James Kinney and Mrs. Fowler, along with H.G. Bauld, formed a partnership that guided the Home through its formative years and transformed negative attitudes concerning the ability of a black institution to care for its own children into positive ones.

Even so, the work of the staff should not be overlooked. Many of the child-care workers, who were women, and the farm hands and maintenance workers, who were men, took an active interest in the welfare of the children.

James Bundy's granddaughter, Frances Harper, remembers how her grandfather would come home from work every day down the Cherry Brook Lane. "He would always tell stories about what the 'little ones' did that day," she recalls. "He loved the children at the Home, and they loved him."

Bundy, who began working at the Home in 1921 and continued for forty-three years, was a versatile man. He served as organist and choir master for the Cherry Brook Baptist Church for forty-six years, and also played the organ for Sunday School classes at the NAHCC. His seventy-six years of life were filled with service to his community.

Daily Life

During its first two decades of operation, the Home often had to deal with as many as forty-five residents at a time, ranging in age from infants to teenagers. Thus, an orderly, disciplined routine was necessary for the well-being of the residents, who in the 1920s and 1930s were called "inmates." Although the word "inmate" is today associated with jails and prisons, at that time it was used to refer to residents of other types of institution as well and carried less of a stigma.

The building was designed to allow separate quarters for boys and girls, with the staff housed between those wings. Upper and lower dormitories, bathrooms and playrooms were provided for male and female residents, and, there was sleeping space for their supervisors. Each dormitory was 26 feet by 18 feet and slept sixteen. There was also a nursery for infants and toddlers. Kitchen and dining facilities completed the building's facilities.

As in most institutions, the daily routine at the Home was invariable. Every morning at seven o'clock the residents were awakened by the sound of a bell, which also alerted them to mealtimes. The boys and girls then washed, dressed, and assembled in the playroom. Before going to the dining room for breakfast, the children knelt beside the playroom benches to pray. Given the Home's close association with the AUBA and the importance of religion in the black community as a whole, it is not surprising that prayer played a large role in the children's routine.

After breakfast the children would attend the one-room school located on the Home's grounds. At first, instruction was given in the main building. Later, the original farmhouse was converted into a one-room school. Although this arrangement was a far cry from the Normal and Industrial Institute of which James Johnston and Moses Puryear had dreamed, it did provide basic education at the elementary school level.

At noon the children would return to the main building for dinner, which was accompanied by prayer. Then it was back to school again until three o'clock.

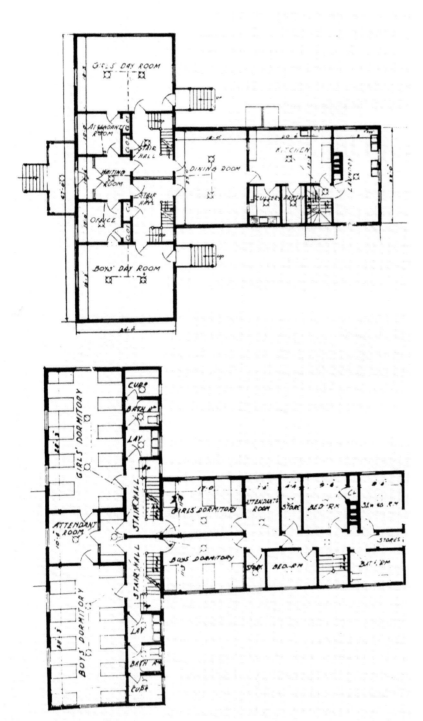

There was more to the children's days than school, however. Every resident old enough to work was assigned specific chores. It was hoped that training in practical manual skills would eventually become available to the boys; in the absence of that, their chores consisted of outdoor and farm labor—cutting wood, keeping up the crops and looking after the livestock. In a rural community, those were good skills to develop. The boys also helped with carpentry and maintenance.

The girls were responsible for the upkeep of the entire Home. Essentially, this responsibility provided on-the-job training for a career in domestic work, which was the only employment available for many black Nova Scotian women during the 1920s and 1930s.

The girls learned by doing. They scrubbed the floors in the playroom, kitchen and dining room daily, and those in the dormitories once a week. As well, they learned cooking, washing and sew

Floor plan of the NSHCC.

ing from staff members and other women hired for those purposes.

Along with their duties within the building, the Home's girls also performed outside chores. One of their jobs was grading and washing eggs and setting them in flats. They also helped the boys look after the farm animals. When they weren't doing these things, the girls could often be found shelling peas in the "camp," an open-sided, gazebo-style structure located on the grounds.

When school was over and the chores completed, the children would sit down to a supper accompanied by prayers and chants. After supper the older girls would tidy up the rooms and wash the dishes. Bedtime came at seven o'clock for the younger residents, and eight o'clock for the older ones.

Although the Home adhered to no specific religious denomination, Sunday School was still taught on its premises. Because of Superintendent Kinney's affiliation with the Cornwallis Street Baptist Church, many residents attended its services. But they were also free to worship at other churches of their choice.

The residents were not permitted to wear everyday clothing. Upon arrival at the Home, each child was issued a uniform. The girls' uniforms—a plain blue jumper, a blue beret and black stockings—were donated by a Halifax firm that supplied similar outfits for female elevator operators. They were also supplied with navy overcoats made from material imported from England by a wealthy patron of the Home.

Boys dressed casually throughout the week, but on special occasions they wore dark blue blazers and dress trousers. Sneakers were the every-

Girls at the Home received instruction in sewing (top) and cooking.

Bedtime came at seven o'clock for the younger residents.

day footwear of both sexes, with dress shoes provided for outings. The practice of putting the residents in uniform was consistent with the custom of most institutions of the time. The staff of the Home also wore uniforms.

Alfie White, who lived at the Home from 1937 to 1946, remembers the routine to this day.

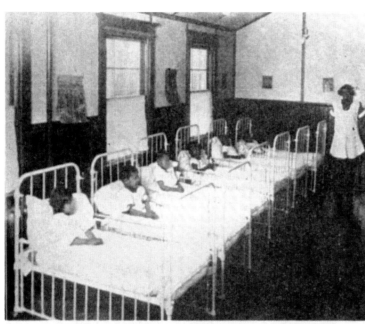

"We all had our chores to do in the morning," she recalls. "We cleaned the dorms, and we also sewed and helped to weed the gardens."

Life at the Home wasn't all work and no play, though. Mrs. White remembers outside groups like the Kiwanis Club bringing in movies and other forms of entertainment for the children. Mrs. White was nine years old when she entered the Home, and she left at 18, the usual age of discharge.

"I couldn't have been treated better," she says. "We would be chastized if we did wrong, but that was the same as in regular home life. I have no complaints."

She remembers that the older children undertook a great deal of responsibility for the younger ones. As well, Mrs. White recalls being "placed out" to do domestic work outside the NSHCC at age 16. That experience prepared her to begin a career in that field once she left the Home.

NSHCC Child Care staff. (From left to right) Mrs. Fred Cromwell, (Inez Dymond), Mrs. John Fowler, Mrs. Lavinia Tolliver, Miss Dorothy Kinney, Mrs. Ada Clayton, (Ada Dymond), Mrs. Earle Bundy, (Miss Florence Shepherd).

"I wanted to get out on my own," she says. "So I went in service at age 18."

"In service" was the term black Nova Scotians used to describe the profession of cooking and cleaning for others. Many of the black women "in service" received their initial training at the Home.

One-Room Education

When the Home's school opened in September 1921, its sole instructor was Miss Gladys Walcott. Miss Walcott, who remained with the Home until 1930, was authorized to teach a full public school curriculum from Grades One through Nine. The subjects she taught included Reading, Language Arts, Writing Skills, History, Geography, Mathematics, Science, Elementary Personal Hygiene, Arts and Crafts, and Physical Education. Before her departure, Miss Walcott was promoted to second-in-charge at the Home.

With responsibility for as many as forty children at any given time, Mrs. Walcott's task was often beyond the capabilities of one person. Accordingly, in 1922 a second teacher was hired: Mrs. Margaret Upshaw. Prior to accepting the teaching position, Mrs. Upshaw had done a considerable amount of fund-raising for the Home. She was also active in the Ladies Auxiliaries of both the AUBA and the Home.

At the time Mrs. Upshaw was hired, she was already teaching at a school in North Preston and was close to the end of that year's term. Tragically, she never set foot in the Home's classroom, as the following newspaper account from 1922 indicates:

Miss Gladys Walcott, teacher.

> *With a heart full of sunshine, a keen brain, and eagerness for service, Mrs. Upshaw ever pursued her duties, and while a month ago she accepted the position of assistant matron and teacher at the Colored Home, she would*

not close her school until she finished her term, her thought being "What would they think of me?" She died carrying along the work she loved, for at the close of school hour Saturday morning last she called to one of the children to assist her in putting on her coat, and immediately dropped to the floor stricken. She suffered a severe stroke, from which she never rallied, and passed away at noon on Monday, May 29th, at the early age of 48.

The Home's school weathered the tragedy of Mrs. Upshaw's passing and went on to hire many more teachers. Some remained at their posts for years; others served briefly but left lasting impressions.

Portia White, renowned concert singer, who once taught school at the NSHCC.

Portia White falls into the latter category. Miss White began teaching at age 17 and was only 20 when she succeeded Gladys Walcott at the Home. Her father, Reverend William Andrew White, was pastor of the Cornwallis Street Church and was Clerk of the African United Baptist Association during the Home's 1915 incorporation.

Although Portia White's stint at the Home lasted only one year, she was remembered long afterward for her skill and efficiency in the classroom and her musical talent.

That latter talent ultimately carried her out of the classroom and into a successful career as a concert singer. By the time of her death in 1968, she had established an international reputation as a contralto. When she sang at New York's Town Hall in 1940, one critic wrote: "Hers was the finest contralto voice to reach this city since Marian Anderson."

To have been compared to Marian Anderson, the black woman who may have been the greatest concert singer ever, was high praise indeed. For all the fame she achieved, however, Portia White never forgot the Home, and the Home never forgot her.

Miss White's immediate successor was Joyce Morgan, daughter of Reverend A.N. Morgan, pastor of the Victoria Road Baptist Church in Dartmouth. In 1940, Joyce Morgan's sister Shirley joined the Home's staff as teacher.

Half-a-century later, Shirley Morgan recalled some of her experiences:

The year was 1940; World War II was in progress. I had just graduated from Teachers College in Truro when J.A.R. Kinney, Sr. invited me to join the staff of the Nova Scotia Home for Colored Children as their school teacher. The students were all residents of the "Home." The school was housed in a separate building on the premises. It was a one-room school with approximately forty children in attendance. The children enjoyed school as it took them away from the institution atmosphere for at least five hours each day. In addition to the regular curriculum there were Bible study, arts and crafts and nature walks.

The staff consisted of a matron, assistant matron, cook, three or four child care attendants, and a teacher. We all lived in the institution with the children. We were always available to them. When the school day ended, I was still involved with the children in some capacity. I might be helping with homework, rehearsing for a concert, conducting Sunday School, etc. The day never seemed to end until playroom lights were out at 9 p.m.

In 1945, Shirley Morgan left the Home to pursue a career in Home Economics. She was later hired by the Department of Education to organize and establish a curriculum for Home Economics in six black rural communities in Halifax County. During her first year in that position, her headquarters were located at the NSHCC.

The NSHCC schoolroom.

Although the teachers were dedicated to their task, the quality of the education they provided sometimes came under question. The Home's school was segregated, as were most schools to which black children had access at that time. Many teachers in all-black schools did not possess formal certification. "Permissive" and "non-licensed" were the terms used to describe such instructors.

Indeed, James Johnston's original vision of the Home included an institute to turn out licensed black teachers. The teachers who eventually served the Home may not have been officially licensed, but they still taught the standard curriculum, along with additional training when possible.

As one indication of the high local regard for the type of instruction the Home provided, some parents paid their children's room and board to attend school there.

The girls at the Home received direct benefits from the training they received. During the Home's early years of operation, young black women were sought after for employment as domestics in well-to-do white households. The Home soon earned a reputation for turning out young ladies who were clean, good cooks and conscientious workers.

Boys, however, did not fare so well in the area of vocational training. Decades would pass before manual trades instruction became available at the Home. In the meantime, they learned gardening and farm operation techniques.

A final aspect of the Home's academic programme was the annual School Closing exercises. Over the years, the Closing Day assumed major proportions, often attracting hundreds of visitors from the surrounding black communities. Prominent citizens from Halifax and Dartmouth also attended, as well as representatives from the AUBA and provincial and municipal governments.

The Closings were long events that allowed the children an opportunity to demonstrate publicly their academic and other skills in the form of plays, singing, oratory, spelling bees, recitations, drills, and oral examinations.

Another element of the exercises was the distribution of prizes and awards for academic and non-academic achievements. Each grade had its own prize winners, with various businesses and individuals donating the awards. Prizes were also given to the winners of the ceremony's spelling competitions.

Specific award categories included: Greatest Improvement, Knowledge of the Scriptures, General Excellence in School Work, Honor Roll, and Special Merit. There was also a series of special Home prizes: Most Useful Girl, Most Useful Boy, Most Obedient and Honest Child, Best Cook and Housekeeper, and Neatest Child. Prizes for Deportment and for Sewing and Mending were awarded as well.

Speeches from dignitaries from the black and white communities were also a major feature of the Closings. Bauld and Kinney always addressed the children, and over the years the words of prominent members of the clergy, the business community and civic government were also heard.

The elaborate Closing exercises served a dual purpose. Not only were students and teachers accorded recognition for a year of hard work; the

Home itself also received favorable publicity on a regular basis. Given that the Home was a non-profit organization dependent on grants and donations for its survival, positive media exposure was a must.

Still, in the teachers' hearts, the smiles on the faces of the children who received prizes and awards meant more than all the publicity in the world.

Life on the Farm

Along with the buildings in which the residents were housed and educated, the Home's farming operation held a high priority during the early years. The farm occupied approximately twenty acres of the Home's land.

Agriculture played a two-fold role in the development of the Home: it allowed the institution a degree of self-sufficiency in food production, and the sale of surplus produce provided a source of income beyond the usual provincial grants and private donations. As the Home's 1929 progress report put it: "The required expense of labor, fuel, food, milk, etc., would greatly increase our operating expenses if our present methods were discontinued."

Children picking peas.

Peas constituted the major cash crop of the farm, with more than one thousand quarts being sent to market by 1927. In 1928 the Home marketed a thousand bushels of potatoes, turnips, beets, carrots and parsnips. Hundreds of chickens were also raised and sent to market, along with the eggs they laid. A small herd of Guernsey cows provided the milk the Home used. The need for additional pasturage for the livestock was a continuing concern and was mentioned in several fund-raising pamphlets.

An early water shortage created a problem that threatened both the farm and the operation of the Home itself. As the number of children in its charge increased, the Home's water supply became inadequate. A proposal to link water and sewerage facilities to a lake on the Home's property required an investment of $6,500.

Once again, the Home's fund-raising machine cranked into gear with James Kinney at the controls. One advertisement, under the headline "Water Shortage Threatens Nova Scotia Home For Colored Children," offered this appeal:

The gravity of the situation is too clearly apparent in the fact that on immediate action depends the continuity of the Home which has done so much for these dark-skinned little ones in training them to take their places as citizens of the future. Is this magnificent work to continue, or must it close its doors as the fruits of its efforts are ripening. Imagine your own kiddies with a meagre supply of water, then do your very utmost, if that utmost is only a little, for these colored little ones are God's as much as are your children.

The wording of this appeal indicates that it was directed toward the white community. Eventually, enough money was raised to ensure a reliable fresh water supply at the Home.

Musical Youth

With fund-raising a constant priority, the trustees soon discovered that the most effective advertisement for the Home was the children themselves. If members of the public could see first-hand evidence of the results the Home achieved, they would be strongly motivated to aid the institution in continuing its work. To that end, Kinney often took selected groups of residents on visits to various local organizations.

The March 28 1928, edition of the *Halifax Chronicle* contained the following description of an appearance some of the Home's children made at a Rotary Club luncheon:

Advertisement seeking funds to alleviate the Home's water problems.

Mr. R.H. Murray, who espouses so many worthy causes, introduced a group from the Home for Colored Children to the Rotary Club on Tuesday. For half an hour they kept the club on the qui vive. They gave some idea of the work the institution is doing. The teacher put some of the children through their tasks. Great long-syllabled words the tiny chaps spelled with ease. Points in grammar seemed to give them little trouble. And when in unison they repeated "The Lord is My Shepherd" and sang some of their bedtime hymns not a few of the eyes of the Rotarians were misty.

They sang some of the old songs and some of the new with a vigor and an enthusiasm which was the envy of all who heard. Samples of the work being done were shown. Curtains made from cheese cloth, embroidered scarfs, night-dresses made from white flour bags, and all so neatly done as to astonish with the result. Dresses in which the children were clothed were made by the pupils. It was all a striking object lesson, and those who heard and saw came away with a vastly different idea of the work which the Home for Colored Children is doing.

This report was reprinted verbatim in the Home's 1929 progress report and fund-raising circulars.

Print media—newspapers, pamphlets and other publications—was an important fund-raising tool for the Home. Later, the Trustees took advantage of a new medium for mass communication: home radio. Although the principle of radio transmission and reception had been discovered in the 1880s, "wireless," as radio was most often called, remained something of a novelty in the early 1920s.

Ten years later, technological advances allowed the medium to become much more accessible to the general public, and in short order radio sets became part of the living-room furniture in most households. And Hal Blackadar, son of one of the original Trustees of the Home, happened to own a local radio station, CHNS.

In 1931, CHNS provided free air time for the first Annual Christmas Broadcast for the Home. Hosted by an on-air announcer named Cecil Landry, the program featured testimonials about the work the Home was doing, appeals for funds to supplement the per diem daily maintenance rate provided by the Government of Nova Scotia, and choral singing performances by the children. In time, those performances became the main attraction of the broadcast.

Eventually, the Home's choir travelled throughout the Maritimes, giving concerts at churches, theaters and auditoriums. "Silver donations" were a small price to pay for an opportunity to hear the children's voices. Kinney, who could count music among his many talents, taught many children how to play the guitar and mandolin, and often played those instruments himself during performances.

The October 23, 1934 edition of the *Amherst Daily News* carried the following report of one of the Home's travelling concerts:

> *A bus load of bright looking colored children attracted some attention on the streets of the town this morning. It was the party from the Nova Scotia Home for Colored Children, who are on a concert tour of this part of the province and will appear tonight in the First Baptist Church. Mr. J.A.R. Kinney, the Superintendent of the Home, is in charge of the group and was enthusiastic over the success of the trip this far. Fully twelve hundred people crowded last night into the Highfield Street Baptist Church, Moncton, to hear them and they were led by the response to announce a matinee recital in the same church this afternoon. Their lodgings had been engaged at St. Regis in Amherst, and they came here but returned this forenoon for the other appointment.*

Some of the Home's theater engagements even included minstrel performances. One such act was the "Tinymites," a pair of five-year-olds, Olive Russell and Charles Grosse, who sang and danced like miniature versions of

Members of staff and Concert Troupe.

"Butterbeans and Susie," a popular black dance team in the United States.

An advertisement for a performance at the Capitol Theatre read as follows:

> *A Minstrel Show, sparkling with music, talented children, comedy that tickles, and sweet Negro melodies will be presented in conjunction with the Revue at the Capitol on Saturday. The theatre doors will open at 10 a.m.*

"Minstrel" has become a term loaded with negative connotations in the history of race relations, conjuring up images of white performers smearing their faces with burnt-cork makeup and acting out offensive stereotypes about blacks. Even worse were the black minstrels who perpetuated parodies of their own people. Eventually, the word "minstrel" became a stereotype in itself.

By the 1930s, though, the sting of the word had lessened. The last major "blackface" minstrel performance was that of Al Jolson in "The Jazz Singer," the first motion picture that included sound.

Given the reputation as a black community leader that J.A.R. Kinney had established over the years, the chances that he would involve the residents of his beloved Home in any activity that would be demeaning to them or their race are virtually nil. In reality, participation in activities that helped to raise funds for the Home would have been a boost for the children's self-esteem.

As well, the skills the children acquired through learning to sing and play musical instruments would last a lifetime. Former resident Phyllis Lucas still remembers how Kinney taught her to play the guitar.

Musical performance as a representation of the Home is a tradition that continues to this day, although on a much reduced scale.

A Memoir

In 1930 a dying mother of five children—a boy and four girls—knew her husband would not be able to care for the family after her departure from this earth. She was aware of the reputation of the Nova Scotia Home for Colored Children, and asked the Home to take in her five together. The Home granted her request, and George Bernard and his younger sisters—Vera, Catherine, Muriel and Mildred—all became inmates at the NSHCC.

George was 13 when he entered the Home, and 18 when he left to live on his own. In 1992, at 75, his memories of those days remained clear.

"I didn't know what to expect when I first got there," he recalls. "I just knew that before my mother died, she told my father to make sure we went there."

Bernard's memories of the Home center around the farm. Large and strong for his age, he was attracted to the farm animals and equipment and enjoyed doing the hard work necessary to run the operation.

"It was right up my alley," he recalls. "They took me out of the school and put me to work on the farm for 50 cents a day. I pumped water, cleaned out the animal barn, took care of the wagons and hauled wood. I did the same work the men did."

Some of Bernard's fondest memories involve J.A.R. Kinney, Sr. and his son Ross.

The Bernard children at the time of their entry into the NSHCC.
(Courtesy Sherleen Bernard)

"Mr. Kinney took a liking to me, somehow or another," he says. "He wouldn't let anybody touch me, or anything. He taught me how to drive. In fact, he even wanted to adopt me. But my father wouldn't let him."

Although Ross Junior was several years older, he and young George became close friends. They spent much of their time working on the farm and exploring the woods that surrounded the Home's property.

The youngsters at the Home went on indoor expeditions as well. Although the boys and girls' wings were separated by locked doors, that precaution didn't prevent after-hours visits.

"We had a key," Bernard recalls with a grin.

Discipline at the Home was strict, as Bernard recalls. In most cases, male staff members like James Bundy were in charge of chastisement. But sometimes the punishment meted out wasn't quite what it seemed.

"When the boys were bad, Mr. Bundy would take them down the basement and strap them," Bernard says. "But most of the time, he'd just hit a board and tell the boys to holler 'Ow, Mr. Bundy! No, Mr. Bundy!' And then he'd let them go. There wasn't any cruelty. There really weren't any bad kids out there at the time. They knew if they did anything wrong what they were going to get for it."

Two of Bernard's sisters played in the Home's travelling band and choir. Along with the in-house training Kinney provided, a music teacher from Halifax donated his time to instruct the children.

George chose to stay on the farm. "I wasn't fond of music at that time," he says. However, he remembers the trips the band used to take all over the province.

"We had a truck, with a tarpaulin over the whole thing," he says. "They used to go to Shelburne and down in the Valley and all different places. They'd all be in the back of the truck, having a great time."

After he left the Home, George Bernard went into the furnace and fuel business. He married Elsie Sparks and raised a family of nine children, two of whom—Linda and Sherleen—later worked at the NSHCC. He now lives in retirement in Cherry Brook.

"My memories of life at the Home are more good than bad," he says. "If you kept your nose clean and did what you had to do, you didn't get in any trouble."

The "Little Colony"

The Home continued to expand its physical plant throughout the mid-1920s. The barn was relocated, and new equipment added. A large, up-to-date poultry facility was built. In 1924, provincial child welfare superintendent E.H. Blois praised the Home as the best-equipped institution in the province. That same year, George Moser became the new caretaker and farm operator.

By 1931 the Home had become a small, self-contained world, or a "little colony" as a contemporary newspaper account put it. The report went on to mention the strawberry and raspberry bushes that flourished on the Home's grounds, as well as livestock which included cattle, poultry and swine.

Within the building, described as "large and commodious," the day-to-day operation was "run on a very modern scale." The article's un-bylined author depicted almost luxurious surroundings that featured washing done "by electricity," an abundance of toys in the playrooms, and "friendly hooked rugs" on the living room floors. In the basement was a collection of airship models made by the boys who lived in the Home.

The article offered the following opinion of the Home's general atmosphere: "There is a place for everything and everything is kept in that place and yet the institutional air is altogether lacking in this home for children of the negro race."

As a final assessment, the author wrote: "Everything about the home, the atmosphere, the teaching, the association tends to the uplifting of the pupil and cannot help to leave an ideal of cleanliness and love of order in the hearts and minds of the little people who would be less well cared for if the people of Nova Scotia did not in this way look after the little children of another race."

Yet for all the business acumen of Kinney, Bauld and the other Board members, financial difficulties continued to be a thorn in the Home's side. As early as 1925 the institution had to deal with a shortfall in revenue resulting from delays in payments from municipalities who had referred children.

Children and Staff of The Nova Scotia Home for Colored Children

By the end of the 1930s, the Home had become a firmly-established institution, with a full complement of children and staff.

On June 4, 1928, the Trustees held a meeting in the Halifax Board of Trade room to discuss the formation of a committee to undertake the task of reducing the Home's debt load. A year later, the committee appointed George A. Smith as chairman. Other members included R.H. Murray, K.C. Scriven and W.R. Scriven.

The debt-reduction committee's work became much more urgent after the New York stock market crash of October 1929 heralded the coming of the Great Depression, an economic disaster that consumed most of the 1930s. All races, all social classes and all institutions felt the heavy burden of the Depression. And the Home's Trustees were determined to keep it in operation, for it was certain that hard times would create an even greater need for its services.

At a January 1931 meeting in the Board of Trade room, H.G. Bauld summarized the Home's financial position. The buildings and grounds were mortgaged, and there was an overdraft at the bank. The cattle herd had had to be reduced because of the high cost of providing fodder.

The Trustees hoped to raise $25,000 for the purpose of clearing sufficient land to plant hay fields that would reduce the cost of feeding the livestock. The money would also help to cut down on maintenance and overhead.

Businessmen who attended the meeting spoke out in support of the Home, pointing out that it was the only institution of its kind in Canada, and its work needed to be continued. A newspaper report quotes D.M. Owen as saying: "The Home is deserving of the very warmest support of all people, not only in Halifax but throughout the entire province."

By March, half of the $25,000 had been raised through the efforts of the Campaign Committee for the Nova Scotia Home for Colored Children. Once again, the wolf at the door had been kept at bay.

Although finances continued to be a problem throughout the 1930s, the Home persevered, even though the staff sometimes had to accept farm produce in lieu of monetary payment when times were lean. By 1939, however, Kinney spoke proudly and confidently about the Home's first two decades of accomplishment. In an article about the Home in a religious publication, he was quoted as follows:

In all these years, there has been but one death, and no epidemics. None of the children who have left us (to our knowledge) has ever been brought before a court on a major charge. A number of the first ones are married and have families, others are scattered over the province and Upper Canada, some even in the United States. There are 45 in the Home this winter.

The single death to which Kinney referred was that of a girl from Cape Breton who was ill when she arrived. She was later taken to the Children's Hospital, where she died.

The Home's work and reputation extended well beyond the borders of Nova Scotia. It took in needy black children from across the Dominion, and a few from bordering American states as well.

Within the Maritimes, the Home's good standing had become firmly established. In 1931 the tenth anniversary of the Home's opening, Nova

Scotia Premier G.S. Harrington provided this endorsement:

> *The work done at the Home for Colored Children during the past ten years has merited the highest praise. Your efforts and those of your associates have made it possible to deal effectively with difficult problems which have required attention, and I am therefore very happy to commend your financial campaign to the sympathetic consideration of the citizens of Nova Scotia.*

Late 1930s NSHCC promotional poster.

The other Maritime provinces shared Nova Scotia's pride in the Home. The *Saint John Telegraph-Standard* in New Brunswick published the following commendation in 1930: "Among Canadian institutions for the benefit of those in need, there is one in Nova Scotia of a very notable character—the Nova Scotia Home for Colored Children."

Frank R. Heartz, Lieutenant-Governor of Prince Edward Island, a province with a very small black population, lent his support to a funding appeal for the Home:

> *This is to certify that I know that the good work being carried on by the Colored Children's Home, situated in the vicinity of Halifax, Nova Scotia, is of inestimable benefit to the Maritime Provinces, and as it is the only Institution of its kind in the Dominion of Canada, it must be of great value to the Provinces outside the Maritimes.*

A.G. Cameron, the Chief Probation Officer of the City of Ottawa, wrote the following concerning the condition of a child he had referred to the Home: "Elmer has arrived safe and sound, we were very glad to see him looking so well. He has made remarkable improvement under your supervision. Please accept our thanks for all you have done for this boy."

After a visit to the Home, William L. Reed, an official of the Massachusetts state government, made the following comments: "It was the good fortune of the writer to visit the Nova Scotia Home for Colored Children a short time ago. The Institution is ideally located and well adapted for the care and training of little children who have been left without the protection of Mother or Father. I can think of no more worthy charity than this little Home."

J.A.R. Kinney and Child Care staff stand on flower-bedecked front steps on the NSHCC.

The roots of what began as a lawyer's dream back in 1908 had now taken firm hold in the province, thanks to the dedication of Kinney, Bauld, the Board of Directors and the staff of the Home. Although financial problems would continue to shadow the Home's operation, everyone connected to it could still take pride in its achievements.

By 1940, Canada was once again embroiled in a world war, one that was even more widespread and destructive than the one of 1914-1918. However, the Home had already survived the Depression, after its founding had occurred on the heels of the First World War. Still, the first year of the new decade would bring a loss as devastating as any to be suffered during the long years of armed conflict.

J.A.R. Kinney's Sermon

*Even in deep snow, find green hushes,
murmurings, oh murmurings,
anticipations of apple blossoms,
then, when the season sings,
apples....*

*We begin, yes, in tremblings
and we end, hallelujah, in beauty.*

*It takes all our lives
to unfold history.*

*Gilt these words:
you are burnished with significance.
Our blackness is Beauty most visible.*

George Elliott Clarke

The Winds of Change: 1940-1960

J.A.R. Kinney's Passing

November 6, 1940, marked a sad and mournful day in the history of the Home and the Nova Scotian black community as a whole. On that day, at the age of 61, James A.R. Kinney passed away at the Victoria General Hospital after a three-week illness.

As news of his death travelled across the province and the country, tributes poured in from far and wide. An article in a Saint John, New Brunswick newspaper provides one example:

The colored people of Saint John are mourning with people of their race throughout the Dominion the passing of J.A.R. Kinney, secretary, treasurer, and superintendent of the Nova Scotia Home for Colored Children which was established, largely through his efforts, in 1921. The institution took care of many little ones and it was said today some Saint John children had enjoyed the privileges.

Closer to home, the homage paid to Kinney was much more personal. His friend and colleague, Henry G. Bauld, said: "The present high standing of the Home is almost completely due to his untiring efforts extending over 20 years. It will stand as a monument to his memory."

B.A. Husbands, a prominent member of the black community and a founder of the Nova Scotia Association for the Advancement of Colored People, placed Kinney in a different perspective:

> *I have known the late James A.R. Kinney for a long number of years, and have always admired him for his energy and enthusiasm in his work for the benefit of his race and the public generally, throughout the Province and often for the whole Dominion. He spent years of his time in the interest of the Nova Scotia Home for Colored Children, and its present success is very largely due to his efforts.*

Another obituary, headlined "A Christian Gentleman," expressed an opinion shared by all, regardless of the color of their skin: "Nova Scotia has suffered a very real loss in the death of this man. To his own people, this loss is well-nigh irreparable."

J.A.R. Kinney as he looked in later life.

Had he been alive to hear them, Kinney would have been honored by all but the last of those tributes. To call his absence "irreparable" flew in the face of his belief in black people's potential for achievement.

Kinney was survived by his two grown children. James Jr., who was called "Ross," had spent much of his life at the NSHCC, and held the positions of caretaker and farm superintendent there at the time of his father's death. Dorothy, who had worked as a child-care attendant at the Home, was a student at the Halifax Conservatory of Music.

The funeral was held at the Cornwallis Street Baptist Church under the auspices of the African United Baptist Association. Although the latter part of Kinney's life had been devoted to the NSHCC, neither the church nor the AUBA had forgotten his decades of service to them.

Reverend William P. Oliver, a young native of Wolfville, Nova Scotia who had become pastor of the Cornwallis Street Church, conducted services that were attended by people from all parts of the province. Rev. Oliver was assisted by Rev. Martin Luther Anderson of Yarmouth County; Rev. A.W. Thompson of Truro; Rev. A.A. Wyse, who was then Moderator of the AUBA; Rev. A.F. Skinner of Bridgetown; and Donald Thomas, a student of theology at Acadia University.

Among the attendees were all the members of the Home's Board of

Trustees. Floral tributes abounded and a special message was sent by Dr. E.S. Mason, secretary of the Home Mission Board of the Baptist Association.

The choir of the church and a special group of ten children from the NSHCC sang Kinney's favorite hymns, including "Rock of Ages" and "Nearer My God to Thee." After the services ended, the funeral cortege proceeded to Camp Hill Cemetery, where Kinney was finally laid to rest.

Thirty-two years had passed since James Johnston first presented the idea of a Home. Kinney had been involved with the Home from its inception, and after the catastrophic Halifax Explosion destroyed the first incarnation of the dream, he was the one who had presided over its rebirth and subsequent development.

For all his many accomplishments, however, Kinney's most indelible impression was left on the children the Home had served. In the words of another obituary: "It is safe to say that no child who ever passed through his hands will fail to cherish his memory."

A memorial tablet dedicated to Kinney's memory was unveiled at the 1943 annual School Closing exercises. The tablet now hangs in the office of the NSHCC Executive Director. A similar memorial plaque at the Cornwallis Street Baptist Church honors his contributions to that institution as well.

Another Passing

Just as it had survived the Depression, the Home also weathered the Second World War with its attendant turmoil and rationing. After the war ended in 1945, however, the NSHCC faced another loss. On February 4 1948, Henry G. Bauld, who had served as President of the Board of Directors since the incorporation of the Home in 1915, died of a heart attack at the age of 88. Like Kinney before him, Bauld was eulogized as one of the primary forces behind the Home's founding.

Reverend W.P. Oliver described Bauld as a "man of passion" who always spoke forcefully in favor of the Home. He was also a tireless fund-raiser who travelled throughout Nova Scotia and New Brunswick on a constant quest to keep the non-profit institution out of the red.

At the official opening of the NSHCC back in 1921, one of the most memorable statements made during the ceremonies was: "If it had not been for Henry G. Bauld, the Home would not be created today."

Those words were well remembered at the time of his death. In an interview nearly three decades later, Muriel States commented on Bauld's relationship with the Home and the black community: "I was surprised that he was so interested in the Home. The Whites did not have a good feeling for us. Mr. Bauld would come out day after day to see how things were going."

Bauld's passing, like that of James Kinney, Sr., left a deep void. However, Bauld's replacement as President of the Board of Directors, the renowned agriculturist Dr. Melville Cumming, proved more than adequate.

In June 1948, Bauld received a lasting posthumous tribute when a new two-room school built at the NSHCC was named in his honor. The school had been planned well before Bauld's death; the Home had received $70,000 to double the space of the Home's initial structure, expand the dining area and replace the one-room schoolhouse.

Nova Scotia Premier Angus L. Macdonald presided over the dedication of the school, which coincided with that year's Closing exercises. During his opening remarks, Premier Macdonald said: "I do not believe any other two-room school in the Province of Nova Scotia can compare to this one, and I would like to congratulate those who have worked to have it erected."

The ceremonies were chaired by Dr. Cumming, and guests included Rev. William P. Oliver, Halifax County Councillors W.A. Evans and M.H. Naugle, Warden W.J. Dowell, Schools Inspector B.C. Silver, School Board Secretary T.W. Mullane, Home Trustee Charles Climo, and Judge R.H. Murray, a member of the original Board and now Honorary President.

Rev. Oliver presented a plaque to be inscribed with the names of the boy and girl who had shown the best leadership qualities that year. Robert Scott and Joyce Davidson were the first to be so honored.

Although the H.G. Bauld School was intended to be a permanent part of the Home, future events decreed a different outcome. Those events would affect not only the school, but also the Home as an institution.

The beginning of a major change in history had occurred two years before the school came into being. On November 8, 1946, a Halifax beautician named Viola Desmond was arrested at the Roseland Theatre in New Glasgow, Nova Scotia. Her offense: sitting in a downstairs seat at a theater in which blacks were restricted to the balcony.

Mrs. Desmond was eventually fined $20 for allegedly "defrauding" the government of a penny's worth of amusement tax. Her case attracted province-wide attention, and the Nova Scotia Society for the Advancement of Colored People raised funds to help Mrs. Desmond with her legal costs. The incident opened a new phase in the conflict that had begun when the Black Loyalists first landed in Halifax.

Historically, black people throughout North America have responded to racial discrimination and exclusion in one of two ways. The first has been to establish separate, independent institutions to serve the black community's needs while maintaining a discreet distance from the white community. The second has involved the use of legal protests and civil disobedience to break down the barriers of segregation, thereby gaining access to facilities and rights that should be available to all citizens, regardless of color.

Each strategy has its positive and negative consequences. Separation can create safe havens and enclaves, but the larger society remains remote and unapproachable. Integration allows access to the mainstream, but swimming against the current of some whites' resistance can lead to exhaustion and cynicism.

Over time, blacks, as individuals and as a community, have tended to swing like a pendulum between the extremes of separation and integration. Richard Preston's black church movement of the nineteenth century and James Johnston's early twentieth century-vision of a black educational institute are examples of the separation option. Viola Desmond's attempt to integrate the Roseland Theatre represents the strategy of inclusion.

As conceived by Johnston and executed by James Kinney, the NSHCC remained well removed from the larger society. Among blacks, it maintained its status as a centrepiece of community pride. Only the church held a higher position.

But the Home's prominence in the consciousness of people outside the black community was beginning to recede by the 1950s. So was the high level of generosity that marked the fund-raising drives of the 1920s. In a 1955 article in the *Mail-Star*, a reporter named Mary Casey wrote:

> *Every Christmas season, hundreds of Haligonians listen to a special broadcast from the Nova Scotia Home for Colored Children.*
>
> *A choir of boys and girls sing Christmas carols and other songs and two or three adult soloists lend their talent to this annual appeal for funds.*
>
> *But beyond this "once-a-year" effort, most Haligonians hear nothing at all about the Home and most people know very little about its operations.*

From the end of the Second World War through the 1950s and early 1960s, however, a movement toward integration swept through the black communities of Canada and the United States. During those years, the very purpose of the NSHCC was brought under question by thoughtful people of both the black and white communities.

The Second Kinney Generation

Ross Kinney, Jr. was as much a product of the Home as the many residents who found shelter there over the years. From early boyhood, he had commuted with his father from Halifax to the institution, and when his mother and sister died, Ross, his father, and younger sister Dorothy took up residence on the Home's grounds.

J.A.R. Kinney, Jr.

"Ross was just like one of the boys," recalls former NSHCC resident George Bernard, a family friend. "You'd never know he was the Superintendent's son."

As a young man, Ross attended the Nova Scotia College of Agriculture. After graduation, he put his training to use at the NSHCC, becoming in turn caretaker and farm superintendent. By his mid-twenties, Ross was already serving on the Home's Board of Directors, of which his father had long been Secretary-Treasurer.

After the death of his father in 1940, Ross Kinney became Superintendent of the NSHCC. The succession was natural, as though Ross had been preparing for it all his life. By that time, the younger Kinney was married to Ida Gray, a native of Hants County, Nova Scotia.

Ida Kinney was once a resident of the Home. She and her future husband had grown up together and fallen in love as teenagers, and their wedding ceremony had been conducted at the Home. At the time, Ross was 18 and Ida 16. Ida worked with the child-care staff and became Matron in 1954, when Elizabeth "Nanny" Fowler retired after thirty-one years of service.

The couple had five children: Edna, Barbara, Ross III, Betty and Patricia. At first, the family lived at the Kinney cottage on the Home's grounds. Later, they moved to Dartmouth, as the cottage was too small to house such a large family. For a time, though, another generation of Kinney offspring grew up as Home children.

To this day, Ross Kinney III retains fond memories of the NSHCC. "I grew up there," he recalls. "It was an important part of my life. I worked on the farm with my father from the time I was ten years old. And the children at the Home were my friends and my sisters' friends. My parents always taught us that we weren't any better than anyone else. Some of the residents I grew up with are still my friends today."

Although Ross was only seven years old when his grandfather, J.A.R. Kinney, died, he remembers him well.

"Every day he would bring me a bag of candy," he says. "He was strict with adults, but kids—he spoiled them rotten!"

Patricia Kinney has similar memories of life at the Home. "Whenever there was a child at the Home who was having trouble adjusting, my mother would bring that child to live with us," she recalls. "I would be like a sister to those children. All the children at the Home were our brothers and sisters, and my parents were their parents."

Although the children attended the H.G Bauld School, their parents later sent them to a private Catholic school in Dartmouth. The Kinneys wanted their children to have as many educational opportunities as possible.

When Patricia Kinney went to the private school, she spent her nights in the Home's dormitory with the girls who were her friends.

"At the school, I learned about the Catholic religion," she says. "One of the first observances I learned was the Name of the Cross. When I returned to the Home that night, I showed it to the other girls, and they did it along with me. It was a ritual that, to my little girl's thinking, would make our prayers magical. And I wanted them to see that what I could do, with the opportunities I had, they could do, too."

When Patricia went to university in Halifax, she worked at the Home during summer breaks, as did her brother and sisters. For all the Kinney children, the Home provided a stable, nurturing environment throughout their formative years.

"It was a happy childhood," Patricia recalls. "It was very secure. We and the residents were all one family."

Her father pursued many community interests in addition to his responsibilities at the Home. He was active in Baptist affairs, holding membership in both the Victoria Road Church and the Cornwallis Street Church in Halifax. He also served as president of the Layman's Council of the African United Baptist Association. The culmination of Kinney's church work came when he was elected Moderator of the AUBA.

Kinney's other activities included the Equity Lodge and other Masonic bodies. As well, he was a founding member and Treasurer of the George

Washington Carver Credit Union Ltd., the facilities of which were located on the grounds of the Home.

In many ways, Ross Kinney's career echoed that of his father. However, their areas of interest outside the home were different. J.A.R. Kinney, Sr. was a businessman at heart, at home in the paper-and-pencil discipline of facts and figures. But Ross preferred the outdoor world of plants and soil, livestock and fodder.

In partnership with his wife, Kinney proved more than able as an administrator. When two Halifax County officials, Warden W.J. Dowell and Councillor M.H. Naugle, visited the NSHCC in 1949, they came away with high praise for the institution. As a contemporary newspaper account put it: "Councillor Naugle said that the Home was certainly a credit to those by whom it was being operated and was serving a wonderful purpose. Adding to his comments, Warden Dowell said, "I was amazed at the set-up. Everything was spotlessly clean."

But it was through his work with Dr. Cumming on the farm that Ross Kinney made his greatest impact on the institution his father had founded.

The Farm's Heyday

The farm's initial importance as a means of income and a source of economic independence for the NSHCC continued throughout the 1940s and 1950s. Under the stewardship of Ross Kinney and Melville Cumming, the farm generated tens of thousands of dollars per year through the sale of eggs, poultry and produce.

Dr. Cumming had been associated with the farm since 1932. Born in Stellarton, Nova Scotia, he graduated from Dalhousie University in 1897, where one of his classmates had been James Robinson Johnston. After graduation, he worked his family farm in Pictou County and became a herdsman on a model farm in Truro. In later years, he attended the Ontario Agricultural College in Guelph and Iowa State College in the United States, where he earned a Bachelor of Scientific Agriculture degree. For four years, he held the position of Professor of Animal Husbandry at the Ontario Agricultural College.

Dr. Cumming returned to Nova Scotia in 1905. Upon his arrival, he became the first Principal of the Nova Scotia Agricultural College, a position he held for the next forty-two years. In 1907 he was elected Secretary of Agriculture for Nova Scotia and held that position for twenty years. Then he was Director of Marketing in Nova Scotia from 1927 to 1934. Eventually he became known as "Mr. Agriculture."

Dr. Melville Cumming, NSHCC President 1948-1966, Honorary Life President.
(Courtesy Nova Scotia Home for Colored Children)

Cumming combined his primary interest in the improvement of animal husbandry and dairying in his home province with a lifetime concern over humanitarian issues. It was the latter that drew him to the Home, where he initiated a scientific experimental produce farm.

The relationship between Cumming and Ross Kinney paralleled the earlier partnership of J.A.R. Kinney, Sr. and Henry Bauld. Through their combined expertise, the farm played a crucial role in the further progress of the Home. By the 1950s, the farm had expanded to seventy acres of land,

200-300 pigs, twenty cows and thousands of chickens. In its best year it had generated an income of $55,000.

Production at the farm depended on the day-to-day toil of the foreman, J. Alexander Johnson; Austin Smith, who was in charge of the barn; Wally Kane, who looked after the hens; and Johnnie Drummond, the carpenter. There were also three full-time workers: Harold "Freddie" Sparks, Henry Louis Sparks and Harry Cunningham. Residents who worked on the farm included Lou Dixon, Aubry Marshall and Larry Leigh. William Colley became a full-time farm hand. Other laborers were hired on a seasonal basis to help with planting and harvesting.

Harold "Freddie" Sparks, agricultural and maintenance worker at the Home.
(Courtesy Wilfred Jackson)

Although James Bundy and James Willis were fortunate enough to own cars, most of the farm workers and other employees at the Home commuted from their homes via shoe leather express. The work atmosphere was strict, yet there was also room for the occasional departure from decorum.

The residents of the Home did their share of the work as well. Generally, boys began working on the farm at 12 years of age, although some started as young as ten. They rose early each morning and went to the barn to feed and clean the animals. At harvest time the boys, and some girls, helped to pick the crops along with the full-time and seasonal hands.

Sometimes the children became a bit *too* involved with the livestock. Jocelyn Boyd lived at the Home for a year-and-a-half during the early 1960s. Although she was only five years old at the time, she retains vivid memories of the Home's rural atmosphere.

"I grew up in Montreal," she says. "During the time I was at the Home, it was a farm, with lots of space. You could play wherever you wanted; you didn't have to worry about cars."

One did have to worry about some of the farm animals, though. Jocelyn remembers an encounter with a bull named "Red."

"The adults warned us over and over to leave the bull alone," Ms. Boyd recalls. "Well, I was an imaginative and contrary child, so when no one was looking, I teased 'Red.' That bull chased me all the way from the field to the front door of the Home! Everybody wondered what 'Red' was doing out there, but nobody saw him chase me, so I never said a word."

Ms. Boyd's encounter with "Red" did not have an adverse effect on her relationship with the NSHCC. She is now the Home's Office Manager.

Freddie Sparks also has a story to tell about an encounter between a Home resident and a farm animal.

"One time I sent a boy to the well to fetch a couple buckets of water," he recalls. "After he drew it up, the big horse that pulled the plow got wind of the water and wanted it. So the horse came after the water, and the boy thought the horse was coming after him. So the boy took off running, and by the time he stopped there wasn't a drop of water left in either of the buckets!"

Because the farm operation required continual care, a rotation system was instituted so two workers would be on duty every weekend and holiday. When a full-time hand was unable to report for work, an older male resident would often fill in.

Two such residents, Charlie Wright and Wayne Kelsie, became sufficiently interested in farm work to take charge of the hen houses. Freddie Sparks, who replaced Johnnie Drummond as a farm hand and maintenance man and continued at the Home until his retirement in 1992, recalls with amusement the rivalry that developed between the two boys.

Charlie Wright

The competition was friendly at first, with each youth trying to outdo the other. Wayne raised baby chicks to maturity, then turned them over to Charlie. Under Charlie's care, the hens laid their eggs. The boys took pride in their respective houses, each claiming his was better.

After a while, though, pride turned into protectiveness, and each ended up refusing to let the other so much as enter "his" henhouse. As Charlie recalls today, the boys eventually cooled off and renewed their friendship. Wayne went on to become a lawyer, and Charlie replaced Freddie Sparks as maintenance man for the Home.

Youthful rivalry aside, the poultry operation was an important part of the Home's economy, and the way it was run reflected that significance. With thousands of hens laying, dozens of eggs were produced daily. A small portion of the eggs were set aside for the Home's use, with the bulk shipped off to the Canada Packers Market in Halifax.

After the eggs were gathered, washed and cleaned, they needed to be stored in a cool place. A twenty-five by eighteen foot egg cellar was located in the basement of the Home. In a smaller room, twelve by five feet, the eggs were inspected for cracks and flaws before being piled up in crates of fifteen and thirty. Whirling fans maintained a low temperature in the egg cellar during summer months.

A one-ton truck owned by the NSHCC and driven by Alex Johnson carried eggs to market in Halifax. But some were kept at the Home to accommodate the local people—black and white alike—who regularly bought eggs there. Generally, the Home's egg market closed at 5:00 p.m., but exceptions were made for those who were unable to patronize the market during regular business hours. In the spirit of generosity that marked the Home's dealings with the public, the market would be re-opened to accommodate latecomers.

Most of the sales at the Home's market were of the four and five-dozen variety—enough to feed the large families parents in rural areas still produced. There were also customers who purchased large quantities of eggs for resale to supermarkets and restaurants.

Eggs were not the farm's only source of income. An abattoir in the piggery was where the livestock was butchered, cleaned and dressed. A walk-in fridge held all the meat processed by the farm for consumption and sale. All farm hands, experienced and inexperienced, took part in the slaughtering operation.

The gardens described in brochures dating back to the 1920s were going strong. Two gardens were in operation: the "special garden," planted for commercial purposes, and the "regular garden," from which 50 percent of the produce was sold and the rest reserved for use by the Home. The one-ton truck carried vegetables to market in a trip separate from the weekly egg run.

All the food that came from the NSHCC was inspected by Canada Packers. If a shipment did not meet standard requirements, a note would be left for Kinney with instructions concerning the disposal of the goods.

By March 1958 the farm had progressed to a point where Foreman Alex Johnson was able to submit the following report to the Home's Board of Trustees:

Our garden crop for the year was good and ample supplies of vegetables were harvested for the Home, including a surplus which was marketed.

We are receiving ample supplies of fresh milk from our grade herd of Ayrshire milking cows, including a quantity of butter made in the Home. They also supply the institution with a quantity of beef and veal, besides a number of growthy heifers in the pasture. We are breeding from the purebred herd sires of the A.W. Evans Farms, Preston East, Hfx. Co., N.S., and are highly pleased with the types of cows and heifers raised; they are a credit to the Institution.

With the removal of the old and the building of the new piggery last year, we are now enabled to produce and finish quality pork, besides supplying the needs of the Institution. Our stock is raised from our own brood sows.

Ample supplies of eggs and fowl are produced for the Home; in addition we move a lot of this stuff to assured markets. Six thousand day-old chicks were raised last year to stock our laying pens.

We would recommend the continuance of land clearing in the hill field. Also, the erection of one permanent hog shelter in or adjacent to pig pasture. We could stand some extension to our poultry brooding quarters to give us more space, especially for winter work.

The farm represented the Home's high point as a self-contained institution. Yet less than a decade later, the commercial farming operation was to be consigned to history.

Bauld School Days

Several teachers at the Henry G. Bauld School made a lasting impression. The first two instructors at the school were Mrs. Patricia Riley and Mrs. Iva Clayton. Mrs. Riley, a daughter of Rev. Wellington N. States, was born in New Glasgow and raised in Dartmouth. She taught the senior grades (four through nine) in one of the building's two rooms, and Mrs. Clayton handled the junior-level children in the other. Previously, Mrs. Riley had taught in the old school building. Both women provided instruction in the full public school curriculum.

Mrs. Riley also took charge of the traditional Closing Day exercises. Knowing that the event was designed to highlight the year's work and to showcase the accomplishments of the children and their instructors, Mrs. Riley was determined to profit from past mistakes.

Early in her career, she had taught at the Cherry Brook School, where she held a public spelling drill. In preparation, she had instructed her pupils to learn a small number of words from a master list of thirty-six.

On the day of the drill, the youngsters performed admirably in front of the assembled crowd—until Mrs. Riley inadvertently asked one child to spell a word on the master list but not among the ones he was assigned.

"But that's not *my* word," the bewildered child protested, much to the chagrin of Mrs. Riley.

On another occasion, the young teacher had intended to impress a group of parents and guests by having a small child tackle a difficult addition problem. She gave the little girl ample time to prepare the question. Indeed, the child had the entire process memorized from calculation to solution. Then her big day arrived.

Patricia Riley, teacher at the Henry G. Bauld School.

When called upon to demonstrate her mathematical expertise, the little girl stepped calmly to the blackboard, took the chalk firmly in her hand and proceeded to solve the problem correctly. However, she had memorized the answer so well that she wrote the numbers out left to right instead of finishing the problem the proper way, right to left.

The unintentional slip-up amused the crowd, so much so that one woman fell to her knees in a fit of laughter. As for Mrs. Riley, the experience was one more step in the education of a teacher.

For the first Closing at the Bauld School, she was determined that there would be no slip-ups, not in front of an audience consisting of the Home's Board of Directors and other prominent members of the white and black communities.

And there weren't. The spelling drill was completed flawlessly—all the students had learned the entire list of words. The children were also drilled in French vocabulary. During that drill, a potentially embarrassing moment occurred. Mr. W. Percy Burgoyne, Secretary-Treasurer of the Home's Board of Directors, took advantage of what he considered an opportunity to further impress the gathering by asking Mrs. Riley if he could drill her students himself.

Without batting an eyelash, Mrs. Riley gave her consent. For the next few moments, Burgoyne questioned the children, and again their responses were flawless. The children had indeed learned their lessons, as had Mrs. Riley.

When she began teaching at the NSHCC, Mrs. Riley was an unlicensed or "informal" instructor. Seeking to upgrade her credentials, she took a four-month leave of absence from her job in 1952 to obtain a teaching license from the Normal College in Truro. This credential enabled her to provide Grade Ten tutoring to students who had finished the nine grades the school offered.

In her school report for the 1957-1958 fiscal year, Mrs. Riley summed up her teaching duties as follows:

Our course of study follows the pattern suggested by the Department of Education, and instruction is given in Language Arts, Arithmetic, Social Studies, Science, Health and Physical Training. Each school day is opened by morning devotions.

During the year we were visited by Mr. Marriott, Inspector of Schools. Mr. Marriott examined written work by the pupils, and also conducted a class in Geography.

Along with her other duties, Mrs. Riley prepared the children for the annual Christmas Broadcast on CHNS Radio. She selected the musical program and trained her pupils for their performance. In earlier years, Mrs. Gladys Borden provided piano accompaniment. After Mrs. Borden had advanced in age and retired from that responsibility, Mrs. Riley took over as pianist.

In 1958, Mrs. Riley left Nova Scotia to accompany her husband to his new military posting in Ontario. In a letter to her, W. Percy Burgoyne expressed his regret at her departure and the difficulty he would face in finding a replacement.

Although the majority of the children from the Home became manual laborers or domestics, some of Mrs. Riley's pupils achieved greater success. One, whom we'll call "Christopher Robinson," became the first resident of the NSHCC to graduate from high school. He later attended Saint Mary's University in Halifax and became an accountant. Joyce Davidson went on to become a stenographer, and Wayne Kelsie was called to the bar as an attorney. Other students of Mrs. Riley's became nurses and secretaries, and many occupied prominent positions in the black community. Mrs. Riley passed away in 1993.

Mrs. Iva Clayton was also well thought of, especially by her colleague, Mrs. Riley, expressing her respect and admiration, once said: "Mrs. Clayton is one of the best teachers I have ever seen...a really fantastic teacher; always fair."

Although she was not a resident of the Home, Mrs. Riley's daughter, Lynn, benefited from Mrs. Clayton's expertise. As a pre-schooler, Lynn accompanied her mother to the Bauld School every day. While Mrs. Riley taught the senior grades, Lynn sat in on Mrs. Clayton's junior classes. This early educational exposure enabled her to enter the public school system in Dartmouth at the Grade Two level.

Another educator of note, Mrs. Gertrude Phills Tynes, taught Domestic Science at the Bauld School. She was born and raised in Sydney, Nova Scotia, and her father was Isaac C. Phills, the first black recipient of the nation's highest civilian honor, the Order of Canada.

Rev. Martin Luther Anderson, long-time fundraiser for the NSHCC.

As the only black graduate of the Sydney Academy in 1948, young Gertrude was encouraged by the Inspector of the Domestic Science Program for Nova Scotia, Mrs. Ruth Binnie, to continue her studies at the Normal College in Truro. She enrolled in a two-year program, even though a teaching license at the time required only a one-year certificate.

After successfully completing the program, Ms. Phills began work as a travelling Domestic Science teacher for black students in the Digby–Yarmouth County School Board. Using a station wagon provided by the Department of Education, she motored to three different locations. When inclement weather brought bad road conditions, she would either pay out of her own purse for lodging in a boarding house, or accept the hospitality of families in the area.

One of the families that hosted her was that of Reverend Martin Luther Anderson of Weymouth Falls. Rev. Anderson, a native of Hammonds Plains, had succeeded J.A.R. Kinney, Sr. as the chief fund-raiser for the Home and had brought the work of the institution to Ms. Phills' attention.

Like Kinney, Rev. Anderson travelled far and wide in search of friends and donations for the Home. From the Annapolis Valley to the South Shore, Cape Breton and then New Brunswick, Rev. Anderson never gleaned less than $4,000 per year to support the Home's endeavors. He would have made quite an impression on the young Ms. Phills.

Soon after her Yarmouth experience, she secured a job with the Halifax County school circuit. The stops on her itinerary included schools in the Prestons, Cherry Brook and Lake Loon and the NSHCC. Ms. Phills, by the way, was not the first specialized Domestic Science teacher at the Bauld School; she succeeded Shirley Morgan and Elizabeth Smith.

During her one day a week at the Home, Ms. Phills, who had by then married fellow teacher Gerry Tynes, taught cooking, sewing and nutrition. Her instruction, along with practical applications within the daily routine of the Home, enabled female graduates to continue the tradition of domestic "in-service" work that had begun three decades earlier.

Eventually Mrs. Tynes was succeeded by Shirley Mentis. Mrs. Tynes went on to teach Home Economics (a curriculum change from Domestic Science) with the Halifax County–Bedford District School Board. A traveller no longer, she held positions at the Graham Creighton and Gordon Bell junior highs, as well as Cole Harbour District High School. She retained her connection with the NSHCC, joining the Board of Directors in 1982 and serving as President from 1985 to 1987. She is now married to Raymond Tynes.

Rev. Donald E. Fairfax

During the leave of absence Mrs. Riley undertook to earn her teaching license, her position at the Bauld School was temporarily filled by Reverend Donald E. Fairfax, pastor of the Victoria Road Baptist Church in Dartmouth.

A native of the Cherry Brook community, Rev. Fairfax was hardly a stranger to the Home. His official association with the institution began when he taught Sunday School there in 1939. But the Home had been part of his life long before that.

"I can remember the Home from the age of 10 or 12 years," he says. "For those of us who had not as yet come into Dartmouth or Halifax to see the

The young Rev. Donald E. Fairfax.
(Courtesy Black Cultural Centre for Nova Scotia)

finer things that existed at that time, the Home was perhaps the nicest thing we had ever seen. We often went there to buy vegetables and eggs from the farm."

The Home served the local black communities in other ways as well.

"At that time, there were no phones in Cherry Brook," Rev. Fairfax recalls. "Most of your messages came to the Nova Scotia Home for Colored Children. Also, during early spring, it was impossible to get through a portion of the road from Dartmouth to Cherry Brook with a horse team, which is all most of us had in those days. Very often the residents of Cherry Brook would come as far as the Home and would leave their wagons there. You could walk on the edges of the field or the road, so we'd unload our provisions and carry them the rest of the way home.

"If one person couldn't carry all the groceries in, he would go and bring the children and older members of the family back to the Home. Naturally, you knew your own wagon, and everything would be there in place. You'd get your supplies and leave the wagon at the Home until the road became passable again. No one seemed to complain...it was more or less a way of life."

Through his visits to the Home and early activities in the Cornwallis Street Church, the young man became acquainted with the Kinney family. James Kinney, Sr. became an important influence in his life.

"Mr. Kinney was very active in the Men's Brotherhood," Rev. Fairfax recalls. "He was very well-respected. My association with him would have been mainly through the Men's Brotherhood. He was a very fine leader and was always anxious to get things done. And he always wanted them done very, very well."

Rev. Fairfax has applied that philosophy to his own life. From humble beginnings, he went on to become a truly self-made man. After dropping out of school at an early age, the 21-year-old Fairfax became interested in the ministry after years of laboring at any job he could get. Through the assistance of the AUBA, he enrolled at the Horton Academy for religious studies.

Later he migrated to Edmonton, Alberta. There, he became pastor of the Shiloh Baptist Church and continued his studies at Alberta College, where he received the Student of the Year award in 1946. The next year, he returned to Nova Scotia, where he received his ordination from the Maritime Baptist Convention. He also graduated from the Halifax Conservatory of Music, majoring in voice.

One of his classmates at the Conservatory was Dorothy Kinney, who studied piano. Dorothy played piano accompaniment for Rev. Fairfax when he sang his first recital at the Cornwallis Street Church.

"She played very, very well," Rev. Fairfax recalls. "I think our people were very happy to see us both performing."

Tragically, Dorothy Kinney, who had also done the Home's bookkeeping, didn't live to fulfill her potential. She died of a sudden illness while still in her twenties.

When he substituted for Mrs. Riley at the Bauld School, Rev. Fairfax taught the junior grades. Before his short tenure ended, he taught the senior students as well, for a total of approximately twenty-five children. Recalling his experience at the Bauld School, Rev. Fairfax wrote:

I was privileged in 1952, for a period of four months, to be a teacher at the Home. During that period, from September to December, it was my responsibility to teach and train the children for their annual Christmas Broadcast. The objective that year was $5000. This amount and more was realized. For one whole month or more the boys and girls, members of the staff and myself were invited to make many public appearances. In those days you felt very proud of the children, for they were able to apply themselves to what they had been taught.

Rev. Fairfax held positions on the Boards of both the NSHCC and the Children's Aid Society (CAS), and it was in that dual capacity that he came to the aid of one of the Home's brightest graduates, "Christopher Robinson," whose name has been altered to protect his privacy.

At the time young Robinson applied to attend Saint Mary's University, the CAS provided tuition scholarships for wards under its care. Two white students at Saint Francis Xavier University in Antigonish had received such assistance.

However, when Robinson applied, he wasn't even considered because the CAS refused to believe that a person from the Home was capable of doing university-level work.

But the CAS hadn't counted on Rev. Fairfax's reaction to such an objectionable notion. Through his persistence and determination, Christopher Robinson received CAS assistance and graduated from Saint Mary's with a degree in accounting.

Rev. Fairfax also remembers Elizabeth Fowler's last years at the Home. "She seemed to have a tremendous power at the Home," he says. "She carried on more or less as Superintendent as well as Matron, because Ross, Jr. looked after the farm. She was a fine person, and I believe she did the best she could do for and with the children. She had worked many years with Mr. Kinney, Sr. to bring the Home to where he had left it.

"With the support of Dr. Melville Cumming, Mrs. Fowler was able to carry on for a number of years. It was a very sad day when she left the Home, for her and for the Home, because the Home was such a great part of her life. But that time had to come, as it comes for all of us."

Although his tenure at the Bauld School was brief, Rev. Fairfax's relationship with the NSHCC continued and was destined to have a significant impact in the years to come.

Noel Johnston's Shopmobile

For decades, industrial and manual arts training for boys had remained an unfulfilled priority at the Home. Lack of funding was the major obstacle, and the male residents received little training beyond the regular school curriculum and their chores on the farm.

In 1950 that situation changed for the better with the introduction of a province-wide Industrial Arts program by the Nova Scotia Department of Education. The only black teacher in the program was Noel Johnston, a Halifax native who had graduated from the Normal College in 1948. He had already taught in Beechville and North Preston schools before the Education Department offered him a new challenge.

Johnston was assigned to bring manual arts instruction to schools in the black communities. As he puts it now: "I was appointed by the Department of Education as the Industrial Arts Instructor for the Colored Schools of Halifax County. Of course at that time there was a tremendous amount of pressure being put on the government about segregated schools. So I had to get rid of that title right quick. I became the Industrial Arts Instructor for Halifax County, with priority for colored schools."

Like Gertrude Tynes, he would be visiting each school once a week. There was, however, a practical problem: how to transport the machines, equipment and materials from school to school.

Fortunately, the province had been operating a program called the "Shopmobile" since 1942. Johnston's Shopmobile began its existence as an empty shell of a bus constructed in Yarmouth. After Johnston and the Industrial Arts Inspector installed work benches and power tools, the bus was almost magically transformed into a mobile classroom that visited black schools throughout Halifax County, an itinerary that included the H.G. Bauld School at the NSHCC.

Johnston was connected to the Home both by ancestry and experience. He is a nephew of James R. Johnston, who had conceived the idea of the Home nearly half a century before. Noel's father had taken him to the Home's Closing exercises during the 1930s.

Another connection came through Johnston's contact with the Kinney family through the Cornwallis Street Church. He recalls James Kinney, Sr. as "a very astute and very strict man. He had his own ideas, and his own way of doing things." But he remembers a lighter side to Kinney's personality as well.

"When the children were going on the Home broadcast, he always used to say, 'If you can't sing properly, sing loud.' The volume would cover up the mistakes."

Although Kinney's children, Dorothy and Ross, Jr., were several years his senior, Johnston became friendly with both.

The Kinneys Senior and Junior had a good relationship, as he recalls. However, like all fathers and sons, they had their moments of discord.

"When Ross was a young fellow, like most young people, he always wanted to go and do his own thing," Johnston says. "Mr. Kinney, Sr., being strict in his upbringing, not only of the children at the Home but also his own family, once told Ross to do something, and if something happened, not to come back home. Ross took the car and something happened—a minor accident.

"Remembering what his father had said about not coming home, Ross drove on to Truro, which was quite a ways off in those days. There was a little problem there, but Ross eventually did come back."

In adulthood, Johnston and Ross Kinney were the best of friends, working together in the church and co-founding the George Washington Carver Credit Union. Johnston welcomed the opportunity to continue their association through his educational work at the Home.

By February 1950 the Shopmobile was ready to roll. Johnston established his headquarters and office at the Bauld School. Every Monday morning he would load the vehicle with supplies and set off to East Preston, the first stop on his circuit. On Thursdays the converted bus would return to the NSHCC for weekly classes.

Once the power tools were hooked up to a source inside the school, the Shopmobile was open for business. Most of Johnston's pupils were boys from Grade Six upward. On occasion, girls would venture in to get a feel for the tools.

The Shopmobile had room for eight to ten students at a time, each with their own work station. Johnston would start them out with basic hand tools until they became familiar with safety procedures. Then they would graduate to power tools. The students selected their own projects and turned out lawn furniture, clock shells and medicine cabinets—an echo of the airship models the boys of an earlier generation had made. Johnston also familiarized his pupils with blueprints and drafting.

The intention of the Shopmobile was to provide a positive experience that would encourage black children to stay in school. At that time, many black children dropped out at Grade Six or Seven, and high school graduates were rare. Because of the importance of his work, Johnston was a strict disciplinarian. If necessary, a tap or two on the hand with a leather strap was administered, not to hurt the child but to let him know he had done something wrong. Back then, it was called "discipline with love."

Sometimes, the students weren't the only ones to learn a lesson or two. One lesson he learned from Ross Kinney caused Johnston to chuckle forty years after it occurred.

Mr. Noel Johnston teaching in Shopmobile No.5 at Lucasville.
(Courtesy National Film Board)

"Me being a city boy, and not knowing all that much about farm work, I didn't know what was going on when Ross sent some knives for me to sharpen. They were getting ready to butcher a steer. I sharpened the knives, but Ross sent them back, saying they weren't sharp enough. I said, 'Goodness gracious, if you run them over your finger, they'll do a pretty good job then.' 'No,' he says, 'they've got to be sharper than that.'"

"So we honed them down until they were so sharp you could cut your breath with them. Ross was quite happy with them, and he invited me over to the barn to show me what they were doing. It was the first time ever for me to see a critter butchered. When they slit its throat, that was it. I took sick. I couldn't eat anything for the next couple of days!"

Johnston recovered from that experience, and for thirteen years his Shopmobile rumbled along the Preston Road, bringing young blacks the chance to learn how to do constructive things with their hands. In 1963 the program was discontinued because of changes in the provincial education system, and Johnston continued his teaching career in non-mobile classrooms.

He influenced many young black people, but not always in the expected direction. Some used the skills he taught to do their own carpentry. One former student built his own house using the basic skills Johnston had taught him. Others, however, were attracted to a different aspect of the Shopmobile.

"A lot of the boys must have been impressed with the fact that I drove in with a big vehicle," he says. "One of the things we used to say to them was, 'You're not allowed up in the front part of the vehicle.' But they'd still be fascinated with the driving controls. I don't think it's a coincidence that many of them became bus drivers when they grew up."

Noel Johnston retired from teaching several years ago. He continues to run the George Washington Carver Credit Union out of his home in East Preston and always has time to lend a helping hand or reminisce.

New Ground

At the end of the 1950s the NSHCC faced challenges equal in magnitude to those that had confronted its founders four decades earlier. During its first decades of existence, the Home was considered an essential response to contemporary social conditions. Those conditions included entrenched segregation of the races and a policy of institutionalizing orphaned and neglected children.

As the 1960s dawned, these conditions were beginning to change. Racial segregation was coming under increasing critical fire throughout North America. And for children in need, foster care was being promoted as a preferable alternative to institutional placement. Social service professionals now believed that long-term residence in an orphanage or other institution could not provide children adequate preparation for life outside the institution. Foster parents were considered a closer approximation to the type of nurturing, care-giving environment only a family could provide.

In the Home's 1955 fund-raising brochure, Rev. William P. Oliver wrote prophetically of how the institution would fit into the new pattern of care-giving:

The economic status of the colored population has not improved sufficiently for their orphaned children to be absorbed into foster homes. Thus the N.S. Home for Colored Children endeavors to provide more than food, shelter and clothing, but also the personal guidance and love so essential to the complete development of the human personality.

Through his work with the church, the NSHCC and the black community, Rev. Oliver was uniquely qualified to assess the changes that were creating a new climate to which the Home would have to adapt in order to survive.

Children at play on swings at NSHCC during the early 1950s.
(Courtesy Black Cultural Centre for Nova Scotia)

"My first involvement with the Nova Scotia Home for Colored Children was in 1937," Rev. Oliver said in a 1985 interview. "In that year, I became pastor of the Cornwallis Street Baptist Church. At that time, the staff and many of the children worshipped there every Sunday. I would also accompany the Superintendent of the Home, Mr. James A.R. Kinney, Sr., and the President, Mr. Henry G. Bauld, on many of their canvassing trips throughout the Atlantic provinces. The Home, at that time, was very closely connected with the Cornwallis Street Baptist Church."

Rev. Oliver went on to say: "I always felt obligated to give whatever assistance I could. During those early years, I was like a chaplain to the

Home and all of their baptisms were conducted by me at the Cornwallis Street Church."

In 1940, Rev. Oliver became the first black Board member to be elected after the Kinneys, Thomas Johnson and Rev. Moses Puryear. He served on several Board committees and participated in the Home's annual Christmas fund-raising broadcasts. In 1980 he was made an honorary lifetime member of the NSHCC Board.

Before his untimely death in 1989, Rev. Oliver's community involvements included adult education, the Nova Scotia Association for the Advancement of Colored People, the Black United Front and the Black Cultural Society. He spent his life on the cutting edge of social change in Nova Scotia, especially during the 1950s and 1960s.

The U.S. civil rights movement had began to attract worldwide attention at that time. That movement had local counterparts in Nova Scotia and other parts of Canada. However, the Canadian version tended to be more polite and less spectacular than its American equivalent.

For example, school segregation in the United States was struck down in 1954 by the federal Supreme Court's landmark *Brown* vs. *Board of Education* decision, which held that racially segregated schools by definition provided unequal educational opportunities for black children. That decision was considered to be one of the catalysts that sparked a massive, interracial and non-violent movement aimed at breaking down the barriers of segregation in other fields. And from that movement, a leader revered to this day came forward: Dr. Martin Luther King, Jr.

During that same year, 1954, laws that provided for segregated schools in Nova Scotia were stricken from the statute book. It was a quiet decision that did not shake the province to its roots or incite street demonstrations. Nor did it lead to the emergence of a Nova Scotian Martin Luther King, although that is certainly no disgrace.

However, the decision did provide a context for an integration movement presaged by the Viola Desmond incident of 1946. Throughout the 1950s the Nova Scotia Association for the Advancement of Colored People and the African United Baptist Association, through its Rural and Urban Life Committee, pressed for improvements in housing, jobs and education for the black community.

The philosophy behind that pressure was desegregation, the belief that blacks should no longer be excluded from access to any aspect of mainstream life nor be confined to the all-black social and economic institutions segregation had forced them to develop. A secondary belief held that those institutions ought to be done away with once the goal of integration was achieved.

Where, then, would a Home for Colored Children, whose very name implied separation of the races, fit into the new ideology? That was a question with which the NSHCC and the black community as a whole would wrestle during the coming decade.

Ironically, children at the Home faced a segregation problem not too far from the institution's gates. In the mid-1950s an immigrant family from Europe opened a store near a riding club.

"They sold fish and chips," Charlie Wright recalls. "But they wouldn't serve black people."

However, the Home's residents found a way to get around that barrier.

"There was a boy in the Home who was light enough to pass for white," Wright says. "When we wanted something from the store, we would hide back in the woods a little ways. Then this boy would go in, and they thought he was white. They'd serve him, and he'd bring ours out with him. They sold him a lot of fish and chips, and they never asked him any questions."

It took more than a decade for the store to break down its barriers and serve black customers. "But they still wouldn't let you play the pinball machines," says Wright.

Even if integration had not become a major issue in the 1950s, the Home would still have needed to cope with a general decline in the number of orphanages in the province, as well as a drop in the population of residents they served.

A 1970 provincial study of five voluntary children's institutions showed that four out of the five experienced a precipitous plunge in enrolment between 1951 and 1961. The Little Flower Institute went from seventy-nine to twenty-six, the Halifax Protestant Orphan Home from forty-eight to twenty-eight, Bairncroft eighteen to eight, and the Home for Colored Children sixty to forty-two. The Bible Hill Protestant Children's Home's small population remained stable at between eight and ten residents.

In addition, three institutions, the Halifax Infants' Home, St. Joseph's Orphanage and St. Paul's Home, discontinued their residential services between 1951 and 1959.

The decline in these institutions' population was not the result of any lack of children in need. The 1950s were the peak years of the post-war baby boom, and a certain proportion of those children would have required care outside their families.

It was the type of care to be provided that came into question throughout the 1950s. The new conventional wisdom held that foster homes would provide a better, more family-oriented environment for children who could not live with their own parents. Institutions were viewed as cold, regimented places that could not provide the close contact children needed.

Thus orphanages and other children's institutions came to be viewed as a last resort to be used only when foster homes could not be found. But for black children in Nova Scotia, the NSHCC had always been the first *and* last resort.

The quality of care for children in large institutions came under question in the 1950s. These youngsters are shown in the NSHCC's nursery.

Ross Kinney made that position clear in an interim report he submitted to the NSHCC Board in January 1959:

Our greatest need at present is the effort to secure minimum requirements in order to pursue desirable goals for the personal and social adjustment of the children entrusted to our care.

For some years we have been seeking information as to the need or trend of Child Caring Institutions, one can almost definitely now say that the pendulum is swinging more to the acceptance of the Child Caring Institutional Services, providing they are rendering a good standard of child care service.

> *Again there is this fact, our problems in Nova Scotia are quite different from Ontario and the other Provinces of Canada in respect to the needs of the coloured race. The largest number of coloured people in Canada are located in Nova Scotia, this being one of the smaller Provinces makes our problems more outstanding in reference to jobs, housing and economics.*
>
> *Consequently, there are many needs that our people would face through these inequities that tends to make the service of our Home very distinctive, in the matter of the care of the Orphaned and Neglected children of the coloured race.*

Kinney's logic was sound. But he could not have foreseen the profound effect the swing of the social service pendulum would exert on the Home. By 1960 the institution that had started as a lawyer's dream would face a period of precarious sailing across the sea of social change.

Home

> The ever-turning, always wild ocean
> Foams in its bed, erases memory —
> The several centuries it softly
> Enrolled black bodies and shackled white bones
> In a silent and mortal liberty.
> We are their witnesses, their memory,
> Who stand on boulders and watch the ocean
> Chafe rocks and shells. Our hearts still chafe from chains
> Of history. Yet we hammer rough boards
> To shape a church, a refuge, a home.

George Elliott Clarke

The Old Order Ends: 1960 - 1973

The Calm Before the Storm

The June 15, 1960, issue of a religious magazine called *The Observer* contained an article by E.L. Homewood entitled "The Lot of Coloured Peoples." In the piece, Homewood investigated living conditions, employment and discrimination among blacks in the Maritimes. He found that "East Coast coloured people are poorest economically and the most discriminated-against Negroes in Canada."

In this assessment, Homewood presaged statistics cited in a later report called *The Canadian Family Tree*. While acknowledging the existence of individual black success stories, the report indicated that the majority were "caught in patterns of living resulting from social disadvantage." The report went on to say:

What this has meant in human terms can be illustrated by the situation in Halifax in 1960. The proportion of the Black population holding jobs in that city was only half as great as the proportion of whites holding jobs; only 6 percent of Blacks had graduated from high school; and of the 134 families living on two "Black" streets, 85 percent lived in inadequate housing.

But Homewood did see some signs of hope. Among them were an increase in the number of black children attending high schools and ambitious plans for urban renewal in Halifax and Saint John, New Brunswick.

Another sign was the Nova Scotia Home for Colored Children, which Homewood visited in the company of Reverend J.D.N. MacDonald of the Woodlawn United Church in Dartmouth. At the time, Rev. MacDonald was a member of the Home's Board of Directors.

Ross Kinney as he looked in early middle age.
(Courtesy Nova Scotia Home for Colored Children)

During the course of the visit, Homewood spoke with Superintendent Ross Kinney. Kinney used the NSHCC's farm as an example of interdependence between the black and white communities: "We have about 75 egg buyers coming here regularly, and most of them are white. We're dependent on the majority group for a living; any minority group is. We've got to co-operate."

Kinney never denied the existence of discrimination and racism. However, he had his own ideas concerning the best means to address those problems: "When there is discrimination we should howl about it. But I don't join any groups. I think too many organizations go around with chips on their shoulders, trying to create issues. There may be little things that are objectionable, and some discrimination, but it's still a pretty good country to live in."

Kinney was not, however, adverse to self-help organizations that placed their chips not on their shoulders but on the table. At the time he spoke with Homewood, he held the position of Treasurer with the George Washington Carver Credit Union, a black financial-assistance association based in the Preston–Cherry Brook area. The Carver Credit Union had been founded by Kinney's friend Noel Johnston.

The NSHCC's physical plant had now expanded to allow the accommodation of up to sixty-five residents, thanks to the addition of the Cumming Annex in 1961. The Annex, which cost $70,000 to build, was named for long-time Board President Dr. Melville Cumming and featured sleeping quarters, enlarged dining facilities, a modernized kitchen and a small gymnasium built into the basement.

The April 28, 1961, opening of the Annex included a speech by then-premier Robert L. Stanfield. In his remarks, Premier Stanfield praised the NSHCC as "a fine example of what can be done by joint participation by government, private enterprise, and self-help."

Other facilities at the Home included boys' and girls' dormitories, playrooms, a gymnasium, main dining room, kitchen, girls' lounge, nursery, staff lounge, staff quarters, hospital room, laundry, sewing room, utility rooms, reception room, and office. Also present were the Henry G. Bauld School and the cottage in which the Kinney family once lived. Now the cottage served as a residence for the Home's caretaker.

The days when a child could gain admission to the NSHCC by means of a knock on the front door had passed at least a decade before the 1960s. And the children for whom the Home cared were no longer primarily orphans. Many suffered from traumatic experiences such as physical and sexual abuse. Some had severe emotional problems, others were runaways.

The Home's administrative routine was coordinated with the provincial Children's Aid Society and Department of Welfare. Those agencies held legal custody of the children admitted to the NSHCC. Prior to a child's intake, meetings would be held between the agency case worker and Home staff. Discussions centered around how the Home could best aid the child in question.

View of the Home showing the Cumming Annex to the left.

Services provided by the Home included custodial care, health (including mental health) care, case work and social planning, boarding home location and placement, supervision, recreation, education and religion. These services were geared toward the total personality development of the child.

Upon admission, the agencies involved would furnish the children's medical certificates, social histories, psychological reports, school records and additional information if pertinent. One month after intake, an assessment of the child's progress and adjustment to the Home would be done. Periodical followups would continue throughout the resident's stay. Case workers from the referring agencies were expected to visit the child once a month to maintain appropriate contact. After the discharge of a child, a close working connection among the NSHCC, the agency and foster families was encouraged.

Some parents whose children were placed at the Home were persistent in finding ways to stay in contact. One Halifax single mother—we'll call her "Esther"—found herself unable to support two daughters and a son. The three children entered the Home in the early 1960s.

"I went out there to see them almost every day," Esther recalls. "Even when they didn't want me there, I was going. I never called, I'd just jump in someone's car and go. I'd stay there until it was time to go to bed. Sometimes the staff would tell me I didn't really have to come back the next day, but I'd show up anyway."

Esther's story is a sad one. One day she went out to the Home and found that the Social Services Department had placed her children into foster care without consulting her. Years passed before she was able to re-establish a relationship with them.

NSHCC children and troops enjoy Christmas party at Windsor Park military base.
(Courtesy Donna Byard Sealey)

The Home continued to accept private boarding arrangements for children who were not wards of the court or the Children's Aid Society. In such arrangements, parents who were temporarily unable to keep their children at home paid the Home a weekly fee—usually about $10—for their care.

In one case, a woman from a well-known Black Loyalist family, whom we'll call "Janet," found herself abandoned in Boston with a child and no source of income. Janet appealed directly to Ross Kinney to accept her son at the Home. Kinney went through channels, but bureaucratic red tape stalled the placement process. In the meantime, Janet's situation became more desperate. Finally, Kinney cut through the red tape and took in Janet's son as a private boarder.

By the early 1960s the private-boarding practice ended because of conflicts with the social service bureaucracy and the beginning of a policy to phase out large orphanages.

However, the relationship between the Home and the social service system was not always—or even usually—antagonistic. The NSHCC held membership in umbrella organizations such as the Welfare Council of Halifax and sent delegations to conventions and conferences, and some individuals within the system developed a positive relationship with the Home.

Jack MacNeil, now Assistant Director of Social Services for Halifax County and a member of the NSHCC Board, placed children at the Home in the 1960s when he worked for the county's Child Welfare Department. His first journey to the Home was memorable.

Group photo of NSHCC residents in the early 1960s. Uniforms are no longer part of the system.

"I guess I had my own stereotype as to what the Home was all about," MacNeil recalls. "I likened it to the old St. Pat's Home, which was a reform school. My first impression when I went to see Mr. Kinney about a placement was it seemed a long way away from Halifax. When I arrived, I wandered up to the farm and looked for Mr. Kinney. But I didn't know what he looked like. So I went over to one of the men working in the field and asked, 'Are you Mr. Kinney?' "

"'No, I work out here,' he said. 'Mr. Kinney works in the office.' So I went to the office, and Mr. Kinney really, truly made me feel comfortable. He showed me the facilities, and we talked about the religious base of the Home. By the time I left, I felt I could have placed any child there."

In some ways, daily life for a child at the Home in the 1960s remained similar to the routine of its earlier days. Institutional life still demanded a degree of discipline and regimentation. The boys and girls continued to sleep in separate dormitories on opposite sides of the main building, and the children continued to contribute to the upkeep of their environment by cleaning the building and helping on the farm.

Larry Leigh (far left) tries his hand at the drums.
(Courtesy Donna Byard Sealey)

The strictness of the staff isn't what John MacNeil remembers, though. "It was a staff that could obviously put their arms around the children and hug them. It was a *home*."

Yet sometimes the children, especially the boys, could have tried the patience of Job, let alone NSHCC staff members. The boys spent much of their free time outdoors—wandering in the woods, climbing trees, building tree houses, inspecting bird's nests and making bows and arrows. They often tormented the female residents by tossing live snakes and frogs into their dormitory. Another stunt involved sneaking into the hen house after bedtime and wringing the poor birds' necks.

Even staff members weren't immune to boyish pranks. On one occasion, some mischief-makers strung a thin wire between two trees in the woods. Then they began to taunt the Matron. She gave chase, only to trip over the wire and end up face down on the ground.

Residents who were not particularly fond of church became rather inventive in seeking ways to avoid Sunday services. One trick was to fake illness in the morning. The Matron or other staff member who attended the child would pop a thermometer in his mouth. Then she would briefly leave the room.

At that point, the child would pull out a previously concealed pack of matches, light them and hold the flame under the thermometer. Then the child would slip the thermometer back into his mouth just before the matron returned.

Upon seeing the elevated temperature, the matron would excuse the child from Sunday services. However, the children had to be careful not to hold the match to the mercury too long. Scorch marks on the thermometer were a dead giveaway. And a fever that was too high would mean a visit from the doctor, with punishment to come when the deception was discovered.

But the staff wasn't always fooled so easily, and they had a few tricks of their own up the sleeves of their uniforms. It was not unusual for staff members to hide under the beds of the dormitories before "lights out" time. At the first sign of any disturbance, he or she would jump out from under the bed and administer punishment, usually corporal.

Larry Leigh, who lived at the Home during that time, recalls that physical punishment was usually deserved. Staff members were strict disciplinarians, but they weren't deliberately cruel. The "spare the rod and spoil the child" philosophy of chastisement was accepted throughout society at that time.

The circumstances surrounding Larry Leigh's admission to and stay in the Home were unique, yet at the same time typical. Entering this world in 1953, he was one of thirteen children born to a Cree from Manitoba and a black woman from Yarmouth, Nova Scotia. When young Larry's father died, his mother was forced to go to work to support her large family.

Unable to afford a babysitter, Anne Leigh left her older children in charge of the younger ones while she was at work. One day, she arrived home to discover that five of her children, including Larry, had been taken by welfare workers. Those youngsters were subsequently placed in the Home.

When he was 11, Larry was adopted by Murray and Edith Langford of Halifax, and as an adult he became a champion body-builder. Eventually, he became floor manager and co-owner of the Gold's Gym franchise in Halifax. Today, Larry Leigh remembers his days at the Home with fondness, especially the opportunity to experience nature at first hand.

White Children at the Home

A newspaper headline from 1963 that read "SEGREGATION ENDS AT COLORED HOME" heralded another change in the institution's policy and orientation. The article described a letter to supporters of the NSHCC signed by President Cumming and Secretary/Treasurer A.D. Grayston that stated the NSHCC was officially opening its doors to "needy white children for whom there is no other place."

"No other place"—the letter did not mention that the NSHCC had been founded to serve the needs of black children for whom there was "no other place" because of a stated policy of segregation at white child-care institutions. This historical reality was swept aside in the Board's zeal to demonstrate that the Home was not itself a bastion of segregation.

Part of the reason for the integration policy involved recognition of a

In the early 1960s, the NSHCC began to accept white children.

social trend that had been gathering momentum since the 1950s—the belief that a massive dose of integration was the only cure for the chronic ailments of the black community. According to that prescription, black institutions like the Home came to be regarded as undesirable impediments to progress.

The following passage from the Board's letter to contributors alludes to that viewpoint: "Perhaps many of our original contributors have ceased sending in donations in the belief that the home should no longer be maintained only for colored youngsters—a thought with which we entirely agree in this enlightened age." The letter went on to note that the

NSHCC would keep its original name for historical reasons: "The Nova Scotia Home for Colored Children' will be retained because it is distinct and the only one of its kind in Canada—and has been so for nearly fifty years after incorporation by a group of white citizens having concern for neglected, needy and unfortunate colored children."

Although the Board's acknowledgement of the need for an end to segregation was necessary and admirable, it should be remembered that the Home came into being as a result of the racism that existed at the time of its founding. Had the NSHCC been advertised as an integrated facility in the 1920s, it would never have received the funding it needed to open its doors. Indeed, the provincial government would not have agreed to incorporate such an institution. In 1915, separation of the races was considered both necessary and desirable.

Even before its integration policy became official it is difficult to imagine the Home actually refusing admission to a white child on the basis of race. The primary reason white children were not admitted to the NSHCC on a regular basis before the Board's announcement was that white families and the social services were reluctant to place them there.

In some cases, of course, children who were white in appearance but had identifiable black ancestry found their way into the Home's care. As the 1960s progressed, the number of children in the Home who either were or looked white increased. The latter children often grew up with identity problems.

The first large-scale admission of white children to the Home came in February 1963. During that month, the Halifax Children's Aid Society referred a dozen whites on an emergency basis following an eviction of their families from Wellington Court. At a special meeting of the Board on February 27, 1963, "the legality and policy under which these children were admitted" was discussed. No conclusion was reached.

A week later, the Board invited Conway Ellsworth, Executive Director of the Halifax Children's Aid Society, to another special meeting. The main topic of the gathering was education. specifically the possibility of moving some of the NSHCC's residents from the Bauld School to other facilities.

The discussion then turned to the emergency placement of white children at the NSHCC. Board President Melville Cumming asked Ellsworth, "Do you need the services of our Home to do your work effectively?"

Ellsworth replied that the Children's Aid Society did use "Home Child Care Centres" in cases where siblings needed to be kept together, for temporary placement and for "periods of adjustment" during which group living seemed advisable.

The exchange that followed was extraordinary, as the minutes of the meeting show:

> *Further stated, his [Ellsworth's] society would be pleased to use the services of the Nova Scotia Home for Coloured Children for children in need, regardless of race or color, should the particular case need the type of care the Home provides. However, if the Home has a policy against the admittance of children of the Caucasian race, he would make other arrangements for their care.*
>
> *After some discussion as to the establishment of the Nova Scotia Home for Coloured Children, the constitution and thinking of today, AGREED on motion of Dr. J.D.N. MacDonald and Rev. W.P. Oliver: "That the Nova Scotia Home for Coloured Children receive for admittance children of the Caucasian Race, under the usual terms; even though conscious of the needs of children of the Coloured Race for whom the Home was founded."*

Had a similar discussion between blacks and whites taken place sometime between 1908 and 1921, and a similar conclusion emerged concerning the admittance of black children to institutions that were officially "whites only," there would never have been a need for a Nova Scotia Home for Colored Children.

Separate and Unequal

One of the most effective weapons in the 1960s struggle for integration was the promulgation of the view that the institutions, businesses and communities blacks built for themselves were by definition inferior. The fate of the Africville community, located on the northern fringe of Halifax, provides one example of how that weapon worked.

Founded in the early 1800s by migrants from the Prestons and Hammonds Plains, Africville became the target of a great deal of negative publicity during the 1950s and 1960s. The people of Africville were hardworking and for the most part self-sufficient, although from time to time children from the community were placed in the Home because their families were no longer able to come for them.

However, despite decades of requests and petitions, the City of Halifax never provided the taxpaying citizens of Africville basic services such as sewers, water lines and paved roads. But the city did locate a garbage dump there.

Conditions in Africville eventually deteriorated, and headlines in Canadian newspapers and magazines called it an "eyesore," a "disgrace," an example of the evils of segregation. Yet the people who lived there called it "home."

Instead of improving conditions in Africville, the city decided that the best solution to its problems would be the demolition of the community and the relocation of its residents to other parts of Halifax. Although Africville's residents did not want to leave, their protests could not withstand the negative image the community had received, courtesy of the news media.

In the mid-1960s, Africville's dwellings were bulldozed and its people relocated, many to public housing. To this day, Africville remains a sore point in Nova Scotia's race relations.

View of Africville, a Halifax black community seen as a symbol of segregation during the 1960s.

But Africville wasn't the only part of black Nova Scotia to acquire negative connotations during the 1960s. "The Concert," an article by William Cameron published in the December 30, 1967, issue of Toronto's *Star Weekly* magazine, illustrates how that perception was applied to the NSHCC. Cameron visited the Home during that year's annual Christmas fund-raising concert and came away with these impressions:

Outside, the older children are slogging up the laneway from the road, coming home from school, passing under the sign: NS Home For Colored Children, in white wooden letters, tacked to the entrance arch where the lane meets the highway. The "E" in "Colored" has been lost and the bottom half of the "R" hangs from the shabby sign by one nail.

A 7-year-old in a tuque marches up and announces that he is Carl—his tone of voice indicates that he is now in charge of me, and that there is to be no nonsense about it. He takes a rubber tire from the side of the road.

"This is my tire."

"Is it?"

"Do you want to see me run with it?"

"Okay."

Carl rolls the tire 20 yards down the gravel road, hoop-fashion, and comes back, picking up a fistful of pebbles.

"You see that tree over there? That's another game. You get to throw five times, and if you hit it you get to throw another five times."

"What happens if you don't hit it?"

He looks at me: Wise Guy. "You want to see me roll my tire again?"

Cameron then ventured inside, where he had an encounter with a young girl in the Home's nursery section:

As I lean over the counter, I meet Pretty for the first time.

She is about 5, thin-legged, but she has already discovered how to use her eyes. She stares over the counter at me, and says, "I'm pretty."

"You sure are."

"Have you got a pen?"

"Yes."

"Can I have it?"

"No. I'm sorry. I need it."

That does not please her; she does a fast circuit around the nursery and comes back.

"Well, can I have a piece of paper, then?"

"Sure." I give her a piece of paper, folded in half. She makes another fast lap around the nursery—the paper is an airplane. She comes back again.

"I'm pretty."

"You sure are."

Then Cameron went to the CHNS Radio fund-raiser, which was held at Saint Patrick's High School in Halifax that year. While the children's chorus sang "White Christmas" for the radio audience, the writer had a revealing conversation with one of the NSHCC's Board members.

> *Al Grayston, the secretary-treasurer of the home, slides into the seat in front of me and begins a running counterpoint. He is a short, gray-haired man, and leans back over his chair while he talks. "My pride and joy is that we have a fellow in college right now—(where the snowflakes glisten)—graduating at the end of this year. But the sad fact, the sad fact is that a lot of these people—(to hear)—don't have the mental capacity of the whites—(sleighbells in the snow)—they're neglected."*
>
> *Grayston lights a cigarette. "Now, some of them repeat Grade 1 twice, Grade 2 twice, and by the time they get finished their potential is that of a basket boy in a supermarket. I'm trying to set up some kind of scheme whereby they can have some kind of vocational training while they're going through their education, so that when they get out they'll have a trade. They won't become charges on you and me by the time their 18. They won't become criminals."*

Grayston also provided a personal interpretation of black history in Nova Scotia.

> "Do you know why Halifax has such a large colored population? Well, they were brought over here, the Maroons, you know, to raise the defence fortifications—there's a hill here that they actually lifted 40 feet, or something like that. And then a lot of them were slaves that were owned by the United Empire Loyalists, and when the Loyalists moved on they just left them here.

Coming from an NSHCC Board member, Grayston's attitudes were appalling, and his ignorance of the history and background of the people upon whose behalf he worked was inexcusable. Any black person who overheard what he said to the reporter would have been justified in thinking, "With friends like these, who needs enemies?"

Within three years, Grayston, who had served as Treasurer since 1960, resigned from the Board under questionable circumstances.

At the end of his article, Cameron did not draw any specific conclusions about the Home. His implication was clear, though. Although the Home had officially integrated four years earlier, it was still perceived as a segregated institution, bearing the full weight of all the derogatory images attached to that designation. And the accepted cure for segregation at that time was to break up black communities and institutions and disperse them into white society.

Before long, the Home's choices would become clear: either adapt to changing times or go the way of Africville.

The Last School Closing

The Home's next major step along the road to integration occurred when the Henry G. Bauld School closed its doors. At that time, it was believed that isolation in a separate school no longer served the needs of NSHCC residents. Because the policy of de facto segregation in public schools that was in place when the Home was founded had been abandoned in the 1950s, the elementary and secondary schools in Halifax County had now become a realistic alternative for blacks.

At the beginning of the 1960s the Bauld School was still filled with pupils. However, some of the older residents had moved on to nearby Graham Creighton High School, which later became a junior high. But the Bauld School's days were numbered. The teacher who guided the students through the final transition was a young woman from Truro named Donna Byard.

Not long before her graduation from teachers college in 1958, Donna came home one day to find Ross Kinney's car parked in her parents' driveway. Kinney was searching for a replacement for the recently retired Patricia Riley and had heard about the Truro woman who was about to finish her teacher training at the age of 18.

"Mr. Kinney asked me if I'd be interested in teaching at the Home," Ms. Byard—whose last name is now Sealey—says. "I said, 'Well I don't have a job and I'm looking for one, but I'll have to ask my parents first.' I talked it over with Mom and Dad, and they said it was okay. So I took the job."

Ms. Byard hadn't had any direct experience with the NSHCC at that time. But her great-aunt had sung at the Home's official opening in 1921, and she knew some people in her community who had lived there.

When she began her teaching tenure, Ms. Byard was favorably impressed with the Home's grounds, buildings and farm, and with the Bauld School itself. However, it took her students a while to decide what to make of their new instructor.

"My first day there, the children had a bit of a squabble over whether or not I was a woman or a girl," she recalls. "Mrs. Riley was a woman, and I was a girl. I was waiting for my nineteenth birthday, so I was only four years older than some of my students."

The dispute was soon settled: whether Ms. Byard was a woman or a girl, she was still the teacher.

Teaching children of different grade levels in the same classroom was a demanding task, but Ms. Byard accomplished it by using techniques similar to those of her predecessors. She did individual reading exercises with her pupils, and in some cases bypassed lower levels of arithmetic if similar principles could be taught with lessons planned for a higher grade. Still, she followed the standard provincial curriculum for primary schools. Ms. Byard often found herself working twelve-hour days and taking the children out for extra-curricular activities.

One of those activities was the annual visit to the Lieutenant-Governors residence in Halifax. "Some of the kids used to get a big kick out of being able to jump on the bed the Queen slept in," Ms. Byard recalls.

Ms. Byard takes serious exception to Al Grayson's previously quoted comments about the supposedly limited learning capacity of black children.

"Out in the country, many black children simply couldn't get to school enough days to pass a grade," she says. "When some of our children came to the Home, it was the first time they'd ever had a chance to complete a whole school year."

The annual Closing exercises continued during the school's waning years. The Board members, the Lieutenant-Governor, and other dignitaries still attended the event, the children still did their recitations and performances, and each child still received a silver dollar.

In Ms. Byard's third year at the Home, construction began on the William Ross primary school at a location just down the road from the Home. With a county school now available for NSHCC residents, the Bauld School was no longer necessary.

Donna Byard at work in the Henry G. Bauld School.
(Courtesy Donna Byard Sealey)

Well aware of the change that was about to come, Ms. Byard approached the Board and asked them to obtain permission for NSHCC residents to attend the new school. That permission was granted. The Home's children would be integrated into the Ross school two grades per year.

"We started with Grades 4 and 5 the first year," Ms. Byard says, "and then the next two years. When I left in 1965, we were down to fourteen students. Eventually all the younger students went to the Ross School."

Throughout the province, the long-sought goal of school integration had now been accomplished, although a few all-black elementary schools would continue to exist into the 1990s. For the most part, black children would be allowed to take their seats in classrooms that had better equipment and facilities. However, the children's adjustment to new surroundings and the reception they would receive were different matters. Ms. Byard knew difficulties would arise, and she tried to prepare her students for them.

"I demanded a lot from them," she recalls. "I had high expectations for them. I remember one of my students, who is a teacher now, not doing so well in her first term at William Ross. But she was one of my best students. So Mr. Kinney spoke to me about it. I told him to give her time to adjust. By the end of the year, she was an 'A' student again. She just had to overcome her fear of going to school with white children."

After leaving the Home, Donna Byard Sealey went on to take a position in special education in the Dartmouth school system. She continues to teach today.

Angus Johnson of Windsor, Nova Scotia, was the last teacher at the Bauld School before it officially shut down in 1967. He was hired in 1965, immediately following his graduation from the Nova Scotia Teachers College in Truro. Johnson submitted his resignation before the closing became official. His final school report listed several recommendations:

Invitation to one of the last Closing Exercises of the Henry G. Bauld School.

The Board of Directors and Staff
of the
Nova Scotia Home for Colored Children
request the honor of your presence
at the
44th. Annual Closing Exercises
and Presentation of Prizes
of the
Henry G. Bauld (Memorial School)
on Monday June 21st, 1965 at 2.30 p.m.

Preferably a man teacher for the next school year, as the staff are all female and the young pupils need a man's influence.

Some physical education equipment should be purchased. Inexpensive items such as bean bags, sponge balls and bats, bowling pins and a rubber mat is essential.

> *Some musical equipment such as song flutes should be purchased.*
> *This equipment should be left at school.*
> *I had a good year at the Coloured Home, with good pupil co-operation.*

With the end of an independent educational institution for black children at the NSHCC, the long-ago dream of James R. Johnston and Moses Puryear had finally ended—its time, like theirs, had passed.

Teacher and children during the last term of the Bauld School.
(Bob Brooks photo, courtesy Public Archives of Nova Scotia)

Down Off the Farm

Another of the NSHCC's mainstays vanished when, at a special general meeting of the Board of Directors held on January 12, 1966, a motion was tabled to abandon commercial farming "immediately."

Dr. Melville Cumming, who had been involved with the farm since 1932, indicated at the meeting that commercial farming was no longer a profitable concern in Nova Scotia. At the time, small farms everywhere were falling victim to changing times and markets. According to Dr.

Cumming, the number of farms in the province had already decreased by 50 percent.

Actually, the farm had been in trouble by 1961. A report on the Home written that year by E.J. Dick, Superintendent of the Nova Scotia Training School, assessed the farm operations as follows:

> *The major portion of farm revenue is from the sale of chickens and eggs. The market prices for these items during the past few years have been low while the cost of feed has been high. The average number of hens kept per year has been 7,000. Approximately $20,000 per year is spent for chicken feed. This is a risky operation unless modern methods are used and the number of hens kept is in the range of 20 to 30 thousand.*
>
> *The farm is not used as a training medium. All the boys who could work are attending day school and leave the Home for school at 8:00 a.m. each school day. The boys also have home work assigned by the school, therefore, other than odd chores they have no time to work on the farm.*

Dick's report recommended the closure of the farm.

At a June 14, 1962, special general meeting of the Board, a motion to close the farm was tabled. According to the minutes of that meeting, discussion became "too heavy for motion that the farm should be discontinued."

In 1963, Ross Kinney reported that the farm had earned a "small profit." And in the summer of 1965, Alex Lamond, General Manager of Linwood Farms, inspected the farm at the request of Board member J.E. Hudson. According to Lamond's report:

> *In regard to the dairy herd and having seen the operational cost plus the income from Woodlawn Dairy, I can see no reason why this could not be put on a profitable basis with a few changes.*
>
> *Secondly, in regards to the pig operation, this appears to be operating on a profitable basis....*
>
> *Thirdly, in regard to the poultry operation as it appears today, this does not seem to be profitable nor do I think the existing buildings to be worth renovating to put on a profitable basis.*

Most of the time, two out of three isn't bad. However, at a September 20, 1965, special meeting of the Board, another motion to discontinue operations was tabled. The vote on the motion was deadlocked: five in favor, five against. The Board then appointed a six-person committee to study the farm situation.

Ross Kinney submitted his final farm report on November 22, 1965. In it, he praised the work of employees Fred Cromwell and William Colley. He catalogued the repair work that would be needed to maintain commercial agricultural operations. And he described his final efforts to save the farm:

In planning to try and hold our position nothing outstanding has been attempted or advanced, we are not in the position to renovate or repair to any extent, as any work done is charged against the farm. However, noting the short space of time we have and the uncertain future, we did have correspondence with the N.S. Dept. of Agriculture through the Minister, the Hon. I.W. Akerley, who made an encouraging reply if nothing else to my letter.

Margaret Wright, longtime receptionist at the NSHCC.
(Courtesy Charlie Wright)

But the Agriculture Department declined to intervene on the Home's behalf.

The minutes of the 1966 special meeting tell the end of the farm's story:

During the past few years there has been a change in general regarding farm income, due to the low prices received, especially for poultry products, paralleled by a strong increase in the cost of poultry feeds. It became increasingly difficult for farm operations to be a financial asset to the Institution.

That assessment stood in stark contrast to earlier days, when the farm report was filled with profit figures. But times had changed drastically, and the decline of the small farm as a way of life and business continues to this day.

Faced with an unpleasant economic reality, the Board voted unanimously to close the commercial aspect of the farm and dispose of "stock and equipment...not needed for future operation."

Although the Board recommended a continuation of private farming to provide for its own needs, the cessation of the profit-making phase of the operation marked the end of an era at the NSHCC, even more so than the closing of the Bauld School.

Since the Home's beginning, its agricultural productivity had been a source of pride and self-sufficiency. Whatever its other financial problems may have been, the Home could at least feed its residents, sell agricultural products for income and provide employment for the surrounding black communities. The demise of the farm dealt a fatal blow to that sense of independence.

However, there was another side to the Home's reputation as a self-contained institution. Although many people in the black community considered the Home accessible, others thought of it as a closed, almost forbidding place.

Margaret Wright, who grew up in Cherry Brook, the black community closest geographically to the Home, recalled:

"All the while I was growing up in this area, I never came to visit the Home. Actually, we were never allowed. During the summer, when they had their end of the year School Closings, we were allowed to go to the school and observe that. It wasn't because of any Home policy. It's just that the kids from our community didn't go there."

Mrs. Wright also remembered attending Gertrude Tynes' Home Economics classes at the Henry G. Bauld School. "You went to the Home Ec room, but you didn't mingle with the residents at the Home."

Years later, when the NSHCC offered Mrs. Wright the position of office secretary, she accepted and remained an integral part of the Home until her untimely death in December 1992.

The 1966 Board meeting that sealed the fate of commercial farming at the Home witnessed another transition as well. Citing "failing eyesight and advanced years," Dr. Cumming tendered his resignation as President. The resignation was accepted with regret, and the Board immediately moved to appoint Dr. Cumming as Honorary Life President. Fraser Ross succeeded him as President of the Board of Directors. Dr. Cumming died three years later, at the venerable age of 93.

The Kinneys Depart

As Secretary of the Board, Ross Kinney attended the meeting that saw the farm's end, and he prepared its minutes. A year after the commercial farming operation closed, Kinney retired as Superintendent, after having served the NSHCC in many capacities for forty years. However, another year passed before the Board formally accepted his decision.

At 56, Kinney was still a relatively young man. And his work at the Home had occupied virtually his whole adult life. But the closing of the farm must have left a deep wound, for even after he assumed the title of Superintendent of the Home, he had spent most of his time looking after the crops and livestock. Freddie Sparks remembers how Kinney would pull overalls over his suit and join the farm hands in whatever work they were doing. Without the farm, the Home would have seemed a diminished place to Ross Kinney.

But the farm's end was only a partial explanation for Kinney's departure. As a member of the Board of Directors and an active participant in black community affairs, he was in a position to have foreseen other changes that would cause the Home to bear little resemblance to the place in which he had spent his childhood.

"The situation at the Home kept changing," says Kinney's friend Noel Johnston.

"Ross had his heart and soul in the Home. He educated all his children at the Home. And now it worked out that you had other players becoming involved and making decisions. First of all, they closed the farm. And to let it just go down to nothing.... We often talked about it, but didn't know what to do. If a board makes a decision, it makes a decision. It was the same with the closing of the Henry G. Bauld School. All of this would have been very disheartening to Ross."

Kinney's daughter, Patricia, takes a different view of her father's decision to leave the Home.

"My father realized his work was done," she says. "For him, it was time to move on, without regrets."

In his last Superintendent's report, Kinney spoke emotionally of the Home's past, present and future:

In the work of the Home for the greater part of my life, I have found it both stimulating and happy and have thoroughly enjoyed the effort, hassles and many challenges to maintain the Ideals of the Founders to provide a home free from the restraints of institutional living, which is difficult in this period because there is no schedule for crisis. We have always done our best to admit children according to NEED, *regardless of race, creed or colour. Our Institution is a Resource and many times we have been under fire with the type of cases Agencies are crying for attention, we have been generally able to hear their cry in the past and offer assistance to which they are entirely grateful. I trust you will be able and equipped to do this in the future. The Home has never been in a higher state of growth and organization and I can highly commend the work to you.*

THE OLD ORDER ENDS

> *I am proud of the work at the Nova Scotia Home for Coloured Children and note the progress over the years to the children entrusted in our care and custody, our programme, facilities, efficient Matron and Staff and the improved personal and real assets on hand. Our endeavors to keep abreast of the trends and advancements in the Child Welfare Field, to assure that we would compare favorably with similar Child Care Centres.*
>
> *It has been a personal pleasure to have been employed with this incorporated Body and consequently, I wish you every success in the future.*

Now, for the first time in more than half a century, the Nova Scotia Home for Colored Children would have to continue without a Kinney at its helm.

But there would still be a Kinney at the Home. Ross' wife, Ida, stayed on for another four years. A 1964 newspaper profile described Ida Kinney as follows:

Ida Kinney with two NSHCC children.

> *Concern for the care and well-being of small children is a vital part of womanly charm; a dominant force in feminine character; the sort of quiet charm and character personified by Mrs. Ida Kinney, assistant matron, Nova Scotia Home for Colored Children, located at the outskirts of Dartmouth. "Mother" to a multitude of youngsters, Mrs. Kinney's interests are extensive, providing an excellent basis for the love, care and guidance of her young charges. In truth, Mrs. Kinney's role can be summed up as active, responsible community service at its most effective level.*

At the NSHCC, Charlie Wright remembers her as "strict, right to the point, tough but fair. If she told you to do something, you'd better do it."

When Ida Kinney finally left the Home, Board President Alice Croft expressed the opinions of many when she wrote:

The Board of Directors of the Nova Scotia Home for Colored Children regretfully accepts your letter of resignation.

Your years of dedicated service to the Home are deserving of consideration and recognition and remembrance and while it is impossible to compensate for the contribution you have given the Home, may you find some consolation in the Board's gratitude and appreciation for the years.

You have touched the lives of many individuals and achieved a balance in the lives of many, and while you may be separated from the day to day tasks of the Home, perhaps on occasion you may feel obliged to return to lend a hand to those who call on you.

Although all five of the Kinneys' children had lived and worked at the Home when they were growing up, none ever felt pressured to succeed their father as Superintendent or their mother as Matron.

"They didn't really want us to follow in their footsteps," Ross III recalls. "When I was growing up, I never expected to become Superintendent of the Home. It just never entered my mind."

By the time their parents left the Home, the children were all adults pursuing their own destinies, as they had been encouraged to do.

Four of the five went to university, a significant accomplishment at a time when the number of native-born Nova Scotian blacks in the province's colleges and universities could be counted on the fingers of both hands. And they were all successful in the careers they chose.

Two of the daughters, Barbara and Betty, have passed away. Barbara worked as an administrator for the Ontario Health Insurance Plan in Toronto. In earlier years, she had served as a teaching assistant at the Bauld School, where she had won School Closing awards as a pupil. Betty Kinney graduated from Mount Saint Vincent University in Halifax, married a Chatham, Ontario, man named Mansfield Robbins and settled in Toronto.

The eldest daughter, Edna, became a teacher and lived for a time in Thompson, Manitoba. She now resides in Truro, Nova Scotia. Ross III is employed as Chief Draftsperson with the Toronto Department of Public Works. The youngest daughter, Patricia, earned two university degrees and a diploma in journalism. She taught at a community college in Toronto and is now a consultant for the Canadian Human Rights Commission.

Placing her family's history with the NSHCC in perspective, Patricia Kinney says:

"My grandfather saw a need and he addressed it. There was no place at all for black children in need to go. So he established the Home. Its very name—the Nova Scotia Home for Colored Children—is an indication of what the need was. But he was also trying to tell society that a child cannot be excluded from the system for reasons of race."

Ms. Kinney doesn't regard her parents' departure from the Home as the end of an era.

"My father finished what my grandfather started. He didn't see the Home as a permanent institution that would go on forever. He always hoped that as time passed, the Home wouldn't be what it once was. Our family never assumed ownership of the Home. It was there to fulfill a need. We knew a day might come when that need would no longer be there, a day when black children could be admitted to any institution in the province without regard to race."

Like her brother, she says her generation of the family was never pressured to continue to work at the Home.

"None of us was ever 'groomed' to step in for our parents, as though we were running a family business. We never saw that as an obligation. We were taught to pitch in and do what we could to fulfill a need, wherever it was."

In terms of fulfilling the need for a haven for neglected black children, the Kinney family left an undeniable legacy of excellence. A 1968 report prepared for Social Welfare of Nova Scotia provided the following evaluation of the Home: "Having reviewed the sound record of the Nova Scotia Home for Colored Children, the opinion is widely shared that there is every indication that the Institution is one of the finest Child Care Centers in Canada, and would be a credit to any community."

In retirement, Ross and Ida Kinney settled in Dartmouth. Kinney continued to visit the Home from time to time but left its administration to his successors. He went on to become a real estate agent and landlord. He also remained active with the church and the Carver Credit Union.

Ross Kinney died in 1981 at the age of 70. Rev. Donald Fairfax officiated at the funeral. Kinney was buried at the Dartmouth Memorial Gardens, located across the road from his beloved Home. Ida survived him by six years, passing away in 1987. A commemorative plaque to Ross Kinney is on permanent display at the Victoria Road Baptist Church in Dartmouth.

There are no longer any Kinneys associated with the NSHCC. Patricia Kinney says: "Our family never considered the Home a 'Kinney thing.' We always knew someone would step in and continue to do whatever was necessary to carry on."

That someone turned out to be a person whose commitment to the Home had lasted virtually all of her adult life.

Mary Paris

Ross Kinney's successor as head of the NSHCC was Mary M. Paris, who had been born in New Glasgow in 1934, the eldest of ten children born to Freeman and Violet Paris. At an early age, she joined the Baptist church and became active in church and community. At the age of 17, Mary had left New Glasgow to become a member of the Home's child-care staff.

"She answered a job advertisement," her younger sister, Cherry, recalls. "She didn't know much about the Home at the time, and her experience with children was limited to babysitting when she was in school. Of course, she was the oldest in a family of ten, which might have had something to do with her interest in the job."

When she answered that "help wanted" ad, Mary Paris found her calling. From the beginning, she poured her energy into the lives of those in her charge with a deep and genuine sense of identification and concern. "The Home became her life," says Cherry, who would herself become associated with the NSHCC in later years.

During her early years at the NSHCC, Mary Paris read widely and keenly observed the residents, many of whom had been adversely affected by the circumstances of their environment. She came to view the Home as a microcosm of the plight of blacks and other oppressed minorities in Nova Scotia and beyond. And she decided the social system as a whole needed to be challenged and changed, not just the Home.

In 1960, at the relatively young age of 26, Miss Paris became Acting Matron of the Home upon the retirement of Ida Kinney for health reasons. Mrs. Kinney had herself recommended Miss Paris for the position. After a period of convalescence, Mrs. Kinney returned as Assistant Matron. The fact that the older, more experienced woman was willing to continue in a subordinate position is a tribute to Miss Paris's character and competence.

During the several occasions when illness forced Miss Paris to take leaves of absence, Mrs. Kinney stepped in to assume the Matron's duties. But she always made her own position clear, as the following memo she wrote to the Board in 1970 indicates:

I wish to clarify my position as Assistant Matron of the Nova Scotia Home for Coloured Children as of March 17/70.

Due to the fact that Miss Paris, Matron-in-Charge, has returned to full time duty, it is my intention to remain as her Assistant.

I trust that this will clear up any misunderstanding that the Board of Directors and the Board of Management may have had in regard to this matter.

THE OLD ORDER ENDS

Mary was diplomatic as well; she retained the title "Acting Matron" until she succeeded Ross Kinney as Superintendent in 1967. At that point, Ida Kinney took back the title of Matron. Yet even after she assumed the duties of Superintendent, Miss Paris was often referred to as "Matron" or "Matron-in-Charge."

Mary Paris's reputation for kindness and caring continued after her rise in status. Although the number of children resident at the Home ranged from fifty-five to seventy, she knew each one by name and circumstance and attempted to meet their individual needs. She accompanied the children on visits to the Child Guidance Centre and Children's Hospital, and facilitated meetings with teachers and social workers. To use a phrase that wouldn't become common until the 1980s, she was always "there for them."

Miss Paris maintained an excellent relationship with the Home's staff. On many occasions they sought her counsel on matters concerning the Home's operation or on major issues in the outside world. She fought for a higher pay scale for employees of the NSHCC, some of whom were earning less than minimum wage.

Ross Kinney passes the NSHCC torch to Mary Paris.

Although she never finished school, having gone directly to work at the Home as a teenager, Miss Paris possessed a true thirst for knowledge. Her radio was always turned on to the news so she could keep abreast of current events. "Wise beyond her years" is a phrase that fit her perfectly.

Eventually, she became involved in social activism. In that regard, Mary Paris was a spiritual descendant of James Kinney, Sr., who had spoken out forcefully and articulately on social and racial issues in earlier times.

In 1968 she attended a human rights conference and expressed herself eloquently, from the heart. Criticizing the "gradualism" recommended by some members of the white and black communities, she said: "What good is there in saying to them [blacks], 'God bless you! Keep warm and eat well!' if you don't give them the necessities of life?"

At that time the militant ideology of black power had begun to filter up from the United States. In November 1968, former Student Non-Violent Coordinating Committee (SNCC) activist and Black Panther leader Stokeley Carmichael had visited Halifax, causing a near panic among many whites and conservative blacks. Partly as a result of the Panthers' visit, an organization called the Black United Front was formed.

Fear of the militancy black power implied was widespread in Nova Scotia. It even reached as far as the Board of the NSHCC, as expressed in Treasurer Al Grayston's report in the minutes of the Home's 1969 annual meeting:

The Treasurer pointed out that once again a record income from the public had been achieved. He stated that when the letters went out in the Fall of 1968, he was concerned over the fact that certain militant Black Panther leaders from the United States had visited and this might have an adverse effect upon donations. However, in conversation with many donors, he had found they recognized that the Home simply looked after young children who had no association with racism, militant or otherwise.

The Nova Scotia Home for Colored Children as a hotbed of black power militance? Mary Paris put that issue in its proper perspective when she said: "Your enemy is not black power, but ignorance...ignorance of the black man as a human being."

Miss Paris was a pioneer feminist as well. In an address she presented to the Women's Institute of the African United Baptist Association, she presented the principles upon which her life and work were based:

The time has surely come and God knows that it is long overdue when we must redefine our role as women and formulate a plan for complete cooperation and understanding of each other's views. I feel that as a women's organization we have been given a mandate by the people to reach out to everyone as we move forward in our struggle for freedom from want, suffering and the many frustrations that have plagued our people for generations. Never were the words of Abraham Lincoln as apt as today: "The dogmas of our quiet past are inadequate to the stormy present. We must think anew; we must act now."

We live in a world of insecurity, where men everywhere are enslaved by doubt, fear, hate, lust, selfishness, and many other evils. We can help by working to set at liberty those victimized by ignorance, oppression, prejudice, racism, hunger, disease, unemployment and bad housing. God is concerned about the whole of life. Faith, if it does not lend itself to action, is in itself a lifeless thing.

These are difficult and challenging days in which we live, and we must face them with courage and conviction, not counting the cost.

Let us join in creating new endeavors where the strong are just, the weak secure and the peace preserved. All of this will not be done overnight, some of it may not even be accomplished in our lifetime, but please, I implore you, let us begin with a good conscience our only sure reward, with history the final judge of our deeds. Let us go forth in the times like these as freedom's models in a searching world. But remember, before any of these things can be accomplished we must be free within ourselves and in our homes.

For all the battles she fought for the rights of blacks, women and children, Mary Paris faced another, far more personal foe—her physical frailties. She faced surgery over a six-month period in 1968 and took other medical leaves in 1970 and 1971.

Yet even as her health was failing, Miss Paris continued to fight for her Home children. In one case, during the spring of 1971, Alvin (not his real name), a 13-year-old boy residing at the NSHCC, sustained an arm injury during a fight with a teacher. The school called Miss Paris, who took the boy home. At the time, Alvin refused to disclose his injury. In her report on the incident, Miss Paris wrote: "I went out and [Alvin] was sitting in the car. I didn't say anything to him at this point as I have learned from past experience that when a person is angry or upset communication is usually at a low ebb."

Only after returning to the Home did Alvin admit the extent of his suffering. After taking Alvin to the hospital, Miss Paris had him examined by Dr. A.N. Lamplugh, a Westphal-based physician. Dr. Lamplugh had been making house calls at the Home for several years and continued to care for its residents until 1978.

In a report requested by Miss Paris, the doctor stated: "This boy has sustained a severe soft tissue injury to his forearm, which in the absence of any underlying bony injury, indicates that very great force must have been used to produce such a disability."

Through further investigation, Miss Paris learned that a woman teacher had intended to strap Alvin because of an infraction of classroom rules. Alvin refused to be strapped, and a male teacher was brought in to administer the punishment. In the ensuing struggle, Alvin managed to take the strap away from the teacher. The teacher then kicked Alvin in the arm to get the strap away from him.

School officials determined that both teachers had acted appropriately under the circumstances. That explanation satisfied neither Miss Paris nor Board President Alice Croft. They took the case to Carl Perry, who was then Superintendent of Halifax Municipal County Schools. After a one-hour meeting, Perry conceded that the incident was "a deplorable thing and there is no question that errors in judgment were made by both teachers."

Miss Paris won young Alvin's battle. However, her health continued to deteriorate, and in the fall of 1971, she once again had to be hospitalized. Alice Croft was one of many who hoped for the best, telling the Board: "I am pleased to report Miss Paris is now home in New Glasgow and feeling much improved."

But that hope was not to be fulfilled. On November 7, 1971, Mary Paris finally succumbed to her illness. She was only 37 years old.

Gone Too Soon

Mary Paris's passing, like that of J.A.R. Kinney, Sr. thirty-one years earlier, left a void at the Home that would not be easy to fill, as this quote from a letter of condolence from Rev. Donald D. Skeir indicates:

> *It is not possible for us to adequately relate the services that Miss Paris rendered to our Home over the nineteen years she was associated with it. The true value of her services can only be understood by the hundreds of young people whose lives were moulded by her example and counsel.*

At her funeral, which was held at the Second United Baptist Church in New Glasgow, speeches and Bible readings were given by Revs. Donald D. Skeir, William P. Oliver and Joseph Mack. Rev. H.D. Thomas officiated.

When Rev. Donald Fairfax preached her eulogy, he spoke of her time as Matron of the Home:

> *...a position she filled so well, gaining the respect and admiration of people in all walks of life who came in contact with the Home. It was always a delight for her to meet many distinguished visitors such as the late Governor General of Canada, Mr. Vanier and Mrs. Vanier, who were delighted to meet such a gracious young lady.*
>
> *One of the fond memories I have of her is that her first love was the children who were committed to her care. Hundreds of young men and women, throughout Nova Scotia and many parts of Canada, will remember her for her great concern and dedication to them.*

Though only a young woman, she was often faced with many problems which often demanded her to make difficult and demanding decisions. To be sure, her decisions would always be in the best interest of the children. She was particularly interested in raising the standard of living at the Home, thus introducing an awareness of higher education.

Miss Paris's younger brother, Rev. Peter Paris, who is now a professor of ethics in the Theological Seminary at Princeton University in the United States, delivered a final tribute that included these words:

It may be that a young woman goes to work at the young age of 17 as an aide in an institution established for children who have been hard hit by the circumstances of life. It may be that such a young woman pours herself into the lives of those children with a deep sense of identification and genuine concern, reads and studies as much as she can pertaining to the well-being of those children, comes to see the impact of certain institutional structures and arrangements on the lives of those children, and following long years of experience and insight, comes to know the impact of the entire social system on those children.

At this point, and long before, she is no longer content simply to apply band aids, but sees the necessity of challenging the entire social system that makes for oppression in whatever form.

Mary Paris
(Courtesy Cherry Paris)

That challenge was not a vain one. To this day, more than twenty years after her death, Mary Paris lives on in the memories of those who knew her.

Rev. Donald Fairfax describes her as "very sensitive to the needs of the children, able to give them the warmth and love they needed. She filled a great, great gap, and the Home was the richer for it."

He also says she could be assertive when circumstances warranted. "Mary Paris fought for the well-being of the children," he recalls. "She would approach the department of welfare and battle for the children, and that in itself was very, very beautiful."

Donna Byard Sealey says: "She was a mother figure to the children. Each child at the Home was like her own, and when I first started teaching there were about sixty-five of them."

Charlie Wright recalls her as a "soft, gentle woman. You'd have to do something very, very bad before she'd correct you. She'd never, ever raise a strap to punish you."

Mary Paris' own words serve as her best epitaph. In a 1967 report to the Board, she expressed her views on staff salary and the future of the Home in terms that were far from uncertain:

> *In twelve years our salaries have increased from $65 per month to $100 per month. This only proves to show you that our strides have been limited in this field. Our salary structure is pathetic when you look at the picture and see that our cook is paid more than our supervisor.*
>
> *I can only repeat as I have in the past that we only get what we pay for. What value do we put on our operation at the Home if we only pay meagre salaries to people who are expected to perform the impossible?*
>
> *I strongly feel that unless administration recognizes the severity of this problem, there is only one way we can go and it is certainly not ahead. I have faith in past experiences in working with those who direct the N.S. Home that you will honestly and with much care and foresight deal with these problems and work them out for the mutual benefit of all concerned.*
>
> *I assure you if I were not concerned for the Home and the Home only and for all it stands for I would not even bother to be here today. But because I do care and believe you care, I have faith in the future of the N.S. Home and the great task that is set before us.*
>
> *Let this be our Centennial project and let us go down in history as being known for people who had a reputation for recognizing the core of the problem, and then setting forth to accomplishing the results. May we be a signpost on the highway of life, rather than a rut out of which the wheel cannot turn.*

Those words would prove prophetic in years to come, and the Board of that time would have done well to heed them. Had it done so, the Home's future might have followed a different path.

Mary Paris's passing was only one of many adversities that would face the Home over the next few years, but it was the one from which it would have the greatest difficulty recovering.

The Foster Home Problem

In the immediate aftermath of Mary Paris's untimely death, her sister Cherry succeeded her as Acting Matron of the Home. Then Portia Provo, a native of Cherry Brook, took on the Matron's position. Mrs. Provo had previously worked under Mary Paris at the Home as Supervisor of Boys and Girls. In that position, she had assisted in attending to the needs of the children, planning their activities and taking them out into the community.

Portia Provo was succeeded in 1973 by Mrs. Ada Clayton, who was in turn replaced by Cherry Paris, who had come back to the Home after furthering her studies. By then, with a restructuring of the NSHCC staff, the Matron's role and title had been supplanted by a new position called Child Development Supervisor.

Children ice-skating at the Home during the 1960s.

However, Cherry Paris's tenure lasted only eight months. In 1974 she moved to Bermuda with her husband, Charles Swann. She later returned to Nova Scotia and is now Regional Supervisor of the provincial Human Rights Commission's office in Digby. She is also a founding member of the Digby–Annapolis Women's Network.

Cherry retains warm memories of her time at the NSHCC. One of her fondest recollections involves Christmas time, when children, who did not have families to go to, spent their holidays at the Home.

"We did everything we could to make it a good time for the children," she recalls. "We collected gifts, made a traditional dinner and lit candles. It was a special time for them and us."

But the times, special and otherwise, continued to change. Throughout the 1960s and 1970s, social service agencies' preferences for placement in foster homes over institutions increased. The theory behind such preferences was that foster homes were more like natural homes. However, the circumstances surrounding foster care for black children were becoming a cause for concern.

Because of depressed economic conditions within their communities, many black families who were willing to host children from the NSHCC did not meet the standards required by the Children's Aid Society and the Department of Social Services. The only alternatives were to keep the children in the Home or to place them with white families. But an increasing number of black children placed in white foster homes were beginning to experience adjustment problems of varying degrees of seriousness.

In an article on the history of the NSHCC, Rev. Donald Fairfax assessed the foster home situation as follows:

What we need is an opportunity to do what is best in the interest of Black, orphaned and neglected children through the Province of Nova Scotia, many of whom have lost their identity, having been placed in foster homes that are inferior and unable to meet the needs of black children.

Until now, the black population of Nova Scotia have been most patient, the reason being that many are not aware of the situation that exists among the orphaned and neglected children of their own race. There are alarming situations in some of the foster homes. A study must be made as to some of the deplorable conditions encountered by black children and unless something very constructive is done, we could face a racial crisis in this very province.

Rev. Fairfax was circumspect about describing the "deplorable" conditions to which he referred. Others say some children were treated as servants by foster families who saw child care as a source of income and cheap labor.

In one case a teenage boy from the NSHCC was placed in a foster home that already had several children. After he'd seen where he'd be sleeping—on the floor—and listened to the house rules and long list of chores, he walked back to the NSHCC and announced that he would not be leaving until he turned 18. Social Services bowed to his determination.

Jocelyn Boyd, a former NSHCC resident who became the Home's office manager in 1993, was too young to walk away from her white foster family in Montreal. The effects of the placement linger to this day.

"I would honestly say it had a devastating effect on me," she says. "A lot of people who took in foster children only took them in for the money, and a lot of them were quite racist. It was common for you to be called a nigger, or stupid, or ugly. I was lucky enough to have spent time with my mother, who had taught me that I wasn't an ugly child or a stupid child. But if you're told that from early childhood till the time you're 15 or 16, you're not going to have much of a chance, because you're going to believe it by then."

NSHCC children enjoy outing at Windsor Park military base in 1963. The child in the front row with the Coca Cola bottle is Jocelyn Boyd, who is now the Home's Office Manager.
(Courtesy Donna Byard Sealey)

Jocelyn persevered despite those circumstances, and by the time she turned 17, a business college in Montreal offered her a scholarship. She turned it down.

"I refused the scholarship because taking it meant staying in the foster home," she says. "I went out and got a job and my own apartment rather than stay there. I would have been destroyed."

In all, Jocelyn spent five years in three white foster homes. She remains cynical about the families' motives for taking her in.

"They had a built-in babysitter," she says. "Somebody that could clean the house and be a little maid."

Some aspects of Ms. Boyd's foster home experiences may have cut across racial lines. And some white foster families provided the care and attention children needed regardless of what color they happened to be. Still, for many black children placed in white foster homes, the racial element added to the stress of an already difficult situation.

Another unforeseen consequence of the foster home system was the high turnover rate for placements. Board President Alice Croft mentioned that problem in a September 6, 1971, memo to Board members:

At the meeting held with the Department of Welfare officials on August 2nd, Dr. Norton, Psychologist at the Children's Hospital, discussed a number of cases with which he has had to deal at the clinic in connection with the hospital and he definitely feels one of the greatest problems he has to face are the children who have been moved from one foster home to another and in some cases the child has been very severely disturbed as a result of so many moves. Therefore, this is just one more reason why the Nova Scotia Home for Colored Children is a much better place to put a child.

Other problems occurred in the area of interracial adoptions. Halifax writer Kimberley Covey, who spent a short time at the NSHCC as an infant during the early 1960s, talks about the circumstances of her adoption by a white couple from Montreal:

"They responded to an ad in a Montreal paper placed by the Nova Scotia Children's Aid Society. The ad said: "Wanted—Homes for Negro and mixed-race children." It reminded me of the Humane Society trying to find homes for puppies....

"My mom and dad were good to me. But he was 60 when I was adopted—old enough to be my great-grandfather. And my mother was 47. I don't think they would have been allowed to adopt a white child."

Another difficulty was that light-skinned and mixed-race children tended to be preferred by foster and adoptive families, making their darker-skinned peers feel unwanted. Color sensitivity has always been a problem within the black community as well as the white, so it's not surprising that the child-care system—including the Home—would reflect a bias toward children with "fair" complexions and straight hair. It also follows that lighter-skinned children would be more likely to experience identity problems in white foster or adoptive environments.

There was another side to the race-consciousness story, however. Wayne MacKay, a law professor at Dalhousie University in Halifax, wrote the following defense of interracial adoptions in the November 6, 1977, issue of *The Halifax Loyalist*, citing a 1963 study performed by Edith Roskie in Montreal:

> *Black children in white families were very clear about racial identity and demonstrated no ambivalence or confusion about their color. The study also indicated that being raised in a white family did not generate negative feelings about their own race. Perhaps the importance of being raised in the black culture has been over-emphasized. In summary, the facts that are used to oppose transracial adoption have not to date been substantiated.*

Because of a shortage of black foster families, children such as this late-1960s NSHCC resident were often placed in white foster homes.
(Bob Brooks photo, courtesy Public Archives of Nova Scotia)

Although MacKay's arguments sounded convincing, Roskie's study wasn't the final word on the issue. A 1979 study of the NSHCC prepared by Diane Smaggus and Blair Blakeney for black educator Savannah Williams painted a different picture of how black children's ethnic identity fared in white foster and adoptive homes:

When placing black children in white homes, many problems arise. A majority of the black children are placed in middle-class white families. These parents do not promote cultural awareness in their homes, so the black child grows up not knowing anything or very little about his culture. Aside from the lack of cultural awareness, the white parents also have problems managing their children's hair and skin types. Their hair can vary from light, loose curls to very kinky hair, which could be very difficult to control if not taken care of properly. White parents of black children usually have no idea of these problems, so they wash and comb [black children's] hair as they do [that of whites]. What happens is that these children grow up not able to care for themselves, because they were never properly taught.

Black people also have skin problems whites do not encounter. Their skin is prone to keloids, which are thick scars which can develop after a cut or burn. Keloids are treated with different methods such as injections, X-rays, and dry ice treatments.

To intensify problems even further, black kids in white homes label themselves as "colored," "brown," and even "white." This shows that these white parents don't even tell their children that there are differences among people. It therefore seems the acceptance of black children in these homes is more a matter of proper attitude than having parents of the right skin color, but with the above information it seems to me they don't even have the proper attitudes to raise a black child properly.

From a realistic perspective, the viewpoints expressed by Mr. MacKay and Ms. Williams represent opposite extremes that are not necessarily applicable to individual cases. Undoubtedly some black children were able to maintain their identity in white foster and adoptive homes, as the Roskie study indicated. And, undoubtedly, other black adoptees grew up as "white" children with dark skins. Most black children in trans-racial placements would have fallen somewhere between those poles.

The Williams report also addressed the shortage of black families willing to foster or adopt children. It concluded that economic and social factors were the primary explanations rather than commonly held assumptions of lack of interest and information. In specific terms, the report said:

Why do very few Nova Scotian blacks adopt? The most obvious reason is that many black families do not have the economic resources necessary to adopt a child. Because of their socio-economic position, black communities often have a significant number of single-parent families who are rarely allowed to adopt.

The report also cited an American study that suggested a suspicion among blacks of dealing with red tape, bureaucracy and long waiting periods. There was also a high expectation of rejection, an attitude that carried over from experiences in schools and workplaces.

However, the report overlooked the informal, extended-family childcare network that had always existed within the black communities of Nova Scotia. Rather than go to social service agencies or the NSHCC, grandparents, aunts, uncles, or even distant cousins would take in each other's children in times of need. But the increasingly interventionist policies of social services and Children's Aid obstructed that informal network.

Not to be outdone, the Home itself struck a Casework Committee to prepare a report addressing the issues of interracial adoption and the role of the NSHCC within the structure of the social services network. Jules Oliver, a Board member and son of Rev. William P. Oliver, chaired the committee.

In an April 1971 letter to F.R. MacKinnon, then Deputy Minister of the provincial Department of Public Welfare, Oliver wrote:

The Board's position is simply that the Home should remain for the health and welfare of our Black children; only revitalized to include many areas for the future development of the Black Child, e.g., therapeutic, educational and placement needs, etc.

The Board's position is based upon the fact that we prefer the Black child to be placed in Black foster or adoption homes. The matter of racial, cultural and self-identification is one of the most crucial aspects in order to ensure a "positive, healthy and mature" development of a Black child. We are of the conviction that this factor has been too long neglected.

By September 1971 the Casework Committee's report was complete. Oliver concluded that the Home was "in a very difficult position" because the province seemed determined to phase out orphanage-style institutions and replace them with a combination of foster parents and therapeutic group homes. At that time, the NSHCC did not fit into either of those categories.

In one part of the report, Oliver recounted an interesting exchange he had with Kevin Burns, Director of Child Welfare for the Department of Public Welfare:

Mr. Burns indicated that White parents are becoming much more liberal and that there has been a steady increase in White parents adopting Black children. I asked Mr. Burns would Black parents have the right to adopt White children. His answer was "no." I challenged him on this matter and the only argument he could put forth was one of statistics and that is: since there are more Black children and less adoption or foster care by Black parents, there is no other alternative but to allow them to be adopted by White parents. It was pointed out that the answer to my question and the inconsistency in his logic makes one question whether psychological and racial genocide is being practiced.

Clearly, the practice of interracial adoption was a one-way street, and the Home was on a collision course with the social services establishment. To this day, the debate over placing black children in white foster and adoptive homes continues.

Edie Gray's Children

An exception to the misgivings of Rev. Fairfax and others concerning foster home care was Miss Edith "Edie" Gray, who in 1959 began to raise foster children who had lived at the NSHCC. An unmarried woman with many friends and relatives who had become parents and grandparents, Miss Gray regretted the absence of children from her life. The boarders she had taken into her home had only partially compensated for that lack.

On Thanksgiving Day in 1959, she sat down to dinner with her boarder at the time, black community leader B.A. Husbands. She looked at the large turkey on the table and decided the bird was far too big for two people. She then phoned Matron Ida Kinney at the NSHCC and asked if it would be possible to bring some children over to share Thanksgiving dinner. Fine, Mrs. Kinney replied, as long as the children were returned by suppertime.

The dinner turned out to be such a delight for the children and Miss Gray that she seriously considered raising them herself. When she returned them to the Home, she asked Mrs. Kinney about the possibilities of becoming a permanent foster parent. Mrs. Kinney explained that the youngsters were wards of the Children's Aid Society (CAS), which had the final say in custody matters. However, she assured Miss Gray that her name would be highly recommended for consideration.

A social worker from the CAS inspected Miss Gray's eight-room home and found it eminently suitable for child-raising. But her single status was a major obstacle. At the time, unmarried persons were considered unsuitable as foster or adoptive parents.

Miss Gray persisted, urging the CAS to give her the opportunity to prove she was a fit parent. She also pointed out that few people, married or not, were willing to take in children who were not their own.

Edith Gray (center) with her five adopted children (left to right) Gerry Morrison, Loretta Johnson, Juanita Johnson, David Johnson and Roy Williams.
(Courtesy Edith Gray)

Finally, Mr. Blois agreed to a trial placement. Miss Gray wanted four children, two boys and two girls. Another little boy caught her eye as well, and she ended up with five youngsters in tow. Their names were Roy Williams, Gerry Morrison, and Loretta, David and Juanita Johnson.

The CAS provided for the children's financial needs; Miss Gray gave them a stable and loving environment. During their first Christmas with Miss Gray, though, one of the girls, Loretta seemed depressed. She told Miss Gray she wanted to return to the Home.

"Why?" Miss Gray asked.

"We get to hang up stockings at the Home," Loretta replied, glancing pointedly at Miss Gray's bare mantel.

From that year on, all five children received a full stocking on Christmas morning.

Edith Gray took great pleasure in the children and treated them as her own. "They were my pride and joy," she recalls. "I took them everywhere."

A woman who believed in honesty, Miss Gray never allowed the children to believe she was their mother. To them, she was "Aunt Edith," or just plain "Aunt." But she did things for them only a real mother could.

On one occasion she gave two of them a birthday party in the hall of the Cornwallis Street Baptist Church. All the neighborhood children and their parents were invited to share in a celebration with balloons and a magician.

The children attended church on a regular basis. Always well-groomed and tidy, they wore white linen outfits, and the girls' hair was braided and be-ribboned. Miss Gray took great pride in their appearance.

Although they no longer resided at the NSHCC, Miss Gray's wards still participated in the annual CHNS radio broadcast. Their section of the program included the naming of the sixty-six books of the Bible, which they had memorized in only a week's time. Then they recited a poem that began with the line: "God loves little children no matter what color they may be." Their finale was the song, "He's Got the Whole World in His Hands." The children were well disciplined and made a lasting impression on the audience.

An extremely strong-willed woman, as evidenced by her battle to overturn the barriers against single foster parents, Miss Gray always stood by her children. All she asked was that they be open and honest enough to come to her with their problems. In her personal philosophy, everyone was equal, regardless of race or other differences.

Once one of Miss Gray's boys was expelled from school for a racial incident that ended in a fight. The boy had a white girlfriend, and a white male student found that objectionable. Although both boys threw punches in the fight, the white boy was not expelled.

When Miss Gray called to school to find out why her child was the only one expelled over the incident, she was informed that the other boy's mother made substantial yearly donations to the school and was also a member of the School Board. For that reason, certain "allowances" had been made for him.

Edith Gray responded that social status was no basis for expelling one child and not the other. She also said that if her boy wasn't permitted to return to school the following day, she would pay a personal visit and settle matters in her own way.

Shaken by Miss Gray's display of determination, the teacher apologized and promised to rectify the situation. The next day, Miss Gray's ward was back in the classroom.

Although the children have long since grown up and moved away, they all remain in close contact with their "Aunt Edith." She taught them independence, but they were never neglected. For Miss Gray, the upbringing of those five children was a labor of love.

"If I had it to do over again, I would do the same thing," she says. "Of all the things I've done, I don't regret anything. The key to my life is love."

The love in Edie Gray's heart proved more than enough to meet the needs of the five children she took in. But it would take more than love to carry the Nova Scotia Home for Colored Children through the difficulties it would soon be facing.

Loyal

*The first believers
lusted after liberty —
a road, a roof, a rose.*

*But this is how history
actually commences —
among stones, among thorns.*

*Our first believers
dreamt of poetry
but planted potatoes.*

*They knew this truth:
the line of verse follows
the row of potatoes.*

*The song-bejeweled voice
trails the muddy plough:
Swing low, swing low sweet....*

George Elliott Clarke

A New Attitude: 1973-1979

The Mandate Changes

By the early 1970s it became clear that the NSHCC's survival would depend upon a change in focus. The turn-of-the-century identification of orphanages as primary care-givers for troubled children had become passé within the social service profession. Long-term, self-contained child-care facilities were now viewed as final rather than first resorts. Adequately adjusted children who could handle personal responsibility went to foster homes; those who could not ended up in group homes or public and private institutions.

Disturbed children, violent children, withdrawn children—children with chronic and complex emotional problems made up an ever-greater proportion of the residents of most institutions that had not already closed down, including the NSHCC.

The Home had hardly become irrelevant, however. The black community still needed a place where troubled children could develop a sense of belonging and identity. However, major changes would be necessary before the Home could begin to fulfill that need.

In February 1973, the Board, with financial assistance from the Department of Social Services and the Catholic Social Services Commission, hired the community consultant firm of Rafuse, Dwyer & Marentette to conduct a comprehensive survey of the Home. As Board President Alice Croft said in her report to the African United Baptist Association's annual meeting that year, the purpose of the consultants' presence was "to endeavour to try and upgrade and change the concept of the Home to make it more in keeping with present day trends toward Child care."

The consultants' final sixty-seven-page report painted a portrait of an institution that was in a state of transition but without direction. In its introduction the report's authors wrote:

NSHCC Board members Rev. Donald Skier, Rev. Donald Fairfax, Mrs. Alice Croft and Ian Forsyth.

To some considerable extent, this report is a continuation of previous studies done on the Home, which include the National Study Service report of March, 1970, entitled Children With Special Needs, and a series of reports in April and May of 1970 by the Nova Scotia Human Rights Commission. The former report, known as the "Hall Report," concentrated primarily on the continuing role and function of voluntary child caring institutions within the framework of child welfare services in Nova Scotia. This report was commissioned by the Nova Scotia Department of Social Services. The latter series of reports emanated from investigations by the Nova Scotia Human Rights Commission of complaints of unfair and unequal treatment to staff by the Home at that time. The Commission's reports concentrated primarily on internal administrative problems resulting in a series of recommendations to the Board.

The present evaluation attempts to combine these two approaches evaluating both the progress made in alleviating past problems and the present operation of the Home.

After two months of direct field observation, the consultants' ultimate assessment of the Home comprised a mixed bag of positive and negative impressions.

Financially, the institution was on a relatively even keel, although the report did note that "many of the agencies who have children in the Home are very slow in paying their per diem rate." The report recommended a renegotiation of the per diem rate and a broadening of efforts to solicit funds from other sources and an overhaul of the Home's accounting system.

However, the evaluation of the NSHCC's staff and administration raised some disturbing questions. The report's language was blunt:

There is considerable agreement among Board members that the Home's major objectives are to provide care, warmth and an increased opportunity for emotional, social, and educational development for Black children away from their natural families. There is, likewise, considerable agreement that the Home is not meeting those objectives at the present time.

Among the staff—interim Matron, the child-care workers, the maintenance people and the cooks—morale appeared low. As the report put it:

Generally, staff are apathetic and dissatisfied with their working conditions. Their dissatisfaction is centered, primarily, on salary and fringe benefits; lack of good personnel practice and policies; lack of direction by the Board; and lack of adequate job descriptions.

That assessment reflected a change in the nature of the Home's authority structure. In the past, operational control was centered at the top, i.e., the positions of Supervisor and Matron. And the J.A.R. Kinney Senior and Junior father-to-son succession as Superintendent led to a direct, hands-on style of management from which the Board could maintain a distance. In tandem with the Matrons, the Kinneys did the hiring and firing at the Home; thus, staff accountability rested in their hands rather than the Board's. And, of course, the Kinneys' membership on the Board provided a direct link to the Home's ultimate authority.

To a lesser extent, Mary Paris continued the tradition of leadership from within the NSHCC after Ross Kinney retired. Although she was not a member of the Board, she attended its meetings on an ex-officio basis.

Tragically, her life was cut short before a changeover to a different authority structure could commence. In the absence of the leadership of a Ross and Ida Kinney or a Mary Paris, the conditions the consultants encountered should not have been surprising.

In fact, those findings had been anticipated by the Hall Report three years earlier. The scope of that report was broader than that of Rafuse, Dwyer et al., because it covered five voluntary child-care institutions: Bairncroft, the Bible Hill Protestant Children's Home, the Halifax Protestant Orphan Home, the Little Flower Institute and the NSHCC.

The Hall report mentioned the same staff pay and experience problems the Rafuse, Dwyer consultants found. However, the stature and influence exerted by Mary Paris would have counterbalanced the morale problems that emerged later.

As for the Home's physical plant, the Rafuse, Dwyer study concluded that the building that had been such a source of pride in the 1920s and 1930s had become inadequate for the changing needs of the residents. According to the report:

The building is difficult to supervise because of its physical layout. The top floor is not used and is consequently a liability in terms of maintenance and upkeep, offering no return. The dormitories are very much traditionally institutional, allowing for little or no privacy, personal possession or individuality. This also dictates the stereotype of routine and total group movement (regimentation).

In other words, facilities that were state-of-the-art in 1921 had, in the report's opinion, become state-of-the-past in 1973.

Perhaps the most telling comment of all came in the consultants' assessment of relations between the Home and the black community: "It is our feeling the awareness of the Home in the Black community is predominantly an historical awareness *not* a functional one."

To the extent that this conclusion was valid, the change in the black community's image of the Home paralleled changes in the Home itself. From its early days as a relatively independent institution on a par with the province's black churches, businesses and schools, the Home had by the early 1970s sacrificed its independence to become part of the provincial child-welfare bureaucracy to which it had been conceived as an alternative.

The consultants recommended sweeping changes in policy and philosophy for the Home, including:

- *The creation of an Executive Director position to replace that of Superintendent,*
- *The construction of new facilities that would be suitable for group homes rather than institutions,*
- *Implementation of training for staff in the areas of child development,*
- *A public relations program to improve the Home's image in the black and white communities, and*
- *Better communication between the Board and the staff.*

Yet for all the shortcomings the report listed, it also endorsed the need for an institution like the Home. Two years earlier, the NSHCC and the Social

Services Department had agreed in writing that although white children were welcome at the institution, its primary purpose was to take in black children for whom foster homes were not available: "This policy, although reinforcing the premise that a Black child should be placed in a White foster home only as a last resort, emphasizes in fact that the Home is to be used only as an alternative short term placement of Black children when no Black foster home is available."

That mandate was much narrower than the "care, education, and training of the members of the Afro-American race" mentioned in the Incorporation Act of 1915. However, given the racial difficulties that continued fifty years after the Home's inauguration, that responsibility remained sufficient to ensure the institution's survival.

Despite the groundswells of change that were occurring around them, in 1973 the Home's residents (twenty-eight black and six white) found time for outside pursuits. As Mrs. Croft reported to the AUBA:

> *During the summer the children have enjoyed many outings through the generosity of friends of the Home and at this time I should like to mention just a few. All children attended the Circus. "The Singing Milkman" show put on in Lower Sackville recently was attended by all children as guests of the Sackville Lions Club. The East Preston annual Sunday School Picnic was enjoyed as well as a trip to the Wildlife Park.*

Still, to paraphrase folk-rock singer Bob Dylan, "The times, they were a' changin'."

From Superintendent to Director

Although some of the Rafuse, Dwyer study's conclusions must have been somewhat unpalatable, the Board accepted the majority of the report's recommendations. At a meeting on July 30, 1973, a motion carried that enabled the Board to: "propose the upgrading of the present institution on a temporary basis with the gradual establishing of Group Homes on this property as the need arises and with the understanding that this proposal will be subject to review."

Following up on that motion, Board members met with Dr. F.R. MacKinnon, Deputy Minister of Social Services, to negotiate an increase in the per diem rate and lay the groundwork for a request for provincial funds to upgrade the Home's facilities. B. Housser of the Social Services staff was assigned to assist in the preparation of a specific proposal.

Another recommendation the Board embraced was an increase in communication with the black community. At a July 7 meeting at the Home, the Board discussed future policy with representatives from the Black United Front, the Nova Scotia Association for the Advancement of Colored People, and the AUBA. All these organizations offered both moral and financial support for the Home's change in direction.

The NSHCC's restructuring plan began in earnest later that year, when the Board advertised in the local newspapers for an Executive Director, one of the major recommendations in the community consultants' report. An indication of the extent to which the Board was committed to a new direction may be found in text of the want ad:

> *This is a new post being created by the Board interested in changing a long-established institution responsible for the care of black children into a new concept of child care.*
>
> *The Executive Director should have a degree in Social Work, child care or a comparable area, and would be working closely with the Board, the Department of Social Services of the Nova Scotia Government and other Children's Agencies to effect far reaching changes in the care of black children in Nova Scotia.*
>
> *This is an exciting new post with ample room for original thinking, innovative changes and leadership and will be a challenge to any person interested in child care.*

One of the applicants was William Robert Butler, who had served as Executive Director of the Halifax Paraplegic Association, the Association for the Mentally Retarded, the Neighborhood Centre, and Special Services. He was also one of the founders of the Kingsmeadow Sports Dinner, an annual benefit for the mentally handicapped.

Butler was no stranger to the NSHCC. In his capacity as Executive Director of the Neighbourhood Centre, a social services office in the North End of Halifax, he had come into contact with staff and children from the Home. But his initial experience with the Home had a different source.

"My first contact with the Nova Scotia Home for Colored Children would have been when I was with the Paraplegic Association, and I was a member of the Northwest Rotary Club," Butler recalled. "And we did a 'fishorama.' We used to bring a lot of children in from the Home for the fishorama. I was delegated by the club to take a number of cars and station wagons over to the Home to pick up the kids for the event. At that point, I met Mary Paris. That would have been about 1961."

When the Executive Director's position at the Home became available twelve years later, Butler applied without hesitation.

"I think I was primarily interested in the fact that they wanted to develop a child development program," he says. "And they were particularly interested in developing some sort of new residential complex. Also, I was interested in minorities. I once wrote up a report which I hoped the provincial government would pick up—they didn't—in terms of coordinating everything that would be of help to socially disadvantaged minorities."

Butler wasn't the only applicant for the job. The process by which the position was filled was summarized in the following memo submitted by Dr. John Savage, a family physician who was a member of the NSHCC Board and acting chairman of an ad hoc committee assigned to select an Executive Director.

Bob Butler, first Executive Director of the NSHCC.

Advertisements were placed in the Halifax Chronicle-Herald, *the Canadian Welfare newsletter, "information" of the Canadian Association of Social Workers, and the Toronto* Globe and Mail.

The initial interviewing of some six people who applied to the advertisement in the Halifax paper was done by Mrs. Croft, Mr. Brindley and myself with the assistance of Mr. Allen Dwyer. Many applications were also considered in addition to those who were interviewed, and many were thus weeded out at the initial stage.

Following a flood of replies to the advertisement in the Toronto Globe and Mail, *it was decided that rather than bring six or seven people down from Ontario and other parts, it would be better if a small committee was to go up to Toronto and interview people there.*

Accordingly, on September 7th and 8th, the Reverends Fairfax, Mack and myself went up to Toronto, where we stayed at the Skyline Hilton and interviewed some six people. Following this, we sat down again with Mrs. Croft and Mr. Brindley, and it was decided that of the numerous applicants the best suited for the job of Executive Director seemed to us to be Mr. Robert Butler, one of the five or six people interviewed at the Home originally.

Born in Newfoundland in 1924, Bob Butler was the son of a clergyman and a nurse who had established a pastoral/social/medical ministry in the remote parts of the province. After attending elementary and secondary schools in Newfoundland, he earned his Bachelor of Arts degree at Dalhousie University in Halifax and then did post-graduate work in psychology.

Upon completion of his studies, Butler was employed by the Halifax YMCA. Then he relocated to Montreal, where he taught Public Relations at Sir George Williams University. In 1959 he returned to Halifax, where he continued his career in community service work until he saw the NSHCC's search committee's advertisement.

When the Board offered Butler the job, he accepted. Although most members agreed he was the correct choice to see the NSHCC through its period of transition, the decision wasn't unanimous.

"I did not want that change to come," Rev. Fairfax says. "Women had always done a tremendous job. It didn't matter whether he [Butler] was white or black, he should have been there as an Executive Director with less control over the children. That was a job that belonged to women—the care and the love of children. He certainly could never have been a father image to those children."

But Rev. Fairfax's opinion didn't reflect the majority's view. And with the hiring of Butler, the changes anticipated at the Home would soon become reality.

New Directions

By the time he began his duties, Butler had already developed definite ideas on how a group institution for troubled children should operate, and what its physical layout should be.

"I had worked with the Paraplegic Association and the Association for the Mentally Retarded, and I had developed a residential construction program which the provincial government pulled out of," he recalls, "when I realized the idea was to create a developmental program for children coming out of what was pretty much a traditional orphanage, and I had the experience of getting the funding into place, and everything ready to go. So when the situation at the Home came up, I had something to offer that was already packaged."

Butler specified his ideas in a draft constitution, and at the Home they were applied in a practical way. According to Butler's plans, the Home would be divided into two sections: a Receiving Center and a Group Home. The Receiving Center would provide a preliminary psychological and behavioral evaluation of each child referred to the Home. After the initial assessment, three options would be available: referral to another agency or institution, placement in a foster home, or a period of residence in the NSHCC's Group Home.

Duration of residence at the Group Home would depend upon each child's specific needs and circumstances. Some would stay only until other arrangements could be made; others might remain for several years. Flexibility was essential; without it, the individual child could be lost in a shuffle of paper.

Funding was another requisite. Few professional child-care workers would be willing to spend the time and energy necessary to deal with "problem" children at the salary levels offered by the Home. Accordingly, by 1977 the daily rate of Social Services funding per resident had increased from $3.50 per day to a more realistic $14.29.

Some of the older workers remembered a time when "quiet" children were the norm. Indeed, when the institution opened in 1921, its stated policy was to refuse accommodation for children who were "mentally defective or delinquent." But by the 1970s the "quiet" children were placed in foster homes, not institutions. Now the Home was taking in difficult children, but there were fewer workers available to take on the demanding care of such children.

Also a social services evaluation had forced the Board to upgrade qualifications for permanent employees. Previously, the majority of employees were residents of the Preston–Cherry Brook area and other historically black communities, and the primary qualification was the trust of the Superintendent in their ability to care for the children. Now, a "piece of paper" that few residents of the area possessed was required just to get one's foot past the personnel interviewer's door. Resentment over this change was bound to occur.

Butler set his tone from the beginning with a memo on staff development:

> *As you already know, the N.S. Home for Colored Children is about to embark on a new program, and there is no question that the changes to take place will be considered revolutionary.*
>
> *There is no question either, that this requires a whole new approach to all matters relating to staff, all the way from responsibilities, understanding and ability through to assessment of qualifications and training.*
>
> *The task is going to be a demanding one, and while every effort will be made to help staff better equip themselves for that task, we have to recognize that the Home exists for one purpose only...to provide a child*

development program for the children that is second to none. The Board has taken the position that the children always come first, and that the staff is here to serve them.

The memo also indicated that the Home was moving toward a smaller but more qualified staff, and more training would be required.

Racial tension also played a role in the growth of discontent among the staff. Although 1960s-style black power militancy never became entrenched in the province, a heightened sense of ethnic identity and awareness characterized the early 1970s. Younger blacks became more assertive, and some members of the older generation rethought their commitment to 1950s-style integration, with its accompanying dismantling of black institutions.

This change in attitude coincided with the arrival of Butler, the first white person ever placed in direct charge of the Home. The results, while unfortunate, were also inevitable. Butler himself was aware of the shift in racial realities.

"The amazing thing to me was that for so many years, it was a majority white Board operating the Home, with the token black person, and there was a black person as the Director of the Home," he recalls. "And the opposite was true when I went in there. The majority of the board was black, and they appointed a white person as Director."

But Butler felt he could handle racial tensions that might come his way. That impression was heightened during the period of transition during which he worked with Cherry Paris Swann, the Home's outgoing Matron.

"When Cherry Paris was leaving, one of the things both of us commented on was that things worked so well between us that we never had a cross word between us," Butler recalls.

As Butler began the task of transforming the Home, several principles dominated his thinking. He believed, correctly, that the Home's days as a relatively isolated institution—a "little colony"—were over. He encouraged NSHCC residents to participate in social and recreational activities in the outside community. These activities included Brownies, Canadian Girls in Training, sports groups and military cadets.

He did, however, object to the placement of the "Nova Scotia Home for Colored Children" sign on the grounds. In Butler's opinion, it was not helpful to advertise the fact that the residents were living in an institution.

"It was a number on a street that was a home for some people," Butler says. "When I went in there, they had these big signs with the provincial government crest on the corner—The Nova Scotia Home for Colored Children—which essentially said this is a Nova Scotia government-operated facility. That's what I was against. You don't say, 'Here are black children who are set aside.' It's just a street number."

Butler also believed the sign would reinforce the negative attitudes toward the Home already held by many. The very existence of such attitudes provided an indication of the extent to which the social climate in the province had changed since the great outpouring of pride and goodwill that accompanied the Home's opening in 1921. Back then, separate institutions for blacks were commonly accepted. But in the aftermath of the civil rights movement, those institutions came under increasing critical fire. In part, Butler's program of integrating the Home's residents into the outside community was a response to such criticism.

Butler believed that the Home should accommodate only black children. He viewed the residents as members of a close-knit black community and he felt they needed a sense of cultural identity. Could that identity remain intact in the presence of white children? Butler wasn't certain.

In an article in the December 1, 1973, *Mail-Star* soon after he was hired, Butler's philosophy on integration was presented as follows:

> *Mr. Butler believes that present ideas of total integration of blacks and whites are often over-simplistic.*
>
> *He says children such as those at the home are happier with their own people than if they were put in white homes.*
>
> *He says they integrate in schools, sports, and community activities, but they like to feel they can come home to their own ethnic group where they share history, identity and culture.*

Today Butler says: "When the Home was started, it started as a children's aid society for black children. And that, I thought, was a very commendable thing to attempt. I was convinced that the white society was calling the shots, and they didn't understand the value of black culture or the strength of the black family."

Butler also felt that racism played a role in the placement of black children in institutions and foster homes. A 1974 presentation from the Home to the Nova Scotia Family and Child Welfare Association demonstrated that view in no uncertain terms: "It is felt that over the years, the black race in Nova Scotia has not been afforded the opportunity of self-determination and decision as far as the care of their own children are concerned."

One underlying factor in this position was a belief that social service authorities placed too much emphasis on economics without acknowledging the circumstances of black history and culture, and as a result economically disadvantaged black families were often not allowed to keep their own children. Also, some black families who were willing to take in children from the Home had been rejected because they were perceived to have an inadequate socio-economic status.

"I had the feeling that probably half of the children in the Home that I saw could have been placed in foster homes, if the social services department had acknowledged the fact that there were suitable black homes for them to be placed in," Butler says.

In many ways, Butler agreed with blacks who believed that identification with black culture and heritage was the key to the development of a more positive self-image among the community's children. Ironically, a philosophy with which Butler was compatible would eventually contribute to his downfall.

For all his strong opinions, though, rules didn't have to be ironclad in Butler's book. In deference to the reality of the black situation in the province, he was willing to circumvent established procedure in the best interests of the individual people involved. He once took in a child who'd been living alone in the woods, saving the admission paperwork until after the youth's comfort and safety were assured.

In the summer of 1977, Butler hired Sherleen (Sherry) Bernard to work with him as Child Care Coordinator. Although she had spent much of her life in Ontario, Ms. Bernard remembered the Home well. Her older sister, Linda Bernard, had worked there and, in the 1920s and 1930s, her father, George, and his four sisters had been raised at the Home.

"I went to school in Ontario for a child development program," Ms. Bernard recalls. "Then I came back here and applied for the job at the Home. My goal at that time was to work with black children, and where else would be better to do that than the Nova Scotia Home for Colored Children?"

Despite their differences in philosophy and background, Butler and Ms. Bernard worked well together. Long before he hired Ms. Bernard, however, Butler was proceeding with his plans.

In an interview with the *Chronicle-Herald* on December 9, 1976, Butler summed up his child-care philosophy and his future plans for the Home:

For children who have encountered difficulties in their young lives, happiness is living in an atmosphere where encouragement replaces criticism, where approval, acceptance and friendship replaces ridicule and hostility.

Not only is the board of the Home emphasizing the importance of developing closer human relationships, it also recognizes the need for cheerful physical surroundings, and therefore plans to start the construction of new, more home-like community residences which will be modern and more in keeping with the present-day needs of children.

By fall of the next year, the old Home building gave way to those new structures, and the changes Butler had been hired to implement were complete.

A New Board

In the March 14, 1978, proceedings of the Nova Scotia House of Assembly, Liberal MLA A. Garnet Brown made the following remarks about the NSHCC:

> *Perhaps like no other, this institution reflects what is happening in our society today, which I think helps to make all of us have some hope for the future. Less than ten years ago, I am told, the Home's Board of Management was comprised for the most part of men from the white community. In fact, there were never more than two Black citizens serving on the Boards at any one time and no women. Today, it is just the opposite—only two white citizens serve on that Board, which also now includes four female appointees, thus making it a more truly representative of the community it serves.*
>
> *Also, another sign of the times, is that the old policy of only appointing female staff to provide care and understanding to the Home's young people has now gone by the boards, for today, the staff is also representative of the community the Home serves.*

Brown's speech was part of the process that resulted in passage of legislation to fund the construction of two new buildings: a Receiving Center for short-term intervention and a Group Home to house longer-term residents. When the buildings opened, Butler's plans for change would be fully implemented.

The change in the racial balance on the Board of which MLA Brown spoke had occurred gradually. As early as 1969, the question of increasing the number of blacks on the Board had arisen at an NSHCC annual meeting:

> *Dr. Oliver was of the opinion that there were not enough Negro members on the Board and it might be thought there was discrimination, but it was pointed out that last year there were five Negro leaders on the Board but that two had been dropped for non-attendance and another had resigned.*

The Chairman suggested that perhaps we had made the honest mistake of electing leading Negro citizens who may not have time to give the Home the attention it deserves and that perhaps we should look to lesser-known Negroes who might be more actively interested.

Rev. William P. Oliver, in 1986.
(Courtesy Black Cultural Centre for Nova Scotia)

Rev. Oliver's desire to have more blacks directing the affairs of a black institution is understandable. It should be remembered, however, that the presence of three black members on the first NSHCC Board back in 1915 was a significant event in Nova Scotia's history. Those first black members—J.A.R. Kinney, Moses Puryear, and Thomas Johnson—had wielded influence far beyond their numbers.

Over the years, many distinguished members of the black community have served on the NSHCC Board. Among them are clergymen such as Revs. Oliver, Martin Luther Anderson, Donald E. Fairfax and Donald D. Skeir. George McCurdy and Dr. Anthony Johnstone, both of whom also served as Executive Directors of the Nova Scotia Human Rights Commission, served on the Board, as did Gordon Earle, who later became provincial Ombudsman of Manitoba. Dr. Carrie Best, a holder of the Order of Canada, served on the Board, and so did Corinne Sparks, who went on to become Nova Scotia's first black judge.

In 1973, Wayne Kelsie became the first former NSHCC resident to be named to the Board. Ten years later, he was elected Board President. He also served as Treasurer.

The white community has also provided notable Board members, foremost of whom were long-serving Presidents Henry G. Bauld and Dr. Melville Cumming. Businessmen such as W.J. Stairs and W.D. Piercy; judges such as Robert H. Murray and Elliott Hudson; politicians such as Dr. John Savage, who later became Mayor of Dartmouth, Leader of the Nova Scotia Liberal Party and Premier of the province, and Tom McInnis, who became Deputy Premier as a Conservative; and academics such as Professor Graham Murray all contributed greatly to the continued development of the NSHCC.

Mrs. Alice Croft served as the first woman President from 1970 to 1973 and remains an honorary Board member today. She joined the Board in 1964 at the request of her friends, Mrs. H.P. MacKeen and Mrs. Donald McInnis, both of whom were Board members. Mrs. Croft was involved in many of the decisions that led to the NSHCC's transition from orphanage to group home, and she saw the institution through some difficult financial times.

"I remember making many a trip to the Royal Bank, trying to get loans to keep the Home going," she recalls.

However, the increase in the number of blacks on the Board had its down side as well. Because many whites still regarded blacks as either culturally or inherently inferior—or both—the competence and acumen of the new Board members was questioned. The detractors had apparently forgotten the major role J.A.R. Kinney Sr. and others had played in the founding and maintenance of the Home.

John Savage, Premier of Nova Scotia and former NSHCC Board Member.
(Courtesy *The Daily News*)

Still, in 1974 the NSHCC reached a major milestone when the Board elected its first black President. Appropriately, that honor went to Rev. Fairfax, whose services to the NSHCC were legion. He still considers his accession to the position a great honor, but it was also a great responsibility.

"By this time, practically all of the whites who had been involved on the Board had left," Rev. Fairfax recalls. "Being President of the Board was not an easy task. Many black people came and joined the Board, representing various segments of society. Prestigious as the position was, all that glitters is not gold."

Rev. Fairfax served from 1974 to 1977, when he was succeeded by Rev. Donald D. Skeir, a longtime friend and colleague in the AUBA. Born in Halifax in 1927, Rev. Skeir was originally a member of the same African Methodist Episcopal Church that sent a contingent of Boy Scouts and Girl Guides to the Home's opening ceremonies in 1921. During his high school years, he joined the Cornwallis Street Baptist Church, where he became acquainted with the Kinney family.

Rev. Donald D. Skeir, second black NSHCC President.

After graduating from high school, young Skeir followed a call to the ministry and earned a divinity degree at Acadia University in 1950. Three years later he became pastor of the churches in the Preston–Cherry Brook communities, succeeding Rev. A.A. Wyse.

Rev. Skeir's early memories of the NSHCC are not as intimate as those of some other important figures in the history of the institution.

"My concept of the Home in those days was a place that was off-limits," he recalls today. "Very few people were even able to get into the Home as visitors. One of the most significant things was the School Closing ceremonies. As a young boy, I had the opportunity to go there with my parents on those occasions. As for knowing much about the Home back then, I didn't have too much knowledge of it."

Rev. Skeir attributes the "off-limits" perception to the policies of the Home's early management.

"Mr. J.A.R. Kinney, Sr. and Mrs. Fowler and some of the Directors didn't open the Home up to the general public as it is now. On the Board of Directors, there were only about three or four blacks; the rest were white. It seemed as though the white people exerted a tremendous amount of influence over the Home, more so than the black community did."

Although many blacks in the surrounding community felt welcome at the Home, Rev. Skeir remembers others who didn't share that view. "I talked to some of the senior members of the Preston area who told me they had never set foot into the Colored Home," he says. "It was one of those places you just drove by. You just weren't a part."

In 1963, Rev. Skeir became a member of the NSHCC Board. At that time, the Board still had a white majority. However, Rev. Skeir believed that the Home's image of isolation in the black community was beginning to change. For Rev. Skeir, the main reason for that change was the shift in the Board's racial representation during the 1970s.

"The climate in the community at that time emphasized blackness," he says. "I think the white community was aware of the fact that black people were at the point of looking after their own businesses and institutions. I think the Nova Scotia Home for Colored Children was caught up in that wave."

The new composition of the Board had both positive and negative consequences. On the positive side, black Nova Scotians now controlled one of their community's major institutions. The negative consequences were primarily a matter of perception. Previously, the world outside the Home had viewed its Board as successful white business people who knew how to run things and get things done. Blacks were generally perceived as not knowing how to run things, regardless of the accomplishments of individuals such as the Kinneys.

Rev. Skeir and other black Board members were well aware of the double standard to which they would be subjected, and the need to overcome overt and hidden prejudice.

"I felt there was a deep sense of dedication among the blacks who were elected to the Board," Rev. Skeir says. "They realized that they had to portray the ability to administrate this institution. They accepted that challenge and they were determined to make it work."

Rev. Skeir praises Mrs. Alice Croft for her contributions toward easing what was a sudden transition. Mrs. Croft stayed on as President after the change, and later supported the black Presidents who succeeded her.

"She never, ever gave the impression that she was patronizing," Rev. Skeir recalls. "She made us feel that we had the ability. That strengthened us and we had a great admiration for her."

For her part, Mrs Croft says: "I enjoyed every moment of my experience working with black people. Color never really entered my mind. I guess it was the way I was brought up."

Mrs. Croft is now Chairman of the Board of Northwood, a senior citizens residence in Halifax.

When the Board nominated Rev. Skeir for its presidency in 1977, he accepted without hesitation. "I thought it was a challenge, and I accepted the office," he recalls. "Blacks were taking a more prominent role on the Board, and it would be a positive step to accept."

In his President's Report at the NSHCC's 1977 annual meeting, Rev. Skeir reiterated his theme of opening the Home to the black community:

If I may be personal, I should like to say that it has been a great honor for me to serve as President of this Home during the past year. To conceive of a Black man serving in this capacity a few years ago was beyond our fondest dreams. A few years ago, the Home was looked upon by the average Black as a place "out of bounds." A few elite and privileged drove in, but these were few and limited in number. Today, the Home can be considered truly "ours."

Rev. Skeir also reaffirmed the Home's mandate and criticized the social and behavioural theories that were current at the time:

This Home must ever be a home for the homeless, it must ever serve the needs of the Black child not as an experimental guinea pig, but as a human being who is deserving of all that everyone has considering the unfortunate circumstances that sends them to us. If we fail to do that, then we shall have no right to follow in the footsteps of those who have gone before us.

Rev. Skeir's successor, Wayne Adams, is a full generation younger than his predecessors, and he recalls the Home from a different perspective. He remembers the times his father, who was a friend of Ross Kinney's, took him on visits to the Home's farm during the late 1940s and early 1950s.

"I remember the huge barns, and the cattle and horses," he says. "And the barns were modern. There were pipes that fed water to the animals. I was also impressed with the chicken house, so much so that I kept my own chicken in the backyard as a pet at home in Halifax."

Born and raised as the youngest of three children in a North End

Wayne Adams, Member of the Nova Scotia Legislative Assembly.
(Courtesy Black Cultural Centre for Nova Scotia)

Halifax family, Adams studied auto mechanics at the Halifax Regional Vocational School. He later attended the Nova Scotia Institute of Technology, becoming a master mechanic.

After working at Citadel Motors, Adams operated his own service station in Lower Sackville, a suburb of Halifax. Eventually, Adams' interests turned to journalism and broadcasting. From 1965 to 1968, he wrote on a freelance basis for the *Dartmouth Free Press*. After two years of knocking on doors, he landed a position at CJCH and never looked back.

One of Adams' major accomplishments during the 1970s was "Black Journal," one of the longest-running public-affairs radio broadcasts ever to serve the Halifax–Dartmouth area. Running from 1971 to 1977, the program focused on the achievements of Nova Scotia's black community. In 1975 the program won a national award for human rights in broadcasting for its promotion of a positive image for blacks. In collaboration with Rocky Jones and Sharon Ross, Adams also developed "Black Insights," a television program for CBC that ran from 1977 to 1978.

Adams' adult association with the NSHCC dated from 1970, when he worked at the CHNS radio station as a night news editor. CHNS had aired the Home's Annual Christmas Broadcast since 1931, and Adams helped with it. Prior to his employment with CHNS, Adams had been a sports broadcaster and news editor at CJCH, another Halifax radio station.

In 1976, Adams became a member of the NSHCC's Board of Directors. Adams and Revs. Fairfax and Skeir served on the Board during the process that led to the decision to construct the new Group Homes.

Selecting a Site

During the last five years the NSHCC operated at the old site, Butler came to agree with the view that the building wasn't suitable for a group home's needs. "You're not able to deal with children as well in a large setting as you are in a smaller one," he says.

Rev. Skeir agreed. "At the time, I felt there was a need to get away from that building up there. It was too isolated and too big. You could almost get lost in that place."

The children at the Home had concerns of their own. Tracey Dorrington, who was an NSHCC resident from 1972 to 1984, remembers feeling uncomfortable in the old building.

"It was a little creepy," she recalls. "The older kids used to tell us there were ghosts in the shadows. I never saw any ghosts, and I didn't want to."

Butler also felt the building was becoming an economic liability. "In those days, even though things weren't as expensive then as they are now, there was somewhere around eight to ten thousand dollars going through the roof in heat every year," he says.

The Board delegated Butler to propose a site and obtain the funding for the new structures. He chose the location of the old George Washington Carver Credit Community Centre, which was on Home property. The main advantage Butler pointed out was the site's proximity to Dartmouth water lines. The old Home had depended upon two wells for its water supply but had no connection to municipal facility.

"One of the main practical reasons why the buildings were located where they were was because they were at a spot on the property of the Home where water would be accessible," Butler recalls. "There wasn't a problem with the well at the old Home, but there was a concern. If one of the children left the toilet running, we'd be concerned. We had to be constantly watching that we weren't using too much water."

With a site located, the next step was to design the two buildings. The Halifax architectural firm of Aza Abramovich Associates Ltd. provided the final plans.

After the location was finalized and the plans for the buildings were drawn up, a public invitation to tender for the project appeared in November 1977. The successful bid came from the J. Whalley Construction Company of Elderbank, Nova Scotia.

The majority of the Board agreed with Butler's decisions on building and site selection. But there was still some dissent, some of which was based on the old Home's tradition.

"I never wanted that move," Rev. Fairfax says. "I always spoke out against it, because the old building was far too beautiful to let go and just not be upkept. I did not want the two buildings built where they are presently. I fought against that. However, I didn't get enough support from the Board."

Another objection raised against the new site cited a lack of available play space for the children, as opposed to the acres of grounds at the old building. As well, the old building sat at a distance from the road, reducing the possibility of traffic accidents.

However, the principal source of opposition was the site's reputation as a swampy, water-filled area, especially during the spring season. Some critics wondered why anyone would want to place buildings there.

"They are in what we knew as the Long Swamp," Rev. Fairfax says. "There were times during the spring of the year when you had to go through the fields, and you could not have gotten past a portion of the Long Swamp. It was a bog."

To an extent, Noel Johnston, founder of the Carver Credit Union, agrees with Rev. Fairfax. "The original George Washington Carver Credit Union building was located where the present homes are now located," he says. "At that time (the early 1950s), it was the Credit Union Hall. When the two-lane road going past it was widened to four lanes, the water backed up into the building's basement. The land was basically a swamp, but we didn't have a water problem in the basement until then."

And the problem became worse, not better, as the Highways Department refused to take responsibility for the flooding.

"The water in the basement froze, and forced the bottoms of the walls out," Johnston recalls. "We ended up having to sell the building. And then the Home built in the same location that we were having the water problem."

However, not everyone on the Board agreed that the location was a swamp. Wayne Adams was one of the skeptics.

"I kept saying, 'I don't think that's a swamp,'" Adams recalls. "The swamp was on the other side of the road."

But if the area wasn't a swamp, what was the source of the water problem that forced the George Washington Carver Centre to close?

"It was a wet area because of the drainage," Adams says. "It had a lot of clay, which had to be removed in order to install a septic system."

Butler was never aware that the local people considered the area a swamp. However, he did discuss the sewage situation with the contractor, Whalley Construction.

"The contractor asked, 'When I take my water mains out to the street, do I go underneath or over the disposal field where the sewer goes in?'" Butler recalls. "And we brought that question to the municipal authorities. And they said, 'You can't do either one of these.' And they came back with a plan as to where to place the disposal field. They designed the disposal field and septic tank and told us where to place it. And that's exactly what the contractor did."

The plan called for removing the clay and replacing it with topsoil, as recommended by the provincial Department of Health. The topsoil was supposed to prevent any backup from the septic system.

To the people of the area, though, wet land was a swamp, and a swamp was wet land. Despite the contractor's assurances that flooding would not be a problem, doubts concerning the location of the new buildings persisted even as progress toward their construction continued. However, the Board decided to go ahead with construction at that site.

"I think we were influenced by the advice we got from the professionals," Rev. Skeir says. "I don't think there were too many people on the

Board at the time that had any expert knowledge of these sort of things."

The nature of the land wasn't the only objection raised to the new buildings. Child Care Coordinator Sherry Bernard had reservations concerning their design.

"My teachings in child care and the control of situations and being able to monitor situations told me that those buildings were not constructed to be able to do that effectively because you have to keep certain doors closed due to fire regulations," she recalls. "Often you couldn't hear what was going on in another part of the building. The design wasn't conducive to proper supervision."

The funding procedures were far more straightforward than the issues regarding the site and the layout of the buildings. The federal Central Mortgage and Housing Corporation and the Nova Scotia Department of Social Services provided the bulk of financial support for the construction of the new buildings. Butler encountered only one pitfall on the funding path.

"The only problem we had was with what was referred to at the time as a bed allowance," he recalls. "It was essentially a furnishings allowance—so much per occupant. And the Social Services Department wouldn't give me that, even though I knew they were doing it for other group homes that were being established."

The reason the department gave for the refusal was that over the years, the NSHCC had accumulated an endowment fund from bequests made in wills. Furnishings for the new buildings could have come from that fund. However, Butler believed endowment money should be invested for financial security, not used to buy furnishings. The department wouldn't budge from its position, so Butler devised an ingenious solution to the problem.

"I went to Canada Mortgage and Housing, and I said, 'Look, you're mortgaging the Home. You've asked us to stake out a piece of land that belongs to that particular Home. I'm assuming that you've asked to do that, and if the Home ever defaults, and you'd have to take over, you'd assume that the land would be part of the bankruptcy.' They agreed. Then I said, 'Do you mind if I put a value on that piece of land?' They said go ahead. So I put a value on the piece of property, and they gave us the money. And I used that to buy the furniture."

Butler's success was a good omen. In his report to the AUBA, delivered on August 21, 1978, approximately a month before the official opening, he wrote:

As always I feel quite inadequate when it comes to giving in a brief report all that the Home has meant and been in the past year; particularly the past year, since I believe we have reached a milestone in that we have finally *completed bright new facilities, at a cost in excess of $500,000, which are to be officially opened by the Lieutenant-Governor of N.S. on Saturday, Sept. 16, 1978.*

It has been my dream since coming to the N.S. Home for Colored Children, almost five years ago, to provide for the children coming under our care, a home that is second to nothing else in the province, and possibly in Canada, and it's my firm belief that this has now been done.

In less than a month, the new buildings were open and occupied. In less than a year, the course of the Home's history would change forever.

Second Opening

September 16, 1978, marked the beginning of the NSHCC's new era with the official opening of the two Group Home buildings. Lieutenant-Governor Clarence Gosse officiated at the ribbon-cutting ceremony and presented the Home with a portrait of Queen Elizabeth and Prince Philip.

Other dignitaries present included Recreation Minister A. Garnet Brown, who planted a tree; Senator Henry Hicks; Dr. F.R. MacKinnon from the provincial Department of Social Services; and John Stacey of the Central Housing and Mortgage Corporation. Although some of the Home's residents participated in the ceremony, most of the others were busy packing up their clothes and other belongings and moving them into their new quarters.

The attendees heard speeches from Executive Director Bob Butler and former world light-heavyweight boxing champion Archie Moore, who was in Nova Scotia to assist in the training of amateur fighters. Rev. Fairfax provided the opening prayer, and the North Preston Community Club sang spirituals. Rev. Skeir, the Board President, said the new buildings were "an important step in the life and growth of this institution."

Opening ceremonies for the new Homes—(left to right) Wayne Adams, Archie Moore, Garnet Brown, George McCurdy.

Fifteen years later, Rev. Skeir says: "It was a moment that we took pride in. Here was a new facility being erected in the black community. I'm sure that most people shared the feeling that this was a progressive step."

Rev. Skeir's words echo the pride that surrounded the opening of the old building. And on the surface, there were many parallels between the launching of the new Group Homes and the 1921 events that opened the old building. Once again, the province's Lieutenant-Governor presided over the ceremonies. Once again, dignitaries from both the black and white communities spoke from the podium. And, once again, a large number of people from the surrounding black communities gathered to witness history in the making.

Lt.-Gov. Gosse cutting ribbon to open new Home.

But the differences between the two events separated by fifty-seven years were greater than the similarities. The crowd, which numbered about 500, was a far cry from the 3,000 who had marched nearly a mile along a dirt road to reach the old site in 1921. There were no jubilee concerts, no celebrations lasting long into the night in the Prestons and Cherry Brook. No one would say it was the "greatest day in the history of the colored race."

When the old Home had opened, black Nova Scotians, scorned and isolated to the point where even their needy children were not welcome in white orphanages, held their heads up high and shouted with a rush of pride: "See what we have done!"

But in 1978 there were no more orphanages, and blacks were no longer officially excluded from the social service system's facilities. Rather than symbolizing independence, the new buildings confirmed the Home's inclusion into the provincial child care network.

Yet within that network, the new Home still found itself in a separate category. In the September 18 *Mail-Star*, reporter Steve Smith, who had covered the opening, wrote: "The Home is actually the last survivor of the old orphanage system which was phased out in favour of foster homes during the sixties. There were not enough foster homes for black children."

And therein lay the similarity between the old Home and the new. Both institutions were s refuges for black children who had fallen through the holes in the safety net. The reporter's words also indicate that even though the Home had been officially open to white children for more than a decade, it was still perceived as a black facility.

One month after the opening, the move to the new buildings appeared to have been accomplished successfully. In an article in the October 28, 1978, *Mail-Star* headlined "Children Adapting Well to Surroundings," newly elected Board President Wayne Adams indicated that a "family atmosphere" was encouraged in the modern buildings. But he acknowledged that institutional stereotypes continued to exist.

Opening Day crowd gathers in front of new NSHCC building.

Adams hoped that an increase in opportunities for activities outside the Home would help to "remove some of the stigma involved in living in a home which some think of as an institution, which it really is not."

The outside community continued to encroach, however. As the *Mail-Star* story put it:

The one major problem facing the home at this time is a proposal by local businessmen to build a drive-in theatre near the facility. The home and concerned citizens petitioned county council last year and were successful in having the project stopped and will be petitioning again.

If the theatre goes ahead, it will be in full view of the upstairs bedroom windows of the home and could create serious traffic hazards for the children.

Adams represented the NSHCC at the county council's public meeting. The developers argued that the visibility problem could be solved by erecting a buffer between the Home and the drive-in.

"I pointed out that social workers had told us that even if some kind of buffer or fence was put up, there would still be the problem of kids sneaking out to go see the movies," Adams recalls. "And the council agreed with my point."

The developer went on to serve a notice of appeal to the province against county council's decision. However, the appeal was never followed up, and the drive-in was never built.

Adams would not have much time to savor that triumph. Within a year, the Home would be facing its greatest crisis since the Halifax Explosion had leveled its first cottage in North End Halifax back in 1917.

The Strike

Hindsight indicates that the strike that nearly destroyed the NSHCC should have been anticipated. Dissatisfaction among the child-care staff had been gathering steam for several years. The unrest had many sources: the change from orphanage to group home, the problem behavior of many of the children, the low salaries staff were paid.

"What I began to notice was that the really hard-to-manage kids in the system were being placed in the Home," says Sherry Bernard. "Which was putting a real strain on the staff."

As well, some of the staff's complaints centered on Butler's style and emphasis. Sheila States, who is now Assistant Child Care Supervisor and had worked at the old Home, says:

"I was mainly in charge of housekeeping, and I would like to have seen the place cleaner. The children came first, but he (Butler) wasn't that interested in how the place looked. He said that wasn't his main aim. I wanted it to be both the house and the children. Other than that, I couldn't really say bad things about the man."

However, Butler had his reasons for de-emphasizing the tradition of spotless tidiness that had existed since the Home's beginning.

"The Board wanted to have the Home open, so that anyone could go through it anytime," he recalls. "Well, my home isn't ready anytime for somebody to knock on the door and say they'd like to come through it. I wasn't worried about the condition of the Home; I was worried more about interfering with the privacy of the children."

Mrs. States also remembers having reservations about the new buildings. "They looked good from the outside, and we were glad to get down here," she says. "But then the trouble started with the sewer and water. We were upset about that, because we thought it was built properly. We came down here and got bigger problems than we had at the old Home. We had floors lifting, and the children had to move upstairs."

Tracey Dorrington says the children shared those concerns. "The buildings really looked up-to-date, and it didn't take us long to get used to them," she recalls. "But when the flooding started, we helped to clean it up. I didn't mind, though. We got extra allowance for doing it."

But the problems with the new building were only part of an overall set of difficulties. Through April 1979, the Board's Personnel Committee had been wrestling with demands for better pay and working conditions from the staffers, who believed they were getting minimum pay for maximum work. There was also talk of unionization, something that had never before been considered. In the meantime, Butler was negotiating with the government for more funds to satisfy the workers' grievances.

Mrs. Sheila States, NSHCC Child Care Worker and Assistant Child Care Supervisor.
(Courtesy Sheila States)

"I had drawn up a salary scale for the Home after researching the salary scales in other group homes," he recalls. "And we were way, way down. When we went to the provincial government for our grant every year, we had to build in what we were going to raise, build up a budget, and establish a per diem rate. And our per diem rate was way under what other group homes were getting that I felt were doing no better than we were."

Butler fought to raise both the per diem rate and staff salaries. But progress was too slow for some. Others considered Butler himself part of the problem. Complaints against him cited an "autocratic attitude" toward the staff and an inability to relate to the residents of the Home.

There were veterans who had been with the Home since the days of the Kinneys and didn't like the changes Butler had implemented. And there were those who did not believe a white man should be in control of an historically black institution, regardless of the "reverse racism" charges that attitude was certain to provoke.

Butler even had discrimination complaints filed against him at the Nova Scotia Human Rights Commission. One of them involved a gift given at a staff Christmas party in which each member, including Butler, drew another's name out of a hat.

"The young lady's name whom I got had just got her driver's license," Butler recalls. "And I got her a key chain with a purple-haired 'troll' hanging from it."

Trolls are ugly, long-haired dolls imported from Europe that have become a fad in North America. It was an innocent enough grab-bag gift, but later another staff member—not the one who had received the key chain—was fired by Butler and subsequently filed a human rights complaint in which she accused him of giving a "monkey" (the troll) to a black person. The provincial Human Rights Commission dismissed the complaint.

"That was the first indication that there may be some feeling that I was discriminating or that there was a difference between the color of my skin and the color of most of the staff," Butler says.

Those differences were clearer to others, though. As Rev. Skeir recalls: "I think it was difficult for Mr. Butler to accept the fact of so many blacks on the Board and the kind of influence they could exert."

Personal clashes were only part of the overall atmosphere of discontent that had developed among the staffers, and Butler remained unaware of how far they were willing to go.

"At that time, there was nobody listening to us," Sheila States recalls. "We had meetings at different staff houses, talking strategy and things we were going to do."

"I don't think Bob had a handle on what was happening in the system," says Sherry Bernard. "There was a definite change in the residents who were getting placed there, and the staff was not equipped to deal with the multiple-problem children that were being placed there. What should have occurred was some really intensive training for the staff, as well as an increase in salary."

Finally, on July 12, 1979, the unrest erupted into the open when eleven of the fifteen staff members went out on strike.

"The people that organized the strike came upstairs and said, 'We're going, we're walking,' " Sheila States recalls. "The last straw was, they weren't giving us the money we asked for, so we had to walk for sure."

The strikers demanded a 15 per cent pay increase, six additional staff members, an extra week of vacation, improved weekend shifts, better overtime pay, and positive direction from the Board and the Executive Director.

"I must confess that I would have struck with them from the point of view of higher wages," Butler says. "But then I heard that they were really striking because of dissatisfaction with the administration, which meant me."

Board President Wayne Adams found out about the strike through a phone call from the media. "Somebody asked me why people were walking around the Home wearing placards," he recalls. "I knew nothing about it."

On the first day of the strike, Adams told reporter Austin French of the *Dartmouth Free Press* that the walkout could not be considered a strike because the workers had no union. He said the "Home's administration agrees with much of what the workers want but is powerless to give it to them."

Adams also said, "It appears very unlikely that the province will be willing to provide any more funds right now although the Department of Social Services has been very encouraging in indicating they will be looking closely at our requests for more assistance in the future."

For Bob Butler, the strike situation provided an opportunity to reaffirm the trust he had placed in the children over the past six years. After the staff walked off the job, the residents were gathered together and informed of the urgent state of affairs at the Home. The older children assembled in the Group Home; the youngsters stayed in the Receiving Centre.

"You will be solely responsible for all housekeeping duties, including cooking and cleaning," Butler told the older residents, some of whom had set fire to the old building, broken windows, stolen, and wrecked the Home's station wagon. And he gave them keys to areas that had previously been inaccessible.

After his talk with the teenagers, Butler went to the Receiving Centre, where the younger children were being tended by non-striking employee Freddie Sparks. Butler and Sparks then attended to the children's immediate needs—cooking, cleaning, laundry.

A few moments later, a knock sounded at the door. It was the older children, who had come to offer their help in caring for the young ones. For Butler, that occasion was more gratifying than the opening of the new Home in 1978.

There were other, more predictable reactions from the children as well. "They were having a ball," Wayne Adams recalls. "Why not?"

"The children came out of the house and were eating our breakfast," says Sheila States, remembering her first day on the picket line. "They were cheering us from their bedroom windows."

But the children's entertainment didn't last long. At the time of the strike, six of the older residents had been placed in summer employment under a federal government program called "Operation Awareness." The program also allowed opportunities for tours and visits to senior citizens. When the walkout occurred, the provincial government took custody of the youths involved in Operation Awareness and placed them in other institutions, foster homes, or with relatives.

Before long, the youngsters who still resided in the Home were also placed elsewhere. After that, the picketers marched back and forth in front of the empty buildings, day after hot summer day.

Near the beginning of the strike, the *Dartmouth Free Press* ran a story that included the following details:

> *The 27 young residents of the Nova Scotia Home for Colored Children have been scattered to temporary housing throughout the province as 10 child care workers have resigned the institution in a labor dispute.*
>
> *The workers are picketing the facility but president Wayne Adams says, that since they have no union, their walkout cannot be considered a strike.*
>
> *Mr. Adams told the Free Press that the Home's administration agrees with much of what the workers want, but is powerless to give it to them.*
>
> *"It appears very unlikely that the province will be willing to provide any more funds right now although the Department of Social Services has been very encouraging in indicating they will be looking closely at our requests for more assistance in the future," Mr. Adams said.*

In the meantime, the strike dragged on. "It was hard," Sheila States recalls. "We tried not to let the administrators and everybody know we were weakening. We had to be strong, but deep down we were feeling pain. To be here that long, and then have to walk out—it was hard."

It was hard on Butler too. From the moment he understood that he was one of the reasons the employees were striking, he knew he wouldn't be able to remain in the Executive Director's position. Finally, on July 31, after a lengthy meeting with the Board, Butler resigned from the Executive Director's position. The Board's 1979 report to the AUBA summarized that process:

> *In coincidence with the walkout, the Board had been dealing with the weaknesses and strengths of the Executive Director's administrative abilities. In this crisis situation, the negatives appeared to be outweighing the positives and following a marathon meeting of the Board with the Director, Mr. Robert Butler submitted his resignation to the President to be effective July 31, 1979.*

"I tried to make a case to the Board for what I believed in," Butler says now. "But there were some on the Board who pushed it for me to leave, that I was at fault. I had no difficulty accepting what they had to say about the impossibility of reversing the situation."

Butler did stay on beyond his resignation date to "carry out detailed remedial changes to a malfunctioning septic disposal system." That problem would continue well after his departure.

An August 3 memorandum from the Board set the stage for an end to the strike. In part, the memo said:

> *During the meetings of the Board of Directors of the Nova Scotia Home for Colored Children with you, the staff of that institution, it was revealed that sources of discontent in your dispute with the Home covers more areas than salary.*
>
> *The Board of Directors has, therefore, decided to institute a complete restructure of personnel functions and positions within the Home in the hope of alleviating all future problems of this nature.*

The memo also invited the strikers to reapply for their positions, for which new job descriptions had been drawn up. With some misgivings, the workers followed this procedure, and the Board accepted all the reapplications.

On August 20, forty days after their walkout, the eleven striking employees returned to work. Upon their reinstatement, they received a 7 per cent pay increase, and some also received a $600 adjustment for an error in the previous year's salary calculations. They returned under the condition of successful completion of a three-month probation period. The question of personnel increases was left open for action at a future date.

Although the strike passed unreported in the Halifax Herald newspapers, the *Dartmouth Free Press* ran a story at the strike's end that read in part:

> *Life at the Nova Scotia Home for Colored Children should be back to normal by Thursday.*
>
> *Home president Wayne Adams said the 11 workers who walked off their jobs one month ago in a labor dispute were all back on the job and the children are being brought back from their temporary abodes.*
>
> *Mr. Adams commended the Dartmouth Free Press and TV station* CBHT *Halifax, for following the line of responsibility in reporting the facts about the dispute but he said other media outlets complicated the situation by making statements that were totally untrue.*

Adams was referring to reports that the administration and staff had used the Home's residents as "pawns" during the dispute. Some staff members also criticized media reports about the strike.

"They said we walked out and left the kids without notice," says Sheila

States. "They said the kids were following the staff; that the staff had gotten the children to come with them."

Mixed emotions greeted Butler's departure. Some members of the staff and Board regretted the loss of his administrative abilities. Others believed his exit was inevitable.

"I thought it was a necessary thing that had to happen," says Sherry Bernard, who had joined the rest of the staff in the walkout. "I felt, and still feel, that the Home should have a strong black director. It's an institution that was designed and developed because other institutions did not want our black children. I have absolutely no regret about Bob being removed as director."

Could the strike have been averted? Rev. Fairfax, who was still on the Board at the time, doesn't think so.

"You had unions to deal with, you had the Department of Labor to deal with," he says. "Mr. Kinney, Sr. did not have this. He could very carefully hand-pick people all over Nova Scotia, very fine people—people who were happy to be there, and who I believe did a tremendous job."

But the days of hand-picking employees were finished. Collective bargaining, with all its advantages and pitfalls, had arrived, for better or worse.

Aftermath

With the strike settled and the staff back on duty, the two buildings awaited the return of their young residents. However, some of the children who had been placed in alternative facilities did not come back to the NSHCC.

As for those who did return, staff members were aware that the bonds of trust that had existed before the strike needed to be re-established. Some of the children were bound to have felt a sense of betrayal because of the walkout.

"They asked us, 'Why did you go on strike?' " Sheila States recalls. "And we told them as much as we could. They said, 'Oh, we know why you fellas went out—you wanted more money.' And we said, 'Yes, it was that, among other things.' They took it pretty well."

Rev. Skeir, who had taken the position of Chairman of the Board's Facilities Committee, summed up the situation at the end of the year in his report to the Home's 1979 annual meeting:

The stress the Home underwent during this past year has necessitated many changes and one of them is the reduction of children, thus we had to close one of the new buildings. This is most unfortunate because these buildings were built to care for and provide a "home" for these children. We trust that this closure will not be of a long duration.

Another concern that we will have to deal with is the ultimate disposal of the old building and the salvaging of furnishings in it. Though this building has a long and historic significance for the Home, yet it may not be easy to find a solution for its use. However, the Committee during the coming months will have to seriously deal with this.

And so the staff, Board and residents took on the task of returning the Home to business as usual. And two of the major players in the strike situation—Bob Butler and Wayne Adams—went their separate ways.

Soon after his resignation, Butler was hired as Executive Director of the Nova Scotia Family and Child Welfare Association, an umbrella social services support group. He went on to become the first President of Canadian Family and Child Welfare. After leaving that position in 1984, he became Executive Director of the Outreach Ministry at St. Paul's Church. Today he and his wife live in retirement in the Spryfield section of Halifax.

Looking back on his six years at the NSHCC, Butler felt no regrets. "I could see why it was very difficult to understand why a white person was there in that position," he says. "And I felt I had done what I was hired for, which was essentially to develop a child development centre out of a traditional orphanage custodial care program."

In fact, he could even see some humor in the ambivalence of his position as the white director of a black institution.

"I'll never forget the time I suggested moving my office from the Home to the old Bauld School," he says. "The Board never criticized me for it. But the question came up, 'What about your role as a father image to the children?' And I said, 'Me? A father image to black children?' So one of the persons piped up and said, 'Well, Mr. Butler, how do you interpret your role?' And I said, 'A black family has hired a white butler.'"

Wayne Adams did not seek a second term as President of the Board. Instead, he plunged into local politics. He was elected Councillor for District 8 in Halifax County in 1979 and has served five consecutive terms in the seat once held by Thomas P. Johnson, a member of the Home's original Board. District 8 includes the predominantly black Preston communities.

For several years, he did double duty as a County Councillor and Executive Director of the Black Cultural Centre for Nova Scotia. The Black Cultural Centre, which opened in 1983, is located on seven acres of property leased from the NSHCC.

Adams made history in 1993 when he became the first black Nova

Scotian to be elected to the provincial legislature. He ran for the Liberals in the Preston riding, which encompasses the historically black communities of North and East Preston, along with Cherry Brook and Lake Loon. The riding had been created in 1992 to give blacks greater input into the political process. Shortly after the election, Premier John Savage named Adams provincial Supply and Services Minister.

In his final report to the NSHCC Board in December 1979, Adams wrote:

> *I want to thank the Board members for having me serve the past year as president of this very worthwhile, vital, and necessary facility. The Nova Scotia Home for Colored Children, I believe, is gone on to be more than an institution, it is a historic landmark on the hearts and minds of black people across North America.*
>
> *I want to say this as sincerely as I can...this Home must never go nor fade away from the moral responsibility that gave it birth.*

The Home wasn't about to fade away. But its future was far from certain. Although Butler had departed, hard feelings endured, and major

Wayne Adams and his wife Nina talk to media after Adams' election as Nova Scotia's first black MLA in 1993.
(Courtesy *The Daily News*)

challenges lay ahead. The staff still had to negotiate a contract, a new Executive Director had to be hired, and referral agencies had to be convinced that the NSHCC had stabilized and was capable of providing proper care for its residents.

Some people who had been deeply committed to the NSHCC began to drift away from it after the strike. Rev. Skeir was among those who reduced their involvement.

"The strike was an embarrassment," he says today. "It reflected the changed attitude that blacks had. I think the blacks were reaching a point where they had to show they weren't going to be dictated to—that they were going to share in the total administration of the Home, whether they were members of the Board or members of the administration."

Rev. Skeir sees a positive effect as well. "I think it made the Board more sensitive to the feelings of the staff. This was never, ever heard of before. The staff had never before expressed themselves in this manner. When this happened, it opened the eyes of the Board to a whole new generation, a whole new ballgame."

Rev. Fairfax, whose association with the Home had by 1979 spanned four decades and continues to this day, recalls the strike's psychological effects in this way: "We lost so very much. We lost love, respect and devotion. We lost the days of Mr. Kinney, Sr. The Home was no longer private; the public had stepped in. This was very sad and painful."

Painful as the experience may have been for all involved, a corner had been turned. It was impossible to restore the NSHCC to the type of institution it had been in the days of the Kinneys, and Butler's attempt to transform it into something different had fallen short.

Still, change had to come to the Home—if not on Bob Butler's terms, then someone else's.

Reminiscing in Tempo

    Remember cheesecloth curtains, blackberries
Breaking lushly, lusciously, into being,
Angels sashaying in flourbag dresses.
Portia White, African Baptist diva,
Lettered us for twelve months; her voice hovered
Golden and shining among sunflowers,
Then scaled to chalked music on the blackboard.
Nan Fowler fussed over our blue raiment
While Kinney and Bauld leashed lightning, rigging
Our country rooms for bright gems of lightbulbs.
Mr. Agriculture led slow Ayrshires
From East Preston; their milk came winter-sweet.
The Home, our Home, houses our history.
    From James R. Johnston and Julia Jackson,
To Mary Paris and Wilfred Jackson,
We are history, all of us who dream:
How much closer can we come to God?

George Elliott Clarke

Picking Up the Pieces: 1979-1991

The Post-Strike Period

The months that passed from the fall of 1979 to the end of 1980 marked the close of one era at the NSHCC and the beginning of another. After the end of the employee walkout and Bob Butler's departure, Sherry Bernard stepped in as Acting Executive Director.

"I received a call from Wayne Adams, who wanted to talk to me about the situation and what they were going to do," she recalls. "And I was asked to fill in temporarily."

Ms. Bernard's task was to reestablish the Home as a viable treatment center. For all the progress she made, however, her tenure lasted only a few months.

"I didn't feel I was ready for that job," she says. "It wasn't where I wanted to be at that time."

Mrs. Jane Earle became the next Executive Director on a voluntary basis. Her husband, Gordon Earle, had succeeded Wayne Adams as President of the Home's Board. Although Mrs. Earle didn't have any direct experience with the Home, she and her husband were foster parents for several children who had once been residents. Her qualifications also included a Master of Social Work degree.

Mrs. Earle undertook the position at a difficult time, with the Home experiencing financial and organizational difficulties. Staff numbers had dropped from fifteen to eleven, and the number of residents had fallen from thirty-nine to fifteen after the strike.

Jane Earle (left) presents award to Crystal Mulder, a non-NSHCC resident who played in a Home-sponsored softball tournament.

"Many children didn't return because some were placed outside the Home," Mrs. Earle told the *Ebony Express*, a Halifax black community newspaper. "And many were old enough to be on their own."

Also, social service workers felt it would be disruptive to return some of the former residents to the Home because they had adjusted well to their new placements.

"Moving children isn't stabilizing; it's the opposite of stabilizing. If there were children who were in other placements and they were doing well, the interest would be to try to maintain the stability as opposed to bringing them back into the Home for the sake of bringing them back," says Bill Greatorex, who is now Administrator of Family and Children's Services at the provincial Department of Community Services. At the time of the strike, Greatorex worked for what was then the provincial Child Welfare Department.

The reduction in numbers caused the closure of one of the NSHCC's buildings. Mrs. Earle attributed delays in placement to difficulties in the referral process. The choice between placing a child in a foster home or an institution had never been an easy one, and the Home's recent troubles added another complication.

"Some children, because of their backgrounds, need to live in a group home situation where they don't feel the presence of a strong authority figure such as a mother or father, but are able to develop themselves through their peer group support," Mrs. Earle told the *Ebony Express*.

Could the Home continue to provide the support necessary to sustain a positive peer-group environment? That was the major question the institution faced as it entered its seventh decade of service.

In an NSHCC pamphlet issued in 1980, Mrs. Earle expressed optimism:

Joan Jones

> *Employer-employee difficulties at the Nova Scotia Home for Colored Children this summer have perhaps had a positive effect in that we have had to take a close look at our operation and are at this point building a more efficient and caring program.*
>
> *At present, we have a black awareness program run by the Black Professional Women's Association in conjunction with the Children's Aid Society of Halifax. It is our hope that in the very near future, a program such as this will operate out of the Home itself.*
>
> *The Nova Scotia Home for Colored Children has a unique history in caring for black children with a program that attempts to integrate black children into the surrounding black communities to give them a sense of their own identity and the proud heritage which is theirs.*

The black awareness program mentioned in Mrs. Earle's report was run by Joan Jones, who had long been active in black community development. Ms. Jones emphasized black history, as well as hair care, cosmetics, black literature, and resources such as the African–American magazines *Ebony*, *Essence* and *Jet*. She also arranged for the children to attend performances of black artists and entertainers who came to Halifax and Dartmouth.

As a friend of Mary Paris, she was well aware of the Home's history. To this day, she remembers her first day on the job.

"Jane Earle told me not to be surprised if some of the children damaged my car," Ms. Jones recalls, "I made it very clear no child was going to damage my car. And they didn't."

Although Ms. Jones' involvement at the Home only lasted one year, she recalls it as a good year. "I enjoyed it, and so did the children," she says.

By the summer of 1980, Jane Earle stepped down to make way for a permanent Executive Director. Her work was appreciated, as the following excerpt from the President's report to the Home's annual meeting indicates.

> *Under her leadership we have seen this Home move from a point of near bankruptcy to a point where we are now paying our way quite comfortably. Following our difficulties last summer we had to close down one of our buildings, lay off some staff, and operate at half capacity due to the decreased number of children at the Home. The enrollment continued to drop until we were down to ten children. However, due to Mrs. Earle's leadership in programming, making contacts with social service agencies and her firm conviction that the Home can and should provide a viable and meaningful alternative for our children, due primarily to these things, the Home started an upward swing to the point that our enrollment has doubled, and we now have an operation respected and utilized by most child caring agencies in the Province.*

The children appreciated her as well. "She would always sit down with us and talk about our problems," Tracey Dorrington recalls.

Mrs. Earle, a white woman, had never intended to stay on a long-term basis because of repercussions from the Bob Butler situation. To avoid a repeat of the racial tensions that had characterized the Butler years, the Board decided that the new permanent Executive Director would have to be both professionally qualified and black. Mrs. Earle departed graciously.

Once again, the NSHCC's top administrative post was vacant. And once again Sherry Bernard stepped in temporarily. After relinquishing the Director's job the first time, she had stayed on as Child Care Supervisor and was content in that position.

"Jane talked to me about filling in after she left," Ms. Bernard recalls. "She also talked to the Board. I agreed to do it, but I still wasn't interested in applying for that job."

The two women ended up working together to stabilize the Home's enrolment and post-strike reputation. In the NSHCC's 1980 report to the African United Baptist Association, Ms. Bernard wrote:

The other very important aspect of the last six months work at the Home has been in the improvement of our image throughout the province. There is no doubt about the fact that our service greatly needed up-grading in order to meet the needs of children placed here. In order to accomplish this, both the former Executive Director and myself working as a team travelled to 13 agencies throughout the province to tell about our expanded program. We also visited child caring facilities to examine various programming services offered, etc. The response to our program was very positive and we have seen that response put into action by the referrals we are getting.

Ms. Bernard soon returned to her Child Care Supervisor's job, which she held until 1989. She is now employed as a probation officer for the Dartmouth Family Court.

During the year that Jane Earle and Sherry Bernard traded places at the NSHCC's helm, the Board conducted a vigorous search for a permanent Executive Director. In the Home's report to the 1979 AUBA meeting, outgoing Board President Wayne Adams wrote: "We have advertised in the Halifax daily newspapers for an Executive Director and the response has been very good. We are seeing some good applications from black people, indigenous and otherwise."

The search would last more than a year before the right candidate was finally found.

A New Director Arrives

Wilfred Jackson, a native of Halifax, had spent several years in Montreal when the opening for the Executive Director's position at the NSHCC came to his attention. Like most members of Nova Scotia's black community, he retained clear memories of the old Home.

"Growing up in Halifax, everybody knew about the Home," he recalls today. "In my younger days, when I used to go to camp in the summer, Ross Kinney always had about a dozen young boys who would come to the same camp that I did, the YMCA Big Cove Camp. So I knew quite a few of the residents around my age who were growing up in the Home."

Both Ross Kinney and the YMCA made a strong impression on the youthful Jackson, although, at the time, he would never have dreamed that he would one day follow in Kinney's footsteps as head of the NSHCC.

In his early adult years he worked in recreation at the Halifax "Y" and furthered his education by studying applied social science at Sir George Williams University (now part of Concordia University) in Montreal under a YMCA Fellowship Program. He played basketball for Sir George while he was a student there, and after graduation he coached the team for three years.

Wilfred A. Jackson
NSHCC Executive Director.

Jackson then began a career at English Catholic Community Services in Montreal, directing a camps and conferences centre program for them. Over his ten years in that position, the camps served several thousand young people, many of whom came from minority backgrounds. Eventually, Jackson became a senior department head with a staff of 250. However, as a Protestant, he was precluded from consideration for the job of Executive Director of the organization. That barrier was on his mind when he came home to Halifax for a family visit in the spring of 1980.

At that time, members of the NSHCC Board visited him and asked if he would be interested in the Executive Director's post. He was told a great deal about the direction the Board hoped the Home would take, but not much about its current difficulties. The Board wanted someone who would be more in touch with the black community.

"After I got back to Montreal, my wife, Olive, and I talked it over," Jackson recalls. "We decided if the call came, we'd take a look at it. Gordon Earle, who was then President of the Board, telephoned me and said they had reviewed my application form and would I be interested in coming down for an interview?"

Jackson accepted the invitation for the interview. He already knew some of the Board members and their families, and received much encouragement from them. Before long the Board offered Jackson the job. After another discussion with his wife, a native of Truro, he decided to accept.

"It was time for a change," he says. "It was a challenge, a chance to come back home again after fifteen years away. I wanted to give something back to the black community."

Like his predecessor Bob Butler, Jackson came into the position with his own ideas on how the Home should be run.

"I was very much aware of the ideals and expectations of people like Mr. Kinney," he says. "I really felt that this Home should be a refuge for black children. There was really an important role to play with community and social services people in making sure that black youths had a place to go to have their needs looked after."

By the time he began his first day on the job, Jackson discovered that the challenges he faced would be greater than he'd anticipated.

His first priority was to get to know the personalities and problems of the children who resided at the Home. Almost immediately, he made a disturbing discovery.

"There was a whole group of kids who really didn't belong in the Home," he recalls. "The Youth Training Centre in Truro, which deals with children who have emotional and mental difficulties, had a practice of dumping all of their kids into this Home during the summer. It was like a summer vacation for them. Of the thirty-odd kids who were here in the summer of 1980, at least fifteen belonged to the Youth Training Centre."

These were youths who spent the rest of the year under medication to control their behavior. Yet they had been sent to the Home without medication. Jackson remembers them as being "totally out of control" and extremely difficult for the staff to handle.

Although the practice had been going on for several years, 1980 was the last summer that children from the Training Centre were boarded at the Home. As for the other children who lived there, Jackson proposed to set up programs that could meet their behavioral and emotional needs.

Jackson had other challenges to meet that did not directly involve the children. As he once described his job in a written presentation, the Executive Director "must wear many hats, and serve many masters. Under the existing structure, the Executive Director must be a professional social worker, an expert office manager, a reasonably adequate accountant, a wizard at public relations, an excellent personnel officer, a top flight planner, a financial go-getter, and chief executive."

That's a plate of duties that might have given even James Kinney, Sr. a moment of pause.

More Problems

One of the most difficult administrative tasks Jackson faced during his first days on the job was the final resolution of the previous year's strike.

"Although the strike was over, negotiations with the Canadian Union of Public Employees had not yet begun," he recalls. "The negotiations were pending the hiring of a new Executive Director. So one the first duties I had was to sit down and try to iron out this contract. Of all the experience I had before, I never had experience in a unionized setting, and I'd never sat down to iron out a contract."

It took two years for the NSHCC and the union to reach a collective

Sherry Bernard passes the torch to Wilfred Jackson.

agreement. Although he had not directly experienced the 1979 strike, Jackson expressed his views of the action in part of an informal written history of the NSHCC:

> *Obviously, there had been a great many obstacles to overcome throughout the history of this proud black institution. However, at no time would anyone ever consider abandoning the children as a means of satisfying their own personal needs.*
>
> *There had been times when there were no funds available, and so the employees and children all had to make do with whatever provisions they could get from the fields. Surely there had been many occasions when due to a lack of funds, the employees had gone without pay checks....*
>
> *The dedication of these employees had been such that nothing could interfere with their getting to work and being with the children of the Home. Each and every person who had ever been employed at this Home*

had done so with the understanding that wages were low. Historically, the care of black children took precedence over everything else. The care of black children by their own race was of paramount importance....

It was never a matter of "Pay me what I am worth, or I will close the whole place down." Although this thought may have occurred to the odd disgruntled employee, it would never have gained the support of the majority—until now, that is. What an abrupt turn of events for a Home that had meant so much to the black community as a whole.

Eventually, Jackson reached a better understanding of the conditions that had led to the strike, and realized that professional job requirements meant professional levels of salary as well.

"When I first got there, the employees were making something like $3.93 an hour. In the first contract, they got over a 100 per cent increment," he says.

The union settlement put an end to the labor/management impasse that had led to the strike, although tensions continue to surface from time to time as they do in any unionized situation. But that wasn't the only problem Jackson had to overcome during his early years at the Home.

Once again, the water problem about which so many had expressed doubt when the new buildings were first proposed rose to the surface. Because of a faulty septic system, the grounds that extended to the woods behind the Home was covered by, in Jackson's words, "about a foot of water that contained raw sewage."

"Since they put these buildings here, the plumbing system never ever worked," Jackson says. "Because of that, there were constant floods in this building. The sewer always backed up. It would be coming from the toilets, from the sinks, up through the floors, into the foundations, and that's how it persisted for some time."

Because of the condition of the Home's back yard, the children could not play there and were confined to the buildings' interior. Recreational activities had to take place off-site. The decision to place the new buildings in their current location had created a health hazard for staff and residents alike. Yet the supposedly deteriorating old Home building had never experienced flooding or sewage problems.

Obviously, those conditions could not be allowed to continue. Within the first year of Jackson's arrival, the grounds behind the Home were drained by a trench dug around the area. Then Jackson and the Board approached the Community Services Department for funds to repair the sewer system.

A new system was installed, but a year later it malfunctioned. Periodic flooding continued over the next three years because the system was too small to handle the demands of both buildings. Eventually, the NSHCC filed suit against the architect who had developed the system. But the architect went bankrupt, which precluded any financial settlement.

Before a new system was finally installed, staff and residents adopted a water-rationing procedure. "We had to set up a schedule: don't flush all toilets at the same time, don't use the dishwasher at a certain period of time, in order not to back up that system," Jackson recalls.

The sewer situation served as a rallying point for the Executive Director, staff, and Board. However, it wasn't the only adversity to confront the Home in the early 1980s.

Highway 7, the four-lane thoroughfare that borders the NSHCC, posed a problem of a different kind. The old Preston Road was unpaved at the time the Home opened, and even in the 1950s it was still a relatively quiet two lanes of gravel. A major increase in Halifax County's population over the next few decades created a demand for better highway facilities. But the fulfillment of that demand led to unforeseen consequences.

By the 1980s, Highway 7 had become a suburban speedway with few traffic signals. Several of the Home's residents suffered minor injuries while attempting to cross the busy highway.

"We petitioned the County and the Department of Transportation to put up some lights," Jackson recalls. But the petitions didn't obtain immediate results.

Lights were eventually installed, including a pedestrian-operated set at the entrance of the NSHCC—but not before 14-year-old resident Catherine Tidswell was killed on the highway in February 1987. Marlene Linda Roy, a daughter of the family who rented the old caretaker's cottage, had died on the highway the year before. Other residents of the Home had received injuries in minor accidents.

"Unfortunately, it took those two deaths for the Highways Department to finally do something," says Jackson. "Since that time, we've gone from having no lights on the highway to five sets that benefit the whole area, not just the Home."

Programs and Promises

Once the septic and traffic problems were brought under control, Jackson began to look at ways to use the facilities at hand to benefit the children. With his background in recreation, some of the first ideas he and Child Care Supervisor Sherry Bernard explored involved athletics.

Previously, the Board had wanted to use a substantial portion of the grounds behind the buildings as parking space. But Jackson pointed out that recreational facilities would be more useful to the residents.

"The kids who were at the home at that time were quite active," Jackson recalls. "We had some really excellent athletes like Tracey Dorrington, who was one of the most outstanding softball and basketball players of her generation. As a 15-year-old, she could play on any men's team in either of those sports. We also had Robert Borden, who was setting age-class records in track and field. To have kids with that kind of talent penned up in these buildings was really an injustice."

Thus it was decided that the space would serve a better purpose as a recreational area than a parking lot. Salvageable playground equipment from the old building was relocated to the new grounds, and the installation of a basketball court provided a new link between the NSHCC and the outside world.

"Young people from the community flocked to the court," says Jackson. "We had thirty to thirty-five residing in the Home, but there'd be seventy-five to one hundred out there playing and being involved."

Later, the NSHCC and Halifax County cooperated in clearing another area for a baseball diamond, which also increased community involvement.

Children from the Home excelled in areas other than sports. Amanda Stevens, a long-term resident of the Home, was crowned Snow Queen of the first Cole Harbour–Westphal Winter Carnival in 1987. Amanda also

Left - Tracey Dorrington

Below - Amanda Stevens
(Courtesy Nova Scotia Home for Colored Children)

represented the National Youth-in-Care Network and went on to attend Saint Mary's University in Halifax. She now lives in the United States.

Another 1980s Home resident, Robyn Atwell, joined a Halifax Police Department training program designed to increase the number of minority-group officers on the force. The rigorous course began in the fall of 1992. A year later, Robyn graduated as valedictorian of her class. She is now a Halifax police officer.

The tradition of outside involvement in programs for the residents continued through the 1980s. The YMCA provided swimming classes. B'nai B'rith took the youngsters on a day-long picnic at Oakfield Park in Elmsdale and sponsored trips to junior hockey games in Halifax. The East Preston Lions/Lionesses Club held a Halloween party for the children, and CFB Shearwater sponsored an annual visit to the base.

In addition, the children themselves organized a spring fashion show and concert that was held at the East Preston Recreation Centre in 1984.

Other initiatives involved preparing the residents for life outside the Group Home environment.

"Many of these kids were not going to go back to anything, so they needed skills to prepare themselves for life," Sherry Bernard recalls. "My energies at that time were directed toward independence programs for the residents."

Despite these and other efforts to provide meaningful programs for the residents, enrolment at the NSHCC declined throughout the 1980s. Three dozen or so lived there after the strike was settled in 1979; enrolment today averages about one dozen. Until recently, the building that was briefly closed for repairs in 1980 continued to serve as a group home for children whose period of residence was anticipated to last at least a school term's duration.

The former practice of placing entire families of children at the Home has also been curtailed. Yet placing families together had certain advantages, as Alisa Stevens recalls.

Robyn Atwell, a former NSHCC resident, addresses audience during graduation from police training program.
(Courtesy *The Daily News*)

Alisa entered the Home in the early 1980s along with two brothers and two sisters, one of whom is Amanda Stevens. Alisa says having her brothers and sisters with her at the Home was beneficial.

"There was always someone to talk to," Alisa recalls. "I remember

NSHCC residents' fashion show.

feeling resentful that we had to be in the Home. The staff was helpful, but we had to work it out our own way. It took me about six months to understand I was going to be there whether I liked it or not. After that, things worked out well."

Alisa's brothers were eventually placed in foster care as part of the move toward deinstitutionalization. She says they regret not staying in the Home with their sisters. The Stevens children were one of the last long-term family placements at the Home.

The decline in the Home's population led to the eventual disbanding of the basketball program. And short-term stays for most of the residents have since precluded the establishment of long-term recreation programs.

Jackson partially attributes the dropping numbers of residents to changing trends in child-welfare philosophy.

"There's more emphasis on prevention now," he says. "The trend now is to keep children in the home. Secondly, if they come into care, the smaller

NSHCC resident Alisa Stevens holds hown first base at the B'nai B'rith Annual Children's Picnic.

the setting the better. The first option is foster homes. Failing that, the next step would be smaller, specialized group homes. There are a number of these that have opened up in the last two years—placement centres, assessment centres, receiving centres. In terms of population, these places have no more than four to six youngsters at any given time.

"On top of that, there are group homes that serve the needs of eight to ten youngsters. And it goes on and on. So what that does, with the intervention of these new specialized-type homes, institutions such as ourselves which had larger populations, is to cause our populations to decline. Youngsters who would have been with us are now going into smaller, specialized areas."

That leaves the Home and other larger institutions playing two roles: first, as a "holding tank" for children who will soon be moved to group or foster homes; and second, a last resort for those who are incapable of adjusting to other settings.

"We're being faced with behaviors that have never before occurred in the history of the Home," Jackson says. "We're getting children who have suicidal tendencies, children who are involved in Satanism, children who are involved with gangs...."

Children with problems of these kinds need specialized, small-group care, which the Home is not presently equipped to provide. Yet these are primarily the children the Home gets, and they're in and out so quickly that the treatment they do receive has little impact.

Alisa Stevens remembers the interaction between long-term and short-term residents during the mid-1980s:

"Most of them didn't fit in," she says. "They just wanted to be by themselves. All we really knew about them was their names. And some of them were so disruptive they kept the staff on edge."

The short-term trend continued throughout the 1980s and shows little sign of changing today. The NSHCC Board recognized the need to adapt to new conditions, as this excerpt from its 1987 report to the AUBA indicates:

> *Last spring our board of directors held a day long retreat to assess our future directions. Faced with collective bargaining, unstable enrolment, site planning, constitutional review, and a myriad of other concerns, the board decided it was time to develop a 5-10 year master plan for the Home....*
>
> *The board of directors outlined items that must be considered in the implementation of any planning strategy. Throughout its history the Home has reflected the changes in society. The closure of large orphanages, the establishment of the Children's Services Act, the shifts in education, the humaneness of the community, the new Young Offenders Act, all have*

impacted on the N.S. Home for Colored Children, and have been instrumental in the movement of this Home into its newer facilities, and its service to a smaller population.

The Board hoped to expand the Home's mandate to include services like a shelter for homeless children, a residential facility for youthful drug and alcohol users, and in-home therapeutic treatment for behavior problems. To date, most of those initiatives remain on hold because of funding problems.

A Woman's Touch

From the inception of the NSHCC in 1921, women have played a major role in the development of the institution. In the Home's earliest days, the Ladies' Auxiliary provided support through fund-raising and volunteer activity. Matrons such as Elizabeth Fowler, Ida Kinney and Mary Paris exercised a great deal of responsibility in the Home's operations and served as role models for the young women under their care. Teachers at

Teacher Donna Byard Sealey with some of her pupils in the mid-1960s. The girl holding Ms. Byard's left hand is Veronica Marsman, who later became the Home's supervisor and a Board member.
(Courtesy Donna Byard Sealey)

the Home's school—such as Gladys Walcott, Portia White, Gertrude Tynes, Patricia Riley, Donna Byard Sealy—were also influential.

In later years the Home's administration came under pressure to provide more male role models for the residents. The last teacher at the Henry G. Bauld School was a man, and during the 1970s more men were hired as child-care workers. However, women have continued to function in important decision-making and managerial positions at the NSHCC.

Sherry Bernard and Jane Earle succeeded in the difficult task of holding the Home together during the strike and its immediate aftermath. After Mrs. Earle's departure, Ms. Bernard continued as Child Care Supervisor. Her responsibilities involved both program development and day-to-day supervision of staff, and she continued in that dual capacity until 1982.

Veronica Marsman
(Courtesy *The Provincial Monitor*)

"That was just too much of a task for one person to do," Ms. Bernard recalls. "After many discussions with Wilfred [Jackson] about it, we were able to hire a second supervisor. And that person was Veronica Marsman. It made a big difference to be able to split that work in half."

In that split, Ms. Marsman handled the child-care operations of the Home, while Ms. Bernard continued to develop and implement life-skills programs until she left the Home in 1989.

Ms. Marsman offered a unique perspective to her position. Along with her younger sister, Gail, Veronica had been a resident at the Home during the mid-1960s.

Ms. Marsman doesn't remember a great deal from those years, but most of what she does recall is positive. She was one of the first pupils to transfer from the Henry G. Bauld School to the William Ross School down the road.

Veronica and Gail often share memories of their experiences at the Home. They remember festive times, when the children played the Mexican piñata game, using sticks to hit a papier-mâché figure filled with candy until it burst. They remember "Santa Claus" flying onto the Home's grounds in a helicopter from CFB Shearwater, and going out trick-or-treating on Halloween.

Sleeping in a dormitory with twenty to thirty other girls wasn't a problem—the sisters had always slept in the same bed in the past. But one occasion caused a sleepless night for just about everyone.

"We heard on the news one night that some man had escaped from jail and was in the Cole Harbour–Westphal area," Veronica says. "We were terrified. We thought this man was going to come up the fire escape to get us. The set-up of the room was that the door opened to the inside. We all slept behind the door that night so he couldn't come in for us."

The Marsman sisters were eventually placed in foster homes. Gail now lives in Toronto. Veronica became a social worker. Before accepting the Supervisor's position at the NSHCC, she worked at the Truro School for Girls. Then she returned to the institution that had once been her home.

But it wasn't the same institution. During her absence, the Home had changed both buildings and mandate and survived the disruptions of the staff strike. From the beginning, Ms. Marsman wasn't satisfied with the new buildings.

"There were lots of problems with the structure of these buildings," she recalls. "The structure wasn't set up for a co-ed population. It's not set up to be supervised properly. Boys are on one floor and girls on another, but the staff room is in the middle. The hallways are on the outside, and there's doors between them. With the doors shut, people can go up and down the stairs and the staff won't even be aware."

She was also concerned about the buildings' construction materials. "If you're talking about an adolescent facility, you don't put up plaster," she says. "You use brick or something that's structurally sound for adolescents who are going to be destructive. That's the type of kids that they were getting. So the Home was constantly spending dollars on renovations."

During her time as Supervisor, Ms. Marsman introduced changes that included upgrading the record-keeping system so that daily reports were made on each resident. She also initiated a separate system for recording major behavioral incidents like running away or destroying property.

"Those were the kind of things the agencies on the outside were looking for," she says. "I was trying to bridge some of the gap that had started to develop between the agencies and the Home."

Ms. Marsman left her job as Supervisor in 1984 to accept a position with the child protection division of the Department of Community Services.

"What I ended up doing was placing kids in the Colored Home," she says. "I had an 'in'; I knew the type of kid who could probably make it there."

However, Ms. Marsman's association with the NSHCC didn't end at that point. In 1985 she became a member of the Board.

"I felt pretty good about being on the Board," she says. "Who else has better insight into the Home than someone who lived and worked there?"

Since serving her two-year term on the Board, Ms. Marsman has continued her work with Community Services and the Association of Black Social Workers. In 1991 she founded a group called Support, Education and Appreciation of Race, Culture and Heritage (SEARCH). The purpose of the group is to provide education about black history and culture to parents of biracial children and white adoptive parents of black children.

The Newest Matron

If Wilfred Jackson is heir to J.A.R. Kinney Senior and Junior's position as manager of the Home, then Althea Tolliver, the current Child Care Supervisor, is filling the shoes of Elizabeth Fowler, Ida Mae Kinney and Mary Paris. In their day, the position was called "Matron." Today, the name has changed, but the responsibilities, which involve overseeing the day-to-day care of NSHCC residents, remains the same.

Mrs. Tolliver's roots run deep in the black community that surrounds the Home. She continues to live in East Preston, the community of her birth. Her mother, Mrs. Edith Clayton, established an international reputation in the craft of basketry, a tradition handed down over generations stretching back to ancient African origins.

Mrs. Clayton taught her craft to all her daughters, including Althea. Althea also retains childhood memories of the old Home. Her uncle, Johnnie Drummond, was the Home's carpenter for many years.

"I can remember as a youngster sneaking into the old Home during the School Closings," she recalls. "The thing that fascinated me most was the layout of the Home, the floors and that sort of thing. Everyone else was gone, so I could explore with nobody catching me."

That fascination had an influence on her choice of careers in adulthood: child care and social work. Previously, she had worked her way up to a supervisor's position at K-Mart, but she had always felt she was a "people person" and wanted to work more directly with people's needs.

To that end, she took a course in child care at the Nova Scotia Institute of Technology. Part of her course involved a ten-week placement at the NSHCC. After she completed her course, Mrs. Tolliver took her first job in 1977 as Program Director at the Home. Her job was to provide recreational programs for the children, who at that time numbered about sixty.

At that time, she worked with the controversial Bob Butler. "Actually, I got along with him quite well," she says. "He wasn't difficult to talk to or work with."

She had more difficulty with veteran staff members, who kept reminding her how much younger and inexperienced she was. Some of those staff members had been there since the Home first opened its doors in 1921, and they were deeply set in their ways.

The old building was then in its last year of use. For Mrs. Tolliver, the building's problems didn't involve decay or dilapidation.

"I think it was the way in which the old Home was laid out," she says. "It was a big building, and they had three floors. The upper floor was closed because it used to hold the nursery, which was discontinued. Heating was always a problem too. And the plumbing was old and became outdated."

She remembers positive and negative aspects to the proposal for a move to new buildings.

"What they began to do, the minute they started talking about new buildings, they let the other buildings deteriorate," she says. "Then it became a dollar factor—either close the place down or build new buildings."

Mrs. Tolliver departed her position in 1978, before the move into the new buildings and the subsequent strike. She studied social work and became involved in community organizing, eventually co-writing a book on black community development in Nova Scotia. However, she maintained an interest in the Home, and during the strike she was asked by a social worker to take in two of the children who were affected. Because her own children were young at the time, she declined.

Her opinion of the strike is to an extent similar to Jackson's.

"I certainly feel that wages were low at the Home," she says. "And I believe in unions to a degree. But I guess, being a people person, that when unions come into a place such as the Home, it takes away from it."

However, Mrs. Tolliver had no problems with the prospect of returning to the post-strike Home.

"I felt it was time for some new changes, a different outlook," she says. "And I'd heard the Home was looking for a supervisor. So I filled out the application and went for an interview."

Althea Tolliver, Child Care Supervisor, with her uncle, the late Johnnie Drummond, long-time carpenter at the Home.
(Courtesy Althea Tolliver)

Wilfred Jackson hired her on the basis of her qualifications and previous NSHCC experience. She thus became a link between the old Home and the new. She sees several differences between the two experiences.

"The old building was so big you could almost lose yourself in it," she recalls. "Or a child could get lost, especially if they went to that third floor."

She also found a lingering resistance to change, as in mutterings of "That wasn't the way Mr. Kinney did it."

The biggest change she sees, however, lies in the problems and circumstances under which children are referred to the institution. The old Home took in children who needed food, shelter and basic care.

"It wasn't so much neglect, as the fact that 'Mom' couldn't afford to look after them," Mrs. Tolliver says. She recalls the story of a friend of hers who was one of nine children of a single parent in East Preston: "She talks about how she woke up one morning and found herself in the Home, and how she was so afraid. But she was only there for a little while."

Today the woman doesn't hold that short stay in the old Home against her mother. Family Services had taken her out of the house and placed her in the NSHCC. The mother eventually got her children back and went to work at the Home.

The children were also quieter and more withdrawn then, Mrs. Tolliver recalls. "You put them in a certain place, and they stayed there. Today, they come in with their own agenda."

Now the problems are more behavioral in nature: drugs, running away, physical aggression and criminal activities. The children tend to be older, too—hard-bitten adolescents rather than the five-year-old waif named "Pretty" who had charmed the *Toronto Star* reporter back in the 1960s. And they're also far more sophisticated, reflecting changes in the surrounding society and the incessant bombardment of television-screen images.

"I can remember the first time we did a workshop with some of the kids on sex," Mrs. Tolliver recalls. "And one of the girls said to me, 'Well, what do you want to know?'"

Renewal and Remembrance

On October 24, 1985, the Home recaptured some of its history by relocating and rededicating its former chapel. During the years since the move to the new buildings, the old chapel had been used by the Black Cultural Society before the construction of its center across the road. Later, it became the office of Watershed Development Association Enterprises, a Preston-area community organization.

The rededicated chapel, located in one of the new Home buildings, was named for Rev. Donald Fairfax, who had been involved with the home for thirty years, beginning as a Sunday School teacher and ending as the first black President of the Board of Directors. He had later gone on to earn recognition as a Member of the Order of Canada.

Dedication of Donald E. Fairfax Memorial Chapel. (left to right) Wilfred Jackson, Gertrude Tynes, Rev. Donald E. Fairfax and Rev. William P. Oliver.

In an article in the October 25, 1985, *Mail-Star*, Wilfred Jackson said: "The chapel will fill an important role within the Home. It is very important in the sense that it was one of the things left behind when we moved here. When the children go out to various churches on Sunday they don't have the feeling of fellowship as they would if going to a service here within their own home. The services are planned for midweek to allow children the chance to attend churches within the community on Sunday."

For Jackson, the chapel would provide a "middle ground" for the residents. To the *Mail Star*, he said: "When they go out into the community churches they are not part of the congregation as they were in their church back in their own community. Because of that they don't get as involved as the regular congregation.... Sometimes it is too formal in the churches within the community and too informal within the residence itself."

When not in use for services, the chapel would be a private space for residents who wanted to "get away from it all." It would also be used as a visiting center for organizations and community youth groups.

Some of the spirit of generosity that surrounded the opening of the original Home was recalled with the donation of Bibles from Gideons International of Canada and the Canadian Bible Society, hymnals and chairs from Canadian Forces Base Halifax, and a piano from the Canadian Martyr's Parish.

Another old Home building reclaimed in the 1980s was the Henry G. Bauld School. In the Home's report to the 1984 annual meeting of the African United Baptist Association, Board President Gertrude Tynes wrote:

> *Our last NSHCC Annual Meeting was held in the Henry G. Bauld Recreation Centre, named in honor of one of the founders of the N.S. Home for Colored Children. For more than five years this building has been idle. In the last three years it was reduced to a state of ruin. However, all of this has changed thanks to two grants from the Department of Manpower and Immigration. Originally used as a school, we have now renovated this facility to serve as a much needed indoor recreation building for our youth, plus a community facility as time allows. Everything within this structure has been changed and upgraded to meet today's standards for community facilities. We have already had several requests for the use of this building, so we anticipate that the completion of this new centre will signal the revival of the old home site.*

Ms. Tynes' optimism about the old Home building was fuelled by the successful renovations of the Bauld School, the old chapel and the caretaker's cottage. However, the restoration of the old building would prove to be a far more difficult task.

The Old Home

When Ross Kinney III visits Nova Scotia, he always drives out to the site of the old Home. And he remembers what the area was like during the happy times of his childhood.

"I used to know this place like the back of my hand," he says. "But everything's overgrown now. It's sad. But the Home had to change with the times."

For the Home's original building, however, those changes have not been for the better. As the 1980s progressed, the old building stood in silent, lonely witness to its own slow but certain dilapidation. Reporter Daphne Ross described it as looking like "the original derelict haunted house" in an article in the April 27, 1985, edition of *The Daily News*, a Halifax-area newspaper.

The old Home building as it looked in the fall of 1993.
(Tony Caldwell photo, courtesy *The Daily News*)

The building should have long since been restored and preserved as one of the principal historical monuments in the province. But that hasn't happened.

Shortly after the new facilities opened, the possibility of the old Home serving as a black historical museum was suggested. However, the new building constructed in 1983 for the Black Cultural Centre took on that role, and the old Home building remained unoccupied.

Other uses were proposed, including a recreation centre, headquarters for the Black United Front, and a junior college; the latter reminiscent of James R. Johnston's original concept for the Home.

H.A.J. "Gus" Wedderburn, a Halifax lawyer who served on the NSHCC Board from 1974 to 1980, recalls another, more unconventional suggestion that was seriously considered.

"We thought of a motel as a fund-generating thing," he says. "From a cursory observation, we figured that there were no motels between Dartmouth and Sheet Harbour. After building the Black Cultural Centre, we would get telephone calls from people in the United States, tourists who wanted to come and wanted to know if there were any black motels in the area. Of course, there were not."

And there still aren't. For many reasons, mostly financial, the motel and other ideas for the building's rehabilitation fell by the wayside.

During the 1980s a lack of funds for maintenance caused the aging wooden structure to deteriorate so badly that Halifax County Council mentioned it in connection with an "unsightly premises" bylaw—a veiled warning to do something about the situation or else.

In response, the NSHCC Board of Directors had the windows boarded up and the outside woodwork painted. However, other problems persisted.

"The age and declining condition of the old home also has the area's fire department worried," Executive Director Jackson told the *Mail-Star* in 1984. And the Board was unable to secure insurance for the building.

The Board attempted to have the old Home declared a historical site by Halifax County, but the County turned down the application because the building didn't meet a set of fixed criteria, including age.

Several suggestions for possible uses for a renovated Home building surfaced over the years, including a recreation center, an office complex, a museum to be run in conjunction with the Black Cultural Centre, and a convention center. Whatever purpose the building might ultimately serve, the consensus was that it needed to be preserved as part of the black community's historical legacy.

"It's extremely important to save the old home site," Jackson said to the *Mail-Star*'s reporter. "It's a fixture in the community because of its history."

Eventually, the Board's Facilities Committee presented the problem to the Nova Scotia School of Architecture. Students were challenged to devise ways to rehabilitate the building's interior while maintaining its original exterior.

Prior to that, drafting students from the Dartmouth Regional Vocational School compiled measurements of the building's exterior in 1985. That information was then passed on to the School of Architecture.

"All work will be done voluntarily and the final drafts will be presented to the Home's Board of Directors around the end of March," Jackson said in the January 8, 1985 issue of the *Mail-Star*.

By June 1985, three proposals were submitted by students in Professor Frank Eppell's second-year architecture class. "Adaptive re-use" was the rubric under which the students worked.

The students included five possible uses in their plans: a conference center, community offices, a recreation/fitness center, a child-care facility, and a crafts workshop. Renovation techniques included a glass wrap-around at the front of the building and a modern addition at its rear.

In the meantime, the Board sought federal funds for the renovation of the building in preparation for future use. However, an application for a $130,000 Winter Works grant was unsuccessful despite the support of then-Dartmouth East MP Michael Forrestal and then-Halifax MP Stewart McInnes. The grant money would have paid for roof repairs, siding, and new windows and doors. In the absence of funds, those much-needed repairs have not as yet been made.

Today the building still sits in silent reproach, like an elderly person who lives alone and never has visitors. The windows are boarded shut, the steps leading to the front door are gone, and signs that warn "No Trespassing" and "Do Not Enter" are nailed to the walls.

The grass surrounding the building is cut regularly, but the old farm fields are overgrown. Foundations from the farm buildings remain visible. On one wall of the brick annex, vandals have spray-painted the initials "KKK."

Although the building hasn't been unoccupied since 1978, its basic structure remains sound—a tribute to the care and skill of the community craftsmen who built it back in 1921. However, the plumbing, electricity and other facilities need to be replaced, having long since been looted.

"In terms of fire and safety regulations, we have to do more to the building now than the original structure demanded," Jackson says.

Wayne Adams remembers a visit with an architect to the building several years ago. The architect's task was to determine the degree of rot and deterioration in the structure.

"He was using these little machines on the wooden beams," Adams recalls. "He wasn't saying very much, but was looking very puzzled. And he finally said, 'It's incredible. Absolutely incredible. This place is as sound as the day it was built.' "

Submissions are still being made to various federal and provincial bodies for renovation funding. Unfortunately, the economic climate has worsened over the past few years, and money has become scarce in both the public and private sectors.

What would it cost to restore the old Home? Jackson's estimate is "anywhere between $250,000 and $5 million." In a cash-strapped Maritimes economy, that's a sum large enough to create serious misgivings. As well, one or more organizations willing to be tenants need to be found so that a long-term lease can be obtained. So far, no prospective tenant has offered a firm commitment.

Former Board President Rev. Donald D. Skeir remains skeptical in the face of lack of progress in restoring the old Home.

"I hear people saying we should convert it into a centre," he says. "But this is going to take a tremendous amount of financing," he says. "And I often wonder where this money's going to come from. Some have suggested that the AUBA use it for its annual gatherings. But that's going to require renovation—and money."

And if the money isn't forthcoming? In the worst-case scenario, the old Home may eventually have to be demolished. If that happens, the process will not go forward without protest.

"We're totally against any demolition of the building," Jackson says unequivocally. "It's too central to our history, and it still has the potential to become a focus for the black community of today."

Rev. Donald Fairfax agrees with Jackson, although he is a bit more pessimistic. "It's one of the most historical buildings, other than our churches, in Nova Scotia," he says. "I don't know if we can ever, ever bring it back and try to restore it. It's gone down, down, down."

Who or what is to blame for this unacceptable state of affairs? Is it the looters from within and outside the surrounding community who have over the years stripped the building of virtually everything of value within it? Is it the provincial government and the NSHCC Board of Directors, who moved the Home into new buildings without having a plan in place for the preservation of the old one? Is it the funding agencies that rigidly adhere to criteria that may not always be fair or appropriate? Or is it nothing more than apathy, pure and simple? The answer probably incorporates all of the above to some degree.

The NSHCC Board of Directors' latest plan for the building is to turn it into a black business centre.

"It would be called the James A.R. Kinney Heritage Complex," says former Board President Donna Smith. "We wrote to the Kinney family and got permission to use the name."

However, that plan is on hold until enough tenants can be found to ensure funding. Funding and marketing continue to constitute the main roadblocks in the path to refurbish the building.

At this point, with precious little money available in the white or black communities in a recession-ridden economy, the only hope for the old Home appears to lie in somehow managing to keep the wrecker's ball at bay until the building becomes old enough to qualify as a national or provincial historic site.

And that's a sad and unnecessary fate for a structure that began its existence as a source of pride for the Nova Scotian black community as a whole.

The Board

Since the day the first NSHCC Board of Directors was formed in 1915, that body has borne responsibility for the long-term direction of the Home. During the time that passed between those early decades and the 1980s, the composition and structure of the Board underwent several changes. From its earliest incarnation as a group of prominent whites from the business community and a few black community leaders, it evolved in the 1970s into a predominantly black group drawn from the clergy and other established leaders.

Today the composition of the Board remains mostly black, with members drawn from more diverse backgrounds. Out of fifteen members, two are white, and five are women. Criteria for nomination to the Board involve specific skills that can be of use to the Home.

"Two of the people nominated this year have experience in human resources, and another in program development," says Donna Smith, who served as Board President from 1991 to 1993 and is now Past-President, "and one has financial background."

Gordon Earle (second from left) with NSHCC residents on a visit to Camp Hill Hospital in Halifax.

The precedent established in 1974, when Rev. Donald E. Fairfax became the Board's first black President, has continued unbroken to this day. From 1980 to 1993 the Board has elected ten Presidents, all of them black.

Gordon Earle held the position from 1980 to 1981. Earle was once considered for the Superintendent's job at the Home when Ross Kinney retired, but Mary Paris took on the position's responsibility, if not its title. At the time he was Board President, Earle served as an assistant to the Ombudsman of Nova Scotia. He later went on to become Ombudsman for the Province of Manitoba.

Two NSHCC Board Presidents, Wayne Kelsie (left), and Rev. Donald Fairfax, compare notes.

From 1981 to 1983, Rev. Fairfax returned for two more terms as President. He had remained on the Board throughout the years that followed his first term, and came back to the position to ensure continuity during a period of restructuring in the Board.

Rev. Fairfax was succeeded by Wayne Kelsie, who is one of the true success stories of the NSHCC. Kelsie spent most of his childhood and adolescence at the Home and was one of the first residents to excel in an academic environment. He went on to establish a law practice in Halifax before becoming Board President from 1983 to 1984. Kelsie now practices law in Labrador.

Gertrude Tynes, who once taught Home Economics at the Henry G. Bauld School, served two terms from 1984 to 1986. Mrs. Tynes is now working on a book about the experiences of the men and women who taught in Nova Scotia's segregated black schools.

Mrs. Tynes was succeeded by James Francois, a native of Barbados who now calls Nova Scotia his home. Francois served from 1986 to 1988. He was familiar with the Home through his work as Executive Director of Watershed Association Development Enterprises (WADE), a black self-help group that focuses on the Preston–Cherry Brook communities. WADE was once headquartered at the Home. Today, Francois serves as Employment Equity Officer for the Canadian Coast Guard.

The next Board President was Brian Darrell, an engineer at Maritime Telephone and Telegraph. Active in community affairs, Darrell lent his name to an annual black basketball tournament that attracts players from Nova Scotia and Ontario. He remained as NSHCC Board President until 1991.

Donna Smith is a pediatrics nurse practitioner and lecturer at the Izaak Walton Killam Hospital for Children. Ms. Smith had previously served on the Board for a year during the late 1970s, and then returned in 1986. She was Vice-President for four years before becoming President in 1991.

Ms. Smith was born in Yarmouth, the hometown of J.A.R. Kinney, Sr. Although Kinney left Yarmouth as a two-year-old, Ms. Smith says his family is still remembered there.

She remembers an incident during her childhood when a black family broke up and the children were sent to the Home.

"There were four little boys," she recalls. "I often wonder what happened to them, but I did know that they did come to the Home. Their mother died, and I think their father must have had some problem with drinking. I never understood why nobody in the community took those children."

Ms. Smith's two terms on the Board reflect contrasting times and experiences. In 1978 she was invited to join the Board by Iona Crawley, who was then the only woman member. The first woman member of the Board was Mrs. H.P. McKeen, who was nominated in 1961. In 1963, Mrs. McKeen's husband, Henry, was named Lieutenant-Governor of Nova Scotia. Black clergymen made up much of the rest of the Board's roster in the late 1970s.

"My first time on the Board was during a period of real upheaval," Ms. Smith recalls. "Bob Butler was Executive Director at that time. There was lots of controversy and problems. They had just opened those two new buildings, and there were problems within the Board itself."

Past Board President Donna Smith with Alice Croft, former Board President and Treasurer.

Those problems, which Ms. Smith says revolved around the decision-making process, caused her to resign her membership before the staff strike of 1979.

How does she compare the current Board to the one she left in 1979?

"Night and day," she says. "It's a younger Board, and their motivations are different. Today's Board is a very cohesive group, and they use a lot of their own work experience in making policy. Their backgrounds are much more diverse, and they're not as hooked into the communities as the members of the first Board I was on."

However, the Board of the 1980s wasn't always a congenial body. The pressure to adapt to changing times that the NSHCC faced during the previous decade continued, and consensus on how to effect that adaptation was hard to achieve.

"Four years ago, the Board was not a good working group," Ms. Smith says. "There were personality clashes, there were differences of ideas. The Board was going off in every which direction. Half the people wanted to sell the land and make some quick money. Other people didn't want to do that."

Eventually the Board set up a new structure. The Executive Committee consists of the Past-President, President, Vice-President, Secretary, Treasurer and Executive Director. Other committees include Facilities, Program, Personnel, Nominating, and Strategic Planning.

NSHCC Board members sing carols at a mid-1980s Christmas party. (left to right) Connie Glasgow, Corrinne Sparks, Susan Downey, Gertrude Tynes, Tom McInnes, Rev. Donald Fairfax, Malcolm MacFarlane, the late Sheila Beals, Matthew Thomas, Veronica Marsman.

"Strategic Planning is a key one at this point, because their whole idea is to revitalize the old Home building," Ms. Smith says.

The Executive Committee is the overall governing body of the NSHCC. The other committees develop plans, which are then presented to the Executive Committee for a decision on further action. "Those are all housekeeping things, but it makes things work much easier," Ms. Smith says.

Another change concerns the period of time members serve on the Board. In the past, some members stayed on for twenty or more years. And the first two Presidents, Henry G. Bauld and Melville Cumming, held that position for a combined total of fifty-one years.

Now, members are nominated for two-year terms, which are renewable at the discretion of the Nominating Committee. The purpose of the turnover is to ensure a constant infusion of fresh viewpoints.

"The idea is to have two-thirds of the Board stay and one-third leave," says Ms. Smith. "And some people go off for a few years, then come back. If you're involved in a situation long enough, you develop a vested interest. New blood and flexibility are what's going to make it move in this age of information."

In terms of division of responsibility, the Executive Director, administration and staff handle day-to-day management of the Home. Long-range planning, policymaking, budget determination, and public relations fall under the mandate of the Board.

Board member Jack MacNeil provides one example of how the body functions: "If a group wanted to rent the Henry G. Bauld School, the Executive Director comes to the Board and asks, 'Should I rent it or shouldn't I rent it, how much money should we get for the rent, what are the restrictions we should put on that school?' The Board would give him direction as to what to do."

The late Mrs. Mayola Johnson at work in the NSHCC kitchen with Sheila States in the early 1980s.
(Courtesy Bruce Johnson)

Through the 1980s and up to the present time, the Board has had to confront issues that affect the very survival of the institution.

"One of the biggest issues is pressure from [the provincial Department of] Community Services," says Ms. Smith. "The most difficult thing for us is that Community Services is changing its focus and its mandate. Basically, they are trying very hard to get rid of institutions. The mandate is now more small group homes. So as a Board we've had to make some decisions to change the way we deal with the kids."

The Board has also had to battle long-standing myths about the nature of the NSHCC.

"The myths are that we're a black organization, that we are not well established, our staff is not well educated," Ms. Smith says. "There may have been some people in the community who have had a run-in with some of the workers. Therefore they have some of these cliché ideas that we're not like white organizations where everybody's papered to death. And it's true. We're not. But I don't think you can ignore a person's work experience."

Bill Greatorex of the Department of Community Services agrees. "Experience is big factor in dealing with these young people if you're not going to be shocked by their behavior," he says. "When a kid becomes upset, you're able to maintain some degree of calmness and help the kid through it."

Another problem area Ms. Smith sees is that the Home is one of the few institutions of its kind to have a unionized staff. Staffs in smaller, more specialized group homes tend to be salaried professionals. Although labor unrest has never reached the level of intensity that preceded the strike, contract negotiations have at times been a source of stress.

James Harper, a former fire fighter who served as NCHCC Treasurer from 1982-1984, says the collective agreement always had to be taken into account in budget preparation.

"It was difficult to be Treasurer of an institution like the Home," he recalls. "Because our funding was based on the number of residents we had, the budget fluctuated from month to month. Private means like donations and will bequests helped but it wasn't enough."

For all the difficulties the Board has faced, the late 1980s and early 1990s also saw plans and progress. One of the Board's more ambitious plans is to make practical use of the property that has lain idle since the commercial farm shut down during the 1960s.

"Whether we do it or whether we lease the land, it would be something that would serve the black community," says Ms. Smith. "And of course we have to realize we're not living in isolation, so we'd have to have something that could serve the predominantly black community, and the white community as well—something like a convention centre, a community college, government offices, so people in this area don't have to go elsewhere to have their needs met."

Such development would ultimately meet the needs of the Home as well. "Down the road, what we'd like to see is financial independence so we don't have to depend on the Community Services Department," says Ms. Smith.

This notion of independence may be an indication that the Home is moving back to the original conception of the 1920s, toward becoming a self-supporting child-care institute. In the 1990s, though, such an institute would scarcely resemble the community over which J.A.R. Kinney, Sr. presided. But it would also be different from what the Home has become today.

In the summer of 1993, the Board elected new officers. Rodger G.J. Smith is the new President; Carol Johnson, Vice- President; Pemberton Cyrus, Treasurer; Donna Smith; Past- President. Other 1993-1994 Board members include: Janis Jones–Darrell, Roger Grant, Darcy Gray, John MacNeil, Michael Mansfield, Rev. Matthew Lucas, Richard Bartolo, Beverly Johnson, Lorne White, Muriel Tupper and Thomas Emodi.

Rodger Smith, a native of North Preston, is a branch bank manager with the Royal Bank of Canada. He studied business administration at Nova Scotia Community College and is active in church and community affairs. He has been an NSHCC Board member since 1986.

"I joined the Board because I wanted to help with decision-making for children in care," he says. "There are a lot of children from single-parent families and children who are not wanted by their families. They need something positive in their lives."

Growing up in North Preston, Smith remembers visiting the old Home often. A relative, the late Mayola Johnson, was the cook at the Home for nearly two decades.

Mrs. Johnson's career spanned the old and new Homes. Her son, Bruce, says more than a few female residents of the Home learned domestic skills by helpng her in the kitchen.

Rodger Smith, 1993-1994 NSHCC Board President.
(Courtesy *The Provincial Monitor*)

"She always had time for the children, no matter how busy she was," Bruce says.

Smith remembers playing with the residents when he went to visit his aunt. "We used to run all over the place," he recalls. "I went to school with many of the residents as well."

As the new President of the Board, Smith has two priorities for the NSHCC.

"We have to keep up with changing community and economic conditions," he says. "The recession affects everybody. We have to be there for children whose home environments are suffering."

Smith's second priority is to instill a sense of pride in the residents. "They have to know they're wanted, despite whatever background they come from. They have to know somebody cares about them."

In that respect, the Home's mission hasn't changed since the day it first opened its doors.

Rainbow

My Mother was tender Rain,
My Father the Sun.

Name me Rainbow.

Call me any one colour,
and you'll be wrong.

I'm all the colours —
harmonized.

Come under my arch,
my arc, my crayon home,

oh children of all colours.

George Elliott Clarke

The Home Today

8

Continuing Tradition

In the 1990s the Nova Scotia Home for Colored Children bore little resemblance to the institution it was fifty years earlier, or even 10 years earlier. However, some long-established traditions continued.

One of those traditions is the annual Christmas fund-raising broadcast, which hasn't missed a year since its inception back in 1931. However, even the broadcast has adapted to changing times and technology. In December 1972, it transferred from radio to another electronic media outlet: television.

During that year, long-time host radio station CHNS shared its airing of the event with CHFX-FM, with a simultaneous broadcast over the Halifax and Dartmouth cable television stations, and Maritime Tel and Tel handled the pledge lines for the first time.

NSHCC Board member Wayne Adams was the initial host and coordinator for the TV broadcast. Rev. Donald Fairfax conducted the NSHCC choir, and other performers included the Mercy Brothers, Juanita Rose Snow, Johnny Gold, Doug Bell, Theresa Cleary, Ralph Conrod and Eric Bowers.

Over the next few years, the Halifax and Dartmouth cable stations continued to simulcast the program with CHNS and CHFX. Eventually the radio broadcast was dropped.

Once the telethon became established on cable TV, it developed a format that has lasted. Program content consists of on-air interviews, auctions, pledges, and entertainment by talent from the Home and the Metro community. The number of NSHCC residents involved ranges from

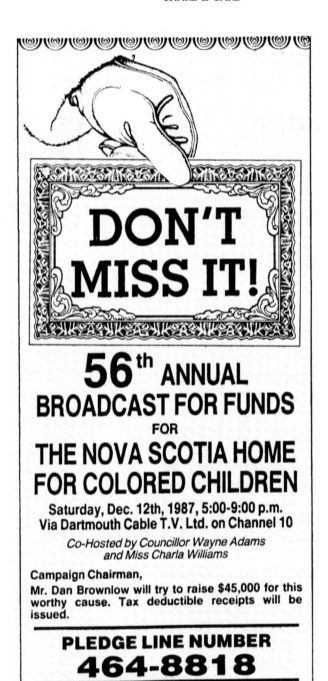

twelve to twenty-five, depending on how many are living there at the time.

Community talent performing on the show has drawn heavily on local church groups, such as the seventy-five-member combined Preston choirs, the Cornwallis Street Church's children's choir, and the renowned Gospel Heirs, a seven-member band from North Preston that sings contemporary gospel and has cut two albums.

Others who have performed or helped to host the broadcast include Four the Moment, a well-known a cappella folk group; Suzanne Herbert-Sparks, a classical singer; Lorne White, a brother of Portia White; Paula Fairfax, a former Miss Halifax and daughter of Rev. Donald Fairfax; and former Canadian welterweight champion Ricky Anderson.

However, the days when the NSHCC boasted its own travelling choir and string orchestra were long gone by the 1970s. The residents' average stay had become too brief to allow for extended musical instruction.

"As far as the kids are concerned, it's very different," says Wilfred Jackson. "In the early years, the children were showcased. The children were here long-term, so you could put together choirs and at one point they had a band. Now, that just isn't there. The children here now are short-term, so there's really no time to train them. Many of the children at the Home now are what you'd consider multi-problemed, so we have to pay more attention to the needs of the children as opposed to trying to train the children to be on air."

However, residents who volunteer to participate do receive instruction and preparation before the broadcast begins.

"We always bring in a volunteer choir director from the community," says Jackson. "The last couple of years, we've had Nina Adams come in, and Don Johnson, both of whom are accomplished singers and musicians and have the patience to work with the children. It's become very rewarding for those who want to participate."

Performances by residents of the NSHCC no longer guarantee sold-out venues and steady streams of donations the way they did in years gone by. As with the passing of commercial farming operations, the termination of the travelling performances and in-house musical training marked the end of another aspect of the old Home's sense of independence.

But the Christmas telethon is still a keenly anticipated event. Campaign objectives range from $40,000 to $50,000. During some years, the objective has actually been surpassed, but others have seen a shortfall. Whatever the final tally of contributions may be, the telethon continues to serve the dual purpose of fundraising and public relations for the NSHCC.

Children performing at annual Christmas broadcast in early 1980s.

Facing page - Newspaper ad for the annual Christmas broadcast.

"The broadcast lends continuity to the type of things we're doing at the Home," says Jackson. "It's one of the times when the community has an opportunity to participate and support what's going on at the Home. Part of the appeal of the broadcast is that there's so many volunteers who get involved with the presentation. So many people—especially the elderly people who've been aware of the Home for these many years—look forward to the broadcast. More than ever, the broadcast is very important to the Home and the community at large."

Although the broadcast represents continuity, the NSHCC is reestablishing other traditions as well. Since 1991 the Home has produced annual fund-raising gospel concerts. The 1992 effort, co-sponsored by Air Nova, IGA Supermarket and CBC Radio, featured prominent local vocalists, including the Gospel Heirs, James Paris, Linda and Tina Carvery, Anne Johnson and the Gospel Friends, and the Cornwallis Street Children's Church Choir.

These concerts are reminiscent of the ones that helped to raise money for the construction of the original Home so many decades ago.

What's in a Name?

Should the name of the Nova Scotia Home for Colored Children be changed? That's a question successive Boards and Executive Directors have pondered since the time the NSHCC was officially integrated during the 1960s. The issue became especially relevant during the 1980s, when the Home faced new challenges.

"Declining enrollment has been a problem," Wilfred Jackson told the *Mail-Star* in July 1985. "From time to time there is not enough, not all the beds are filled, and that means not enough income."

Jackson attributed the enrollment problem partially to the persistent perception that the NSHCC was open only to black children, and the Home's name has appeared to be the major reason for that belief.

Ironically, the Home's residents appear unaffected by the controversy. "The children don't have any strong feelings about it," says Jackson. "As in any other group home, it's the people that they have attachments to. It's not really the name. From a professional point of view, it may be a hangup more with the social workers than it is with the children."

Still, Jackson and the Board hoped to correct those misconceptions by renaming the Home's buildings in honor of persons who were important in its history. The list of candidates for such an honor is a long one: J.A.R. Kinney Senior and Junior, H.G. Bauld, Mary Paris, Elizabeth Fowler, Melville Cumming, James Robinson Johnston, and so on.

"We would keep the Nova Scotia Home for Colored Children as the corporate name," Jackson said in the *Mail-Star* article. "But hopefully it would become known by the other names instead."

In 1986 the Board approved Jackson's renaming suggestion in principle. However, the institution is still formally known as the Nova Scotia Home for Colored Children, and the name continues to be a source of controversy and misperceptions.

Throughout the larger Nova Scotia community, many still believe the NSHCC accepts only black children. Within the social services network, some professionals question the retention of the name in any capacity, saying it creates the wrong impression of the Home.

"Community Services often gets into the issue of the name," says former Board President Donna Smith. "They say, 'You people should really think about being more progressive by changing the name. You might get more children in the Home.' "

And in the North American black culture, there are some who consider the term "colored" outmoded, offensive and inaccurate. Child Care Supervisor Patricia Mugridge received a graphic demonstration of that attitude when some of the Home's staff attended a major conference in the United States.

"When some of the black delegates there heard our name, they almost beat us up," she says. "They asked us, 'What are you doing with a name like *that*?' "

Jackson had an experience that was even more intense when he inquired about applying for a Master's degree program in child and youth care work at Nova University in Fort Lauderdale, Florida, in 1983.

"When I first made contact, I wrote on the Home's letterhead," Jackson recalls. "I didn't get any response. I persistently sent in applications requesting information for about two years. It was only when I finally met some of these people face-to-face, that when they had seen the information coming from the Home for Colored Children, their first reaction when they saw the name was that this was some radical redneck group. They didn't associate it with black people at all. In their impression, the name was outdated, the name was a blot on African-Canadian history, and why anyone was using this term was just beyond them. Their first reaction was that this was some white racist writing to them, and they didn't want that person in their school."

Because Jackson's application met all the qualifications for admittance to the program, the university couldn't come up with legitimate grounds for rejection. He did, however, experience a degree of tension when he arrived on campus.

Once Jackson had explained the history of the Home and the reasons the name was retained, the environment at Nova University became much less hostile. In turn, he learned something about the importance nomenclature holds for some African–Americans.

"They were saying that in some states, the term 'colored' is against the law," says Jackson. "Anything that used to be called that has had to change the name by law."

Ironically, there have been separate African-American child-care facilities that included the term "colored" in their titles. One such institution was the Colored Orphan Asylum in New York City. In July 1863, the Colored Orphan Asylum was burned to the ground by white rioters who were enraged by U.S. Civil War conscription laws.

Times have indeed changed since then, and the word "colored" is no longer fashionable. But the Home's name should not be dismissed so casually. For the generation that worked so hard to establish the Home in the early years of this century, "colored" was deemed an honorable and respectful reference among blacks and whites alike. It was certainly preferable to some of the other terms that have been used to describe blacks, such as "nigger," "coon," "jigaboo," "shine," "jungle bunny," and so on, ad nauseam. Back then, the name of the Home was spoken with pride and self-respect in Nova Scotia's black community.

Some of that old-time pride remains today. "We are probably the only group home or organization in which a group of staff people, volunteer people, professional people actually went out with their own resources and purchased jackets," says Jackson. "And on those jackets is written 'The Nova Scotia Home for Colored Children.' All the members of the Board—black and white—purchased and wore those jackets."

In his Master's degree practicum on the subject of the Home's history, entitled "The Transition of an Orphanage for Black Children into an Interracial Child Care Facility," Jackson offered his own opinion on the name issue:

As a Home for Colored Children, the Home was founded to meet the needs of Black youths who at the time were excluded from all other existing youth services. Since that time, these Colored people have become known as Negroes, Afro-Americans, Blacks, visible minorities, and now People of Color.

As such, there has been constant pressure on the policy-makers to change the name of this institution to reflect these new references to Black people. Point of fact is that all of these references to Black people are simply propaganda devices used by the media and others to divide people into groups.

If that's the case, then it's up to the black community rather than social services and the media to decide what the name of the Home should be. And that decision should take both historical and contemporary factors into account.

Among those with current and past associations with the Home, opinion on its name is far from monolithic, as the following informal poll of people associated with the Home indicates. The question asked was:

"Do you think the name of the Nova Scotia Home for Colored Children should be changed?"

Rodger Smith, current Board President: "I don't think it should be changed. 'Colored' denotes all types of races. The name has historical value. It reminds us of the struggle to get our children into care."

Donna Smith, past Board President: "Although there are pros and cons to it, it's a progressive idea. You'd have to present it to the community in such a way that the community wouldn't get the idea that their heritage is being tossed aside. It's the whole idea of change, and the whole idea of making us look more up-to-date. Today, the name is a misnomer. The children at the Home are predominantly white."

Rev. Donald E. Fairfax, former Board President: "No. Not under any circumstances. I believe that blacks today are more in a position to become part of the Home just through supporting it. We must always be there for our children in their time of need."

Noel Johnston, former Shopmobile teacher: "Basically, I am opposed to any name change. To me, the Nova Scotia Home for Colored Children is something I grew up with. It's a part of our history. To change the name—we would lose a part of our history."

Sheila States, Assistant Child Care Supervisor: "If they change it, what would they change it to, other than taking away something that they had so long? We take in all colors."

Veronica Marsman, former Supervisor: "I always felt it should be changed, despite where some of the Board members were coming from when they talked about tradition and history. But it's now a child-care facility, and it's not solely black kids there. I felt it extremely difficult as a child-care worker trying to place white kids in the Home. I tried to get around it by saying it's a Colored Home for kids of all colors to pacify the parents so they wouldn't say, 'What are you trying to do, set my kid up?' The Home is not the Home anymore. That whole 'Colored Home' concept is gone."

Hope Hume, Child Care Worker: "I've had mixed feelings. It did bother me for a long time. Colored…colored…that's all I would ever think of, the word 'colored.' We have white people in the area that think black children belong in the Home just because of the name. But now that I'm working here, I'm very proud of the name."

Sheila Lucas, Social Worker: "I would like to see the name changed. When anybody asks me, I just say that the term 'colored' refers to all colors. That wasn't the original intention. 'Colored' meant 'black' at that time. There is some stigma attached to that. A lot of people consider this a facility only for black kids, not any other nationalities or ethnic groups."

Rev. Donald D. Skeir, former Board President: "I think the name should be retained for historical purposes. I think the black community and even the white community should be constantly made aware as to why this place came into being."

Hank Simmonds, Child Care Worker: "I think in the community, most people identify with something that belongs to them. You could call it the "Black Home," but there's a lot of white kids here, and that would be a little prejudiced towards them. Sometimes when we take the kids to things like doctor's appointments and sign them in as being from the Home for Colored Children, people ask 'Why do you have a name like that?' "

Althea Tolliver, Child Care Supervisor: "I deal with this question all the time. I have no major problem with the name; it's people on the outside who have the problem. I know the history of the Home, and I know where the name came from."

H.A.J. Wedderburn, former Board member: "In the United States you still have the National Association for the Advancement of Colored People, and I'm the president of the Nova Scotia Association for the Advancement of Colored People. As Shakespeare says, what's in a name? A rose is a rose."

Margaret Wright, former Office Secretary: "In this day and age, it probably should be changed. But I would like to see it stay the way it is, because it is a historic thing. They should drop the word "Colored" and just leave it as the Nova Scotia Home for Children."

Patricia Mugridge, Supervisor: "The reason the Home was given the name was because of racism seventy-five years ago, and kids are still suffering from it now. The name is a reminder that racism is still there. I think the name should stay to remind people that racism still exists. Changing the name isn't going to get us more referrals or more money."

George Bernard, former resident: "I don't think it should change. Where did the black children go before this Home got started? There was no place for them. They couldn't go to the white institutions. That's why Mr. Kinney started the Home."

Alisa Stevens, former resident: "When I think of the word 'colored,' I think of it as a multitude of colors. But when I was at the Home, a lot of the kids were repelled by the name. White kids didn't think it applied to them, and black kids thought it was out of date."

Beverly Wyse, Child Care Worker: " 'Colored' means any race. So it doesn't matter what race comes here. So why should we change the name?"

Jocelyn Boyd, Office Manager: "The Home came into existence because there was racism and segregation, and black children weren't allowed into white institutions. There's still racism today. There's still a lot of places that don't accept black people. Changing the name would almost be like erasing a part of our history. I don't think the past should be erased."

Donna Byard Sealey, teacher at the H.G. Bauld School: "When you look at the changes that are taking place within the black community, I foresee the need for a home for colored children. There's children raising children, cocaine babies.... The notion is, all children deserve a home, but how good are some of these homes? Some of our children are growing up like weeds."

Charlie Wright, Maintenance Worker: "What would be the point of changing it? We don't turn any children down, no matter what their color is."

Sherleen Bernard, former Executive Director: "I'm torn on that question. My father was brought up at the Home, and he's always had good things to say about it. I'd have a hard time giving up on the Nova Scotia Home for Colored Children's name. But I like the idea of naming the buildings after the Kinneys or Elizabeth Fowler or Mary Paris."

Patricia Kinney: "Although the Home was founded as the Nova Scotia Home for Colored Children, we don't use the word 'colored' anymore. I don't really care what they call it, as long as it is an institution that accepts all children regardless of race. That would fulfill the fondest wishes of my parents. They prayed to God that in the future the day would come when there was no need for a separate home for colored children."

Wayne Adams, former Board President: "When I first joined the Board in the 1970s, I made a motion that due to contemporary times, the Home should change the word "Colored" to "Black." That was my baptism of fire. The old guard on the Board wasted no time in letting me know that suggestion was unacceptable. Now, I think the name is important in terms of our history. I do agree with the suggestion of naming the buildings after people who were important to the Home's history. We can't forget those names."

Jack MacNeil, current Board member: "If it were called the Nova Scotia Home for Black Children, I'd be more comfortable than with this term 'colored.' I'm not sure what that means. I don't think it's the best name. I don't think it best describes the children that are there."

Bob Butler, former Executive Director: "I'd favor it being called the Nova Scotia Home for Black Children. And I think there should be a Black Children's Aid Society. I wouldn't see that as a form of discrimination. I would see it as trying to bring a service to black children up to the level that other children have."

Opinions appear to split along generational lines. The older generation, who grew up with "colored" as their preferred term of reference, tends to oppose any change in the Home's name. Younger people, born during and after the post–Second World War "baby boom," are less comfortable with "colored." Others would prefer that the Home discard all racial designations.

Whatever the Home's final decision may be, the process of legally changing its name won't be easy, as Jackson explains. "According to the Charter that we've had since 1915, we cannot go out and change the name," he says. "It has to be a legal process. We were incorporated by a special Order-in-Council, and as such, in order to change the name officially, it has to go before the provincial legislature. We're probably talking about a year-and-a-half to two-year process. From a legal standpoint, we do have a lawyer working on it, but any official change is at least a couple of years down the road."

For the immediate future at least, the institution will retain the name under which it was founded: the Nova Scotia Home for Colored Children. Whatever name is eventually taken, though, to the black community the NSHCC will continue to be known as simply "the Home."

Daily Life in the 1990s

What's a typical 1990s day at the Home like? "There's no such thing," laughs Hope Hume, a child-care worker.

Fellow child-care worker Hank Simmonds agrees. "Every day's a different day," he says.

And for Beverly Wyse, the notion of a "typical day" is too funny for words. "It's a challenge every day to come to work and see what's in store for me," she says. "It keeps the adrenaline going."

Child Care worker Hank Simmonds is caught in a candid moment.

Hope is a native of East Preston, and her grandmother worked as a cook at the old Home. "When I was small I can remember going to the original Home and meeting the Matron," she says.

Hank, who hails from North Preston, began working at the Home one year before the move to the new buildings. Beverly is a descendant of Rev. A.A. Wyse, the man who located the property that was bought to establish the NSHCC. She's worked at the Home since 1984.

What these three and other workers have discovered is that the regimented routine that marked life at the Home in past days is long gone. With the high turnover of residents and the prevalence of behavior and emotional problems, the care the Home provides cannot be cut and dried. The staff must be prepared to adapt to situations that would never have occurred at the old Home.

Generally, the 7:00 a.m. to 3:00 p.m. shift begins with the breakfast wake-up call. "We get their breakfast, make sure they have their books and lunches ready to take with them," says Beverly. "And we make sure everybody's out on time."

Younger children attend the Ross Road School; older ones go to Graham Creighton Junior High or high school at Sir Robert Borden or Cole Harbour. Some are enrolled in special education institutes.

Staff is responsible for the cleaning of the facility, including the residents' rooms. That's a far cry from the days when J.A.R. Kinney, Sr. would boast that visitors could come to the Home at any time and find it spotless and tidy. However, as Rev. Donald Fairfax puts it, "The children's welfare is more important than clean floors."

Lunchtime provides a chance for staff to interact with the residents. "You have to sit with the kids at all times during lunch," Hope says. "I think that's good for the kids. We get to talk about how their morning went."

Then it's off to school again, although there's always one or two who stay home, probably for the same reason residents of the old Home invented elaborate ruses to avoid going to church services.

The later shift, which runs from 3:00 to 11:00 p.m., involves much more interaction with the residents after they return from school. Study and homework time is from 6:00 to 7:45 p.m.. There is, of course, no more farm work to do, but chores of other types are still available.

"We encourage residents of age to do their own laundry," says Beverly. "With supervision, of course."

Especially on weekends, the staff will take the residents out on activities that range from sports and recreation to shopping trips. "Sometimes

NSHCC residents enjoy shooting hoops.

we just jump in the van with them and go someplace to burn off energy," says Hank.

As in the old Home, boys and girls are housed separately. Instead of different wings, though, in the new building the boys' rooms are on the bottom floor; girls' on the upper. Staff members make frequent room checks.

"Crushes happen all the time," says Hope. "You always have some residents trying to sneak upstairs or downstairs. We try to keep an eye on them as much as we can."

Discipline is another matter. Corporal punishment is not only out of fashion; it's also against the law. Non-physical methods of ensuring order and preventing the children from harming themselves, each other or staff now substitute for the strict "spare the rod, spoil the child" regimen of the past. Alternatives include grounding and rescinding of privileges. Hank provides an example:

"Last night, some of the kids were caught smoking outside," he says. "They know it's not right. We give them six smokes a day. So what we did was take away their smoking privileges the next day. Some of them deal with it pretty well, but some of them take a temper tantrum."

Child Care Worker Beverly Wyse (rear right) tries a few dance steps with the residents.

Sheila States, a veteran of both the old and new Homes, has her own perspective on differences in dealing with troubled children then and now.

"They do different things now," Ms. States says. "Same children, but they have more rights now. Before, we could just pull them and take them into their rooms. You daren't put your hands on them now. They know their rights."

Many of those rights are included in the Young Offenders and Child and Family Services Acts. "Surrounding those rights are the things about the type of place and where they can go to, recourses to the law, access to the legal system," says Wilfred Jackson. "Because of the introduction of those types of services, they're also making demands on certain types of services and homes such as ourselves. It's changing our Home and all types of other homes in terms of the small number of kids they can serve and the types of programs offered."

Staff members have mixed feelings about those laws and their consequences. "It's good to protect children who are being physically or mentally abused," says Beverly, "but there are some kids who use the law to benefit themselves."

But the Home isn't totally helpless in the face of the new laws.

"We tell them, we know your rights, but when you're here, these are our rules that you must follow," Beverly says. "We have a set of house rules, and when they're admitted, we go over the rules with them."

Assistant Child Care Supervisor Sheila States with two residents.

Sometimes interaction with the children involves more empathy than discipline.

"I think a child coming into care doesn't want anybody to replace their mother or father," Hope says. "I think they just want somebody there that they can talk to, to try to understand what they're going through. I try to put myself in that child's place sometimes. I try to think on the same level they're thinking on."

Sheila States agrees. "We have to work on them in a different way," she says. "You have to stop and think, 'What can I do for this child?' There's no way you're going to change them right off. You have to sit down and think of a strategy."

Beverly adds: "We try to be there when they want to talk to us. Usually there's one person on the staff that they really take to and confide in."

Remembering her time at the Home in the 1980s, former resident Alisa Stevens says: "The staff was good at what they did. They tried to be our second parents. Some even tried to be our first parents, but that didn't always work."

Chow time at the NSHCC.

The change in the Home's racial ratio appears to have had little effect on the staff's ability to work with the residents. However, the fact that the staff is predominantly black while the population is largely white does create an ironic situation. As Patricia Mugridge points out: "Not too many white kids have been in any kind of institution where the majority of the staff is black."

When larger numbers of white children came into the Home during the early 1980s, some of black residents felt that the staff was intimidated.

"When they [the staff] told us what to so, we'd to it," says Tracey Dorrington. "But the white kids were more defiant, and that gave the staff problems. And we would wonder why the white kids were able to get away with things we weren't."

But Alisa Stevens says only a few white children were disruptive, mainly because they were confused.

"Some of them resented the name," she recalls. "But we got along well with most of them once we got to know them."

Staff members say they don't adhere to different standards in dealing with residents of different races. "I treat them both the same," says Hank Simmonds. "After working here so long, you have to be like that. Same thing with boys and girls."

Beverly Wyse shares Hank's viewpoint. "With me, they get treated equally," she says. "What's color? You go to what's inside the person."

However, given the imperfect state of race relations in the surrounding society, some friction and tension is inevitable. Hope Hume describes one such incident:

"When the movie "Roots" was rerun, some of the kids at the Home watched it," Hope says. "They got mad about the movie—the white kids and the black kids. I told them, 'Just think about it. Don't get mad. The movie's not meant to make anybody mad, just to think about racism.' "

Hope adds: "The black kids weren't really mad at their white friends. They were mad at the white people back then, and they would take their anger out on the white friends they have now. And the white kids were mad because they thought they were being singled out."

Regardless of the frequency with which such problems occur, most white children do not appear to have suffered any ill effects from their stay at a black-staffed group home. According to Wilfred Jackson, "Many white kids have gone out of here kicking and screaming because they didn't want to leave," he says. "Some of them call back and come to visit even when they're in foster homes or back in their own homes."

Jackson's comments echo those of Nanny Fowler from half a century earlier: "They cry when they come and they cry when they go."

Veronica Marsman, a former Supervisor and Board member, offers some reasons why many residents change their minds about the Home.

"The larger numbers take some of the pressure off," she says. "Most of the other group homes only accommodate about eight kids. So the kid isn't being singled out as much. And the staff is down-to-earth. They aren't stuffy people. You're talking with grass-rooters, real down-home people here. And the kids enjoy that."

Ms. Marsman also lists some positive aspects about the Home's location.

"The location is a real advantage for the social workers," she says. "The fact that there was no bus service meant that a kid was isolated, but they're not far from the city. When I was Supervisor, the Home provided transportation to all of their functions. I had worked in another group home before that, and the kids would sign out, hop on the bus, and you wouldn't see them. You wouldn't know where they were or what they were doing. At the Home, you knew where the kids were, and when they went out, the majority of the time they'd be going out with the staff. People outside might complain, but there's more structure at the Home than there is in these group homes with eight kids."

Former resident Robert Loppie agrees. "You couldn't really go anywhere," he says. "There wasn't even a bus."

Bus service from Dartmouth to East Preston and Cherry Brook was instituted in 1992, but the buses run infrequently. It is, however, much easier for a child to simply walk away from the Home now than it was in the past, and it's also more difficult to bring that child back.

The Children

The NSHCC residents in the following profiles were interviewed during the spring of 1992. Their names and the details of their case histories have been altered to preserve the privacy of the children and their families.

With her teased blond hair and off-the-shoulder sweater, "Jennifer" could easily fit in with the cast of Beverly Hills 90210, a popular television series about teenagers. She's living at the NSHCC because she frequently runs away from her family's home.

Jennifer appears bright but somewhat distracted. But when she's asked about her life at the NSHCC, her face lights up.

"I love it here," she says. "It's like really having a home. The people here are like family."

When asked what it's like to live in a place called the Home for *Colored* Children, Jennifer shuts down a little.

"Doesn't matter to me," she says, raking a hand through her hair.

Jennifer doesn't feel like saying much more about her circumstances at the Home. Later, she stands at the side of the highway, waiting for the pedestrian-activated traffic light to change so she can go to the store on the other side. An eight- year-old black girl who lives at the Home holds Jennifer's hand. Older children often accompany the younger ones on trips off the Home's grounds. Jennifer doesn't seem to mind the responsibility.

"Jimmy" is a nine-year-old boy of racially mixed background. He's light-skinned, has curly brown hair and is tall for his age. Jimmy was adopted by white parents. The father passed away, and the mother is now a semi-invalid. Because Jimmy became difficult for his mother to handle, he was placed in the hands of social services.

He's been at the Home about eight months. How does he like the environment?

"Pretty good," he says with a shrug. He also says he gets along well with the staff and other children.

Still, when asked if he'd rather be someplace else, Jimmy doesn't hesitate to say yes.

"I want to go to the K-unit," he says. "It's another home, and it's over by the railroad tracks, and it's just across from where I live."

Jimmy has racial identity problems. When he first arrived at the Home, he refused to believe he was really black. He has made some progress in that area, but hasn't come all the way to full acceptance of his identity. Now he's back with his mother.

Racial identity has never been a problem with "Millie." Her skin is dark, offsetting a pair of large, inquisitive eyes. Millie is 19, but because of her small stature and shy demeanor, she looks four years younger than that. She's actually a year older than the usual cutoff point for residents to remain in a group home, but some are allowed to stay longer provided they are pursuing secondary-school education. Millie is currently in Grade 10.

Millie has been in and out of the NSHCC for several years because of her mother's chronic inability to take care of her. Some of Millie's brothers and sisters have also lived at the Home. Millie enjoys the stability and the various activities the Home has to offer.

"I like swimming and going to the gym," she says in a soft voice. "And I go to a learning center to help me in school."

What about the NSHCC staff? "They treat me okay," "Millie" says noncommittally. "We go shopping sometimes, and do lots of things together. They like to bug you sometimes, though."

Millie will probably remain at the Home until she finishes high school.

"Tyrone" is a tall, loose-limbed 15-year-old with fashionable lines cut into his hair. He comes from one of the oldest historically black communities in Nova Scotia. He was placed in the Home because his mother had difficulty controlling him. Tyrone's been there almost a year. By today's standards, that makes him a long-term resident.

"I thought it was all right when I first got here," he says. "It was new. But after you've been here for a while, your mind changes."

What changed Tyrone's mind? "You don't get that much freedom," he says. "The staff is okay most of the time, but sometimes...."

Tyrone does concede that the Home gives him a chance to pursue his interest in sports, such as soccer and basketball. He wants to be a professional athlete when he gets older, even though he is aware that the odds against success in that field are high.

By the summer of 1992, Tyrone was back with his mother.

In the System But Not of It

Among the various child-care institutions in Nova Scotia, the NSHCC retains a unique status. The last of the old-style orphanages, it is at once private and part of the provincial social services system. Its funding and referrals come from the Department of Community Services.

"Most of the kids who come to the Home are wards of the Department," says Wilfred Jackson. "As such, they can be referred to the Home via any one of the district offices throughout the province of Nova Scotia. The majority of the children would come from the metropolitan area, so they're coming from Halifax Children's Aid, the Dartmouth district office and the Sackville district office for the most part."

Residents "hang out" on swings at NSHCC.

Despite that connection, though, some staff members believe the Home has become the system's stepchild, isolated from the mainstream of the child-care decision-making network and mired at the bottom of a social services hierarchy that includes foster homes, therapeutic group homes, and custodial-care group homes.

That opinion is not shared by Trevor Townsend, the Department of Community Services' Co-Director of Child and Adolescent Services.

"The Home provides custodial care, with a lot of crisis intervention," Townsend says. "The residents stay for relatively short periods of time, then either go back home or move on to another facility. There's definitely a future for this type of care. We are totally overwhelmed by the number of youngsters coming at us. We just don't have enough beds."

Yet the Home's consignment of beds is seldom filled. "I think the Home has been having trouble keeping up with the changing clientele," Townsend says. "I think they've got staff who have been there a long time and who still are wanting to have younger children to care for. Instead, they're getting adolescents who are severely emotionally disturbed, physically aggressive, extremely uncooperative, self-mutilating."

Sheila Lucas was the NSHCC's in-house social worker through late 1992. At that time, she worked directly for the Home, and acted as a link between the institution and the provincial social service system. In that position she attempted to diminish the distance between the NSHCC and the system.

While the child-care workers are responsible for looking after the day-to-day needs of the residents, Ms. Lucas guides them through the maze of paper that leads them into and out of placement. "A lot of my work is behind the scenes," Ms. Lucas says. "Probably about 70 percent of my time is spent on the phone."

She deals with families, guardians, school matters, legal issues, and counselling. In some cases, she does the counselling herself. Much of the time, though, she arranges referrals to private counsellors.

"There's specific things that they would be working on, like anger management," she says. "Or maybe the therapist is acting as a mediator between the child and the family in order to get them back with their family."

On many occasions, though, she finds herself acting as a mediator between the Home and social service workers who harbor negative stereotypes about the Home in particular and the black community in general.

"I made it clear when I started that I expected anybody who dealt with me to deal professionally," Ms. Lucas says. "That's the premise I went on. There have been some problems along the way, and I had to iron those out. That might be because the workers were used to dealing with us here in a certain way. But I wasn't dealing in that way. Things had to change."

The "certain way" to which Ms. Lucas refers involves the belief among some professionals that the NSHCC is an inferior institution to which referrals should be made only as a last resort—a type of "funnelling down" process.

Patricia Mugridge has also dealt with this type of negative attitude in the network. Prior to joining the NSHCC in 1988, Ms. Mugridge worked in group homes in Calgary. She finds that the training and competence levels of the workers in the Home are comparable to those of long-term employees in other agencies. But some of the social services people she has dealt with don't share that opinion.

"I think people thought that they could phone me up and make fun of the facility and make fun of the people and that I would automatically agree," says Ms. Mugridge, who is white. "When I didn't go along with that, they started treating me with the same contempt they treat everybody else."

That contempt takes many forms. "They really feel they can walk on you," Ms. Mugridge says. "The kids don't need a lot of information; they don't have to call you; they can throw kids in here any time they want; your say in program intervention is nil."

She adds: "What I also see is contempt for the workers. "They'll come in and walk right past the workers and either speak to the supervisors or a social worker. In other places, they may want to see the supervisor, but they'll at least greet the child-care workers professionally."

Ms. Mugridge attributes these attitudes to racism—not the in-your-face racism of the 1920s, but the behind-closed-doors racism of today that can be just as devastating but far more difficult to identify.

At the top levels of the Community Services Department, the issue of attitudes toward the Home's staff is a matter of great concern. Alienation of any part of the network is in neither the Department's nor the children's interest.

"The staff that have been there for a number of years came there with very little formal training," says Trevor Townsend. "Most of what they've learned has been on the job. I think the Home has been attempting to provide staff with crisis-intervention training."

However, for Townsend, the level of staff training at the NSHCC is "not unlike pretty well all our other homes. It's pretty well representative of what's going on all over the province."

Yet the impression that the Home's staff is underqualified lingers. One effect of this negative perception is that residents sometimes enter with preconceived notions that have to be overcome before any treatment the Home offers can have a chance to take effect. In some cases those notions come directly from social service workers, but they can be traced to the media as well.

"They think there's a lot of violence out here because of the media coverage and the way people talk," Ms. Lucas says. "When I go to register them at Graham Creighton Junior High School, some of them get scared because they think all black people are violent. After they've been here for a certain length of time, they understand that's not the reality of the situation," Ms. Lucas says.

Hope Hume says, "There are some kids who come in here saying they heard such horror stories about the Home, and then they come here and think it's the greatest place they've ever been at."

Beverly Wyse hints at more sinister motives. "I've heard rumors that they've used this place as a threat," she says. "After the residents get here, though, the tables turn on them because when it's time for the residents to leave, they don't want to leave."

Trevor Townsend is aware of the rumors about negative attitudes concerning the Home. But he says no one has ever approached him directly with complaints.

"I have never personally heard comments like that," he says. "If the Home is feeling that way, its administration needs to get out to the various agencies and try to find out if that's an accurate reflection of how people really feel. And then if it is, to try to change it."

Bill Greatorex agrees. "We need a proactive, positive approach rather than getting defensive about it," he says. "The agencies that are placing in facilities should be talking directly. If it is a matter of perception, then deal with any false perceptions that exist and develop a partnership between the placing people and the receiving people."

Townsend also cites a survey that was circulated among the social service agencies. The only negative response about the NSHCC came from a black social worker who was uncomfortable with the name of the Home.

Nevertheless, if some social service and child protection workers are indeed using the Home as a threat and/or last resort, the practice is at best unprofessional and at worst an example of individual racism. In what way is a troubled child helped by being told that he or she is about to be shipped off to some "terrible" black environment? If this is the playing field upon which the NSHCC is competing with other group homes for referrals, the surface of that field is far from level.

Because of this situation, relations between the Home and some members of the rest of the social services network have become something of a standoff based on mistrust.

As Ms. Lucas puts it: "Actually, the negativity is on both sides. It becomes a stalemate. No side wants to make the first move. People have those perceptions, and it just continues. One side blames the other."

The victims of this stalemate are the children, especially black children. During the past decade the proportion of black residents at the Home has continued to diminish, although not everyone sees that as a trend.

"It's unpredictable," Ms. Lucas says. "When I first came here two years ago, there were more black kids. But many of them were long-term residents who were phased out. The proportion can change in a matter of months."

Still, it appears anomalous that so few of the province's troubled black children would be referred to the institution that was founded to meet their needs. It's almost as though the Home were being deliberately avoided.

"I had heard that some of the black kids that were going into care weren't being referred here, maybe because of the reputation of the Home, or perceptions that the people here weren't qualified to deal with the kids," Ms. Lucas says. "They might say they tried all the group homes and some other group home was the only one that had a bed for this particular child, but that's not the case. We usually have beds. We're the largest group home around."

Althea Tolliver puts it even more bluntly. "Lots of times, agencies don't even let us know that there are black children out there being placed," she says.

Patricia Mugridge touches on another factor. "You don't get a lot of referrals from the communities out here, because they take care of their own," she says. "Most of our black kids come from Halifax or Dartmouth."

The "take care of your own" tradition, including an informal child-care network based on kinship in large, extended families, has existed in the Preston–Cherry Brook area for two centuries. In more than a few cases, adults will speak fondly of a distant relative who raised them "just as if she were my mother."

Today, smaller family sizes and depressed economic conditions in the Maritimes tend to undermine that informal network. The conditions that allowed families of a dozen or more children to thrive in the early part of this century have given way to a cost of living that is so high some families with only one child have difficulty making ends meet, let alone becoming part of an informal foster care network.

"We have to turn it formal," says Ms. Lucas. "If we don't turn it formal, then room and board and those kinds of things are not covered."

Formal or informal, the status quo is unacceptable. Nova Scotia is filled with troubled black children—refugees from a racist society who need treatment, guidance, shelter and hope.

A place exists in which those needs could be met. Yet a wall of social service bureaucracy stands between those children and the place that has been there for them since 1921.

Ironically, some members of local and provincial social service agencies have served on the Board of the NSHCC. One is Jack MacNeil from Halifax County Social Services. MacNeil was elected Treasurer of the Board in 1987 and 1988.

"Sometimes it's been thought that having people who represented outside organizations would be a conflict of interest," Jackson says. "When we were discussing something about the Home, they might be saying the department's policy said another thing. But most people from outside groups serve on the Board because they have an interest in the Home."

Although Board members with influence in the outside network can be helpful, the overall situation still has to be changed. But how?

"That's something we've been dealing with through the Home and the Association of Black Social Workers," Mrs. Tolliver says. "The AUBA also dealt with it this year by sending letters off to the department. One of the things they were asking was that when black children come into care, that the Home be the first agency to be contacted."

Patricia Mugridge goes so far as to say legal action may be necessary.

"Some kids are going to have to take somebody to court to say, 'You placed me in a white family and look what's happened to me,' " she says. "That kind of thing happened in Saskatchewan when some of the native children were placed in white homes."

It may be possible for various representatives from the NSHCC, social services and the black community to pool their resources and reach a state of détente, if not complete harmony, on how to resolve what appears to be an impasse.

Sheila Lucas suggests one way that could happen. "There has to be a lot more openness and willingness to understand differences on the part of white society when they're looking at placing kids," she says. "Perceptions of black people in general, too—hat they're not quite good enough to do the job or measure up—there's a lot of those attitudes that need changing."

Unfortunately, attitudes are notoriously difficult to change. However, the relationship between the Home and the provincial Community Services Department can—and should—be revised.

In 1988 a step in that direction was taken when Wilfred Jackson set up meetings with representatives of various referral agencies. But in his practicum he described the results of those meetings as "less than desirable." Specifically, he wrote:

One of the positive aspects of these meetings was the openness of these representatives to share the views of their respective agencies re: the use of this Home for their wards. Many of the representatives expressed appreciation for the expediency in which the Home responded to emergency placement requests. On the other hand they felt that due to the large population of the Home, and the less than adequate educational background of the employees, the Home was considered the home of last resort for their placements. These workers showed discomfort when expressing the needs of Black youth, and would constantly switch the topic to all children. Attendance at these sessions diminished to the point where we no longer schedule meetings on a regular basis.

Thus do Nova Scotia's two solitudes—one black, the other white—remain separate and unequal.

The Future of the Home

As the 1990s unfold, enrolment at the NSHCC continues to decline. The "break-even" point is sixteen residents; in 1993 only twelve lived there. The overall social-services philosophy of "deinstitutionalization" has gained much momentum and influence since its introduction during the 1960s, and the day of the large orphanage in which children spent virtually their entire childhoods is done.

The staff at the Home is aware of the trend away from long-term institutional care, and to some extent that trend is supported. "I try to see, from my perspective, that the kids aren't here any longer than they have to be," says Sheila Lucas.

Currently, social services departments throughout North America emphasize specialized therapeutic treatment of children who are abused, runaways, or affected by emotional and adjustment disorders. Foster care remains the ideal alternative for youngsters who cannot remain with their natural families.

Yet foster homes are not an absolute substitute for natural homes. The cardinal rule for foster parents is: Don't become too attached to the children you take in. Sooner or later, the children in a foster home will depart. Attachment can lead to painful partings.

Although the demand for foster parents is rising, the supply may be shrinking. In an article headlined "Foster Care Homes Being Rediscovered" in the November 2, 1992, *Globe and Mail*, Lila Sarick wrote: "Child welfare agencies often prefer families in which one parent stays home, especially for children with special needs, which eliminates many potential two-career families." In the same article, Ms. Sarick made a more telling point: "After a decade of neglect, foster care is being rediscovered as the best alternative for children plucked from unstable homes. The agencies are gradually embracing the concept again because they find it cheaper and more effective than placing young people in professionally run group homes and institutions."

The Home no longer hosts large numbers of residents, such as those shown in this mid 1980s visit to CFB Shearwater.

Within that context, large group homes like the NSHCC are viewed as short-term options. Board member Jack MacNeil puts that view in candid terms: "There has been a tendency to use—and I say this with some reservation—to use the Home as a dumping ground."

Where, then, are children who don't make it into foster homes being placed? Over the past few years, smaller units with names like "crisis centers" or "assessment centers" have proliferated. These units serve populations of four to six residents at a time. By contrast, the Home has room for thirty-six when both its buildings are in use.

"The children we used to receive are now going into these specialized units," says Wilfred Jackson. "What we're finding is that we're now dealing with children who are not suitable to those small settings. So we're not only dealing with a smaller population; we're also dealing with behaviors we've never experienced before, like suicidal behavior, involvement with Satanism, and involvement with gangs."

Severe behavior problems demand a smaller staff-resident ratio and a higher degree of professional training for child-care workers. "With only twelve children, our staff is taxed more than ever," Jackson says. As well, the high turnover among residents creates difficulties in developing effective individual treatment plans.

Under those circumstances, success is more difficult to measure than it was during the Home's early days. At that time, feeding, clothing and sheltering the residents were the primary goals, followed by basic education and the inculcation of moral values. Often, the institution had most of a child's lifetime to accomplish its tasks. Today, as Jack MacNeil puts it, the Home is often little more than a "bed and breakfast" for troubled children.

Given such short-term stays, different indicators for success must be used. For example, former residents who return for visits along with their spouses and children often recall the ways in which their experiences at the NSHCC shaped their later lives. Staff members have many stories to tell about these reunions.

"I have community contacts with some people who were past residents of the Home," says Sheila Lucas. "They might be in their twenties right now, doing okay, and managing to get their lives together, and want to turn that around and do something for other kids. So they come back to do a big brother/big sister sort of deal, tutoring or whatever."

"There was a boy who used to live here, and after he moved out, he asked me to be the godfather of his baby," Hank Simmonds recalls. "I was totally caught by surprise. I hadn't seen him for a while, and when he was here, we didn't get along that well. This showed me that I did get through to him when he was living here."

"They constantly come back," Sheila States says. "Looking up the old staff when they're around here visiting on holidays. Even if you had a hard time with them when they were here, they still come back."

"A lot of kids came here roughnecks and left as decent kids," says Beverly Wyse. "Even their parents were impressed with them. We have letters from parents after their kids come home thanking us for what we've done, the changes that have come over the kids since they were here and left. The kids may have been at other places, but when they left here, the parents did notice the difference."

Tracey Dorrington, a former resident who now lives in Truro, says her twelve years at the Home were beneficial. Her two brothers and two sisters also lived at the NSHCC.

"I wouldn't be the person I am today if it hadn't been for the Home," she says. "People like Sheila States, Hank Simmonds and Julie Grosse gave me moral values a lot of people my age just don't have. I learned to respect people. I see too many young people who are ignorant and uncaring. The Home is the reason I'm not like that."

Robert Loppie, who is now an affirmative action officer with the Nova Scotia Civil Service Commission, is another former resident who maintains ties with the Home, where he resided from 1978 to 1985.

"I was one of the hard cases," he says. "Probably one of the baddest kids they ever had. I threw tantrums and was getting on the wrong side of the law."

Robert attributes his problems to being shunted among various foster homes in Nova Scotia and Ontario until he was 12 years old.

"I didn't have any guidance or sense of direction," he recalls. "The Home gave me structure and discipline. We did our own cooking and cleaning, and that helped me become more responsible. We also got a lot of one-on-one attention from the staff."

The Home's basketball program helped to focus some of Robert's energy, and he eventually played on his high school and university teams. He credits the Home for setting his future on the right path.

"It really turned me around," he says. "If it hadn't been for the Home, I wouldn't have come to where I am."

Residents Robert Loppie (right) and Robert Borden ham it up at an NSHCC Halloween party in the early 1980s.

For all these anecdotal success stories, however, it is once again time for the NSHCC to adapt to changing conditions. In a repetition of history, the Home's facilities have again become too large to accommodate current child-care requirements.

One of the two buildings that were erected in 1978 was closed from 1991 to 1993. During that time, it was used for conferences and recreation for the residents. As well, the Fairfax Chapel is located there. However, a new use has been found for the building.

"At this point, what we're looking at is an independence program for the 16-to-19-year-old group," Wilfred Jackson said in 1992. "Right now, based on our research, we find that's the group with the most pressing needs. There's a lot of things we hear about the growing number of homeless adolescents. There seem to be very few resources around for this group. We're hoping we can launch a program that's going to look at this group. They need to learn how to stay off the streets and stay away from drugs and prostitution."

The independence program began in September 1993, and both NSHCC buildings are once again occupied. The Home is considering other services, such as care and counselling for young unwed mothers.

Wilfred Jackson presents certificate to retiring NSHCC maintenance chief Harold "Freddie" Sparks.
(Courtesy Wilfred Jackson)

"Many of our young black girls who find themselves pregnant also find themselves at odds with their parents," Jackson says. "And they get turfed out. Her only option other than abortion is to go to the Home of the Guardian Angel—totally foreign to her. She may have limited writing skills, which would make the paperwork involved difficult for her. This Home could serve as a short-term residence for counselling and practical information, like how to find a job, how to find day care, how to bring up a child."

Yet another suggestion is the use of the Home as a resource to educate black professional foster parents. "One of the things the province is beginning to talk about is professional foster care right across the board," says Jackson. "For us to be able to deal with it from an African-Canadian perspective would certainly be ideal."

In these and other ways, the Home can reestablish its connection with the black community while remaining open to children of all races—a delicate balancing act. Rev. Donald D. Skier, who continues to attend the NSHCC's annual meetings, puts it this way: "I don't like to perpetuate a segregated institution. But on the other side, I do feel that in terms of our history, and how the Home developed, we have a responsibility of retaining the Home. I would like to see more black children brought into this facility. I think there are some things we should hold onto for historical purposes."

For far too many black Nova Scotians, the institution has become little more than a name. In his practicum, Jackson wrote:

> *At this stage, it is still necessary to assure the Black community that there is still an agency that will treat their children with dignity and respect. The Home must be seen as an essential component of the Social Services network, and not as an isolated relic of the past. As remarked by a former employee, this Home has the potential for greatness, if only we could find the funding.*

But what if that funding never arrives?

Already, the annual provincial grant for the NSHCC has been cut. "In Community Services, everybody's budget was supposed to be the same," says former Board President Donna Smith. "Whereas other agencies'

The NSHCC's second building, now being used to house an independent-living program.

budgets stayed the same, ours was reduced. They took into account things like our rental income and bequests in wills. But I wonder if they did that to the Children's Aid Society?"

What if enrolment at the Home falls so far below the break-even point that the institution becomes too much of a fiscal liability for the province to maintain? What if, after seven decades of service, the Nova Scotia Home for Colored Children is forced to close its doors?

"I hope the Home never goes under," says Child Care Worker Beverly Wyse. "It stands for a lot. It's an old tradition, it's heritage, and I'd hate to see it go. For the older people who lived and worked here, it would be like seeing a part of themselves destroyed. It would be devastating for them."

Althea Tolliver has an even stronger opinion on how the black community would react if the Home were shut down.

"I think they'd almost be ready to riot," she says. "The Home means a lot to the black community, even though they don't get involved as much as we would like to see them get involved. But just knowing that it's there is important."

Sherry Bernard agrees. "The Home's been around long enough that it's very difficult to wipe it out now," she says. "The fact that it's stayed shows that there's a need for it, and it would be very difficult to justify not funding the Nova Scotia Home for Colored Children."

The Home indeed has made it through hard times before—harder times than now, according to Sheila States. "I remember in our community church they would ask for money to keep the Home open," she recalls. "We see hard now, but that was harder. Any time they have to take up collections in churches to keep the doors open...."

And those doors need to stay open now more than ever. There's a new type of child neglect prevalent in today's society, that which stems not so much from economic privation as it does from an abandonment of the basic values of parenting.

In the October 1992 issue of *Atlantic Monthly*, writer Anne H. Soukhanov discussed a new term that describes this sad phenomenon, which cuts across racial lines:

> *The term zero-parent phenomenon, which typically arises from drug or alcohol abuse or violence, has exploded in recent decades. According to the U.S. Census, three per cent of America's children were homeless in 1990. The result, in the words of one analyst, is "a new breed of American orphans," urban children who are shuttled between the homes of relatives, neighbors, and strangers. Some experts have called for the creation of a special system of orphanages for these children, similar to those built in the late nineteenth and early twentieth centuries to care for children orphaned by tuberculosis, diphtheria, and influenza epidemics.*

To extrapolate Canadian trends from American data is always a risky proposition. However, the "modern orphans" problem has begun to surface here, although not to the same extent as it has in the United States.

Within that context, Donna Byard Sealey's observation about young black children "growing like weeds" without proper adult supervision takes on a special significance. Is it possible that events have turned full circle? Is it possible that there's a future after all for long-term institutional care for large numbers of "throwaway" children?

If the consensus answer among social services professionals turns out to be "yes," then the two large buildings that constitute the NSHCC would be a logical location for that type of facility.

Sherry Bernard believes that goal could be accomplished through an alliance between the Home and the Association of Black Social Workers (ABSW). "I'd like to see the ABSW heavily involved there," she says. "I'd like to see the Home take over the full care and custody of our black children. The ABSW and the Nova Scotia Home could work together so that any black child in need goes to the Home first."

Ms. Bernard's former co-worker, Veronica Marsman, agrees. "The initial mandate of the Colored Home was to be its own social service agency," she says. "And I like that idea. We need our own social service agency for black kids."

Ms. Bernard's words are an echo of those spoken eighty years earlier, when other voices spoke of the need for a refuge for black children. How much has changed since then? Perhaps everything, perhaps nothing.

In theory, at least, black Nova Scotians no longer face the type of overt racial discrimination that led them to build and maintain the Nova Scotia Home for Colored Children. But in practice, blacks today face different, more subtle forms of racism.

Schools, for example, are no longer segregated, but the dropout rate among black students remains disproportionately high. A report commissioned by Dartmouth federal MP Ron MacDonald indicated that blacks in the Preston–Cherry Brook area continue to suffer high unemployment levels compared to the neighboring white population. And the problems associated with poverty still lead to early pregnancy, drug use, crime and family breakdown.

Sometimes blacks express their frustration with the racial situation in the province in overt ways. In 1989 a brawl between black and white students at Cole Harbour District High School made national headlines. Two years later, another black-white confrontation in downtown Halifax resulted in fighting, window-smashing sprees and charges of racially motivated mistreatment on the part of Halifax police.

The inevitable white backlash has occurred as well. In 1992, violence almost erupted at the Charles P. Allen High School in Bedford when white-supremacist leaflets were found on school property; and Ku Klux Klan literature has been distributed on Halifax streets.

For all the advances individual black Nova Scotians have made during the past few decades—advances that would have made J.A.R. Kinney Senior and Junior and Elizabeth Fowler and Mary Paris proud had they lived to see them—racism and its consequences are still with us. And one of those consequences is a generation of black children with no one to turn to, nowhere to go and no future in sight.

Nearly a century after James R. Johnston presented his proposal for an educational and industrial institution to the African United Baptist Association, there are still lost children in Nova Scotia who need help to find their way Home.

What Band That Sunday Morning?: Helen Creighton and the Home for Colored Children

by Clary Croft

Afterword

Helen Creighton began collecting the folk songs and folklore of Nova Scotia in 1928. Her initial collecting trips took her to the Anglo-Saxon communities near her birthplace, Dartmouth.

In 1942, while attending summer classes at Indiana University's Institute of Folklore, she received her introduction to the study of Black music. Her reputation as a folk song collector had already been established with the publication of *Songs and Ballads from Nova Scotia*, but that work had contained no material from the Black community.

Two of her professors, Herbert Halpert and Alan Lomax, encouraged her to search out material from Black informants. Subsequently, when she returned to her field work later that same year, she actively pursued leads which would introduce her to singers of traditional Black songs.

She collected material from informants in Preston and Cherry Brook, but it wasn't until 1943, when she received a Presto recording machine from the Library of Congress in Washington, that she was able to return to these informants and make disc recordings of their material.

Helen was quick to follow up on leads, and this is how she came to find songs at the Nova Scotia Home for Colored Children. Her diary of October 1942 records her meeting a friend who told of "being at Colored Home and hearing spiritual about angels evidently cumulative going up and up to 17. She had found it very tiresome, but it looks promising to me."

Helen was certainly aware of the existence of the Home. Her personal photograph album had four snapshots of the opening ceremonies held in 1921. Helen was in attendance that day and probably took the photos herself.

On October 9, Helen went to the Home and met with the teacher, Miss Morgan. Then she was introduced to a group of young boys who stood in a row and answered questions pertaining to their Bible studies. Helen noted that the boys were very well prepared and that the row answered as one child.

Photo of old Home's opening day attributed to Helen Creighton.

When Helen asked about songs, she was taken to the music room and introduced to a group of girls who sang with piano accompaniment. She later noted in her diary, "All songs new to me, and ones they had never seen in books. Every girl knew every word thoroughly and sang lustily...enjoyed every minute of afternoon."

With only one course in Black music, Helen felt ill-prepared to make assessments of the material she found at the Home. So she wrote to her former professor, Alan Lomax, requesting his opinion on the songs and games she had collected. He wrote back with encouragement, telling her that all the songs seemed to be genuine folk songs but advising her that some of the material may have been brought to the province through books and not through the more common method of folk-song transmission: the oral song tradition.

It was not until February 8, 1943, that Helen was able to return to the Home and begin her work towards making recordings. Her diary entry for that day illustrates the course of events.

"In aft. called Miss Morgan at Home for Colored Children, and she said to go there at 4 o'clock.... Mrs. Jefferson met me and gave me most cordial welcome. Then the children were brought in, twelve of them carefully selected, and of various ages. One had high voice like natural descant which sounded very pretty. Took songs they had sung for me before and others from paper covered books they had made themselves. Children here from all over Maritimes. In their books there are songs they have never seen written down.... Were some Miss Morgan didn't know. Asked them to teach them to her, so I could get them again...asked about singing games. They mentioned a lot, so I asked Miss Morgan if they could get thoroughly familiar with them, and I would go out again. She thought it would take about a week."

Finally on March 17, Helen returned to the Home to make the recordings. This time there were fifteen children, all girls but one. Helen noted that the teachers had the little ones come in first and present their recitations. These she did not record. Blank discs were scarce during the war, and Helen was making every attempt to collect material she felt was rare or unusual.

However, she did record a number of songs and singing games as performed by the other children. In addition, she recorded a narrative by the Assistant Matron, Mrs. Selena Jefferson, about Admiral Peary's return to Sydney, Nova Scotia, after his famous dash to the Pole. Mrs. Jefferson also recorded an interesting story about the spiritual strength of an Eskimo woman stranded up North for six months.

In addition to Mrs. Jefferson's stories, recorded for speech patterns and historical interest, Helen collected eight songs which she referred to as "traditional jubilee songs" and twelve game songs. The titles given to Helen by the children are as follows:

Songs:
1. Daniel In The Lion's Den
2. Where Shall I Be When The First Trumpet Sounds?
3. I Woke Up This Morning
4. Welcome Table

5. I've Got A Home
6. They Shall Be Mine
7. What Band That Sunday Morning?
8. In That Land

Games:
1. Bluebird, Bluebird
2. Rain, Rain
3. Lazy Bessie
4. The King's Keys
5. Go In And Out The Window
6. I Went To Visit A Friend One Day
7. London Bridge
8. Here We Go Gathering Nuts In May
9. Here Comes One Duke A-Riding
10. Rattlesnake
11. I Wrote A Letter To My Friend
12. On This Carpet

All of the songs were sung with simple harmonies and with piano accompaniment. Helen did not note the accompanist, but it was Miss Morgan.

For the most part, the songs are fairly standard variants of spirituals. The one titled "I Woke Up This Morning" is sometimes called "Stayed On Jesus" or even "I Woke Up This Morning With My Mind Stayed On Jesus." The variant of "Welcome Table" collected at the Home is one of three different versions Helen collected in Nova Scotia. The cumulative song "What Band That Sunday Morning?" was indeed the same song Helen's friend referred to with its increasing number of angels and was the song which had sparked Helen's desire to visit the Home.

The games were all sung unaccompanied. Helen did not note whether any actions were performed during the singing, but during one, "I Went To Visit A Friend One Day," you can hear feet stamping during the final verse.

The child Helen referred to as having a "high voice like natural descant which sounded very pretty" was Olive Russell, aged 13. She is listed as soloist in "Lazy Bessie" and "On This Carpet" and is mentioned in the singing game "Rain, Rain." She and the boy, Arthur Fletcher, are the only children named. This was a common practice with Helen when collecting from a group—she rarely took individual names.

Certainly, none of the singing games were derived from a strictly Black experience. They were common enough throughout the province and elsewhere. Helen herself noted that she used to sing "On This Carpet" and a version of "I Wrote A Letter To My Friend" and called it "I Wrote A Letter To My Love."

When Arthur Fauset collected material in Nova Scotia in the late 1920s, he found variants of "On This Carpet" and "I Wrote A Letter To My Love," both from non-Black informants.

Certainly, one may ask what shaped the music sung by the children at the Home? I cannot hope to cover the history of Black music in Nova Scotia here but there are some influences which shaped the direction of materials selected for the children to learn.

There is no doubt that the children who sang for Helen Creighton were used to performing for guests and even had experience with recording equipment. The popular live Christmas broadcasts over radio station CHNS were already an established feature of Home life by the time Helen collected songs in 1943. Beginning in 1931, when the children were taken to the radio studio, these broadcasts have given them poise and experience not afforded to other singing groups from which Helen collected. In her notes accompanying the audio recordings, Helen noted, "They are accustomed to performing before a microphone, as each year they put on a whole afternoon of songs over the local radio to raise funds for their maintenance."

In fact, even before the broadcasts, the children were given opportunities to show their talents and skills. The Halifax *Chronicle*, 1928, carried an article entitled "Kiddies Are Good Entertainers," where it described the boys and girls from the Home entertaining at a business luncheon for the Halifax Rotary Club. Under the direction of Mr. J.A.R. Kinney and Miss Gladys Walcott, they "won unstinted encomiums as they sang, read, recited, spelled, and demonstrated their needle work and culinary products."

It is clear that a good deal of the material performed by the children was directed by the teachers. Helen notes that she waited for the teacher to rehearse the children in several songs and games before she returned to record them. Perhaps some of the names of the game songs were altered to suit the moral tone of the time—"I Wrote A Letter To My Love" being changed to "I Wrote A Letter To My Friend" being the most obvious example.

Certainly by the 1960s the repertoire chosen for the Christmas broadcasts did not reflect a strong Black tradition. In the 1967 CHNS broadcast originating from the Home, only one song from the era when Helen Creighton was collecting survived. Even that was performed, not by the children, but by an established singing group known as "The Spiritual

Airs" featuring Clyde Jemmott. The song they performed was titled "You Are On My Mind," a version of "I Woke Up This Morning With My Mind Stayed On Jesus." The children also sang standard Christmas songs such as "Silent Night" and "Dear Old Santa Claus."

It was only natural that the teachers and children would move away from repeating the same songs each year. Musical tastes and repertoires change.

Yvonne White, who worked at the Home in the 1960s as contract music teacher preparing the children for the broadcasts, said the children requested specific material and she introduced new songs each year. However, the choice of material was left to the children and Yvonne could tell quite quickly if they liked her suggestions.

One cannot expect a community or group of people to keep their traditions and songs static. Changes, especially with children, come quickly. Thus, by the end of the 1960s, material Helen had found at the Home would be quite foreign to most of the children.

Helen Creighton maintained a constant interest in the traditional music of Nova Scotian Blacks. She petitioned the Nova Scotia government for funds to set up a grant through the Canadian Folk Music Society which, among other things, collected the last Easter sunrise service held in the church at Africville. She served as a project advisor for the 1971 Black Historical and Educational Research Organization (HERO) project which was established "to collect the oral history, folklore, myths and superstitions of the older members of the Black community."

Helen Creighton was a true folklore pioneer, and her contribution to the preservation of the Black heritage continues to be a valuable resource. In 1983 she gave a copy of all her recordings made with Blacks to the Black Cultural Centre. Now, one can sit across the road from the Nova Scotia Home for Colored Children and listen to those sweet, angelic voices from the past.